LEVEL F

SRA Connecting Math Concepts

Columbus, Ohio

The **McGraw·Hill** Companies

Acknowledgments

The authors are grateful to the following people for their input in the field-testing and preparation of *Connecting Math Concepts, Level F:*

Debbie Kleppen
Susan Martin
Sam Miller
Laurie Nowak-Crawford
Chris Thurmond
Linda Van Hook
Tina Wells
Bryan Wickman

www.sra4kids.com

SRA
McGraw-Hill

Send all inquiries to:
SRA/McGraw-Hill
8787 Orion Place
Columbus, OH 43240-4027

Printed in the United States of America.

ISBN 0-02-684689-6

2 3 4 5 6 7 8 9 0 VHG 06 05

The McGraw·Hill Companies

Contents

Program Summary

Facts about *Connecting Math Concepts, Level F*

Placement criterion	Students who have completed either Level E or *Connecting Math Concepts, Level Bridge* and have passed the respective end-of-program test
Format of lessons	Scripted presentations for all activities Program designed for presentation to entire class
Number of lessons	100 (including 9 test lessons and 10 project lessons)
Scheduled time for math periods	50–55 minutes per period for teacher-directed activities Additional 20–30 minutes for independent work (homework)
Weekly schedule	5 periods per week
Teacher material	*Teacher's Guide* *Presentation Book* *Answer Key*
Student material	Program material: *Textbook* Additional materials: calculator and ruler Project Lesson materials: protractor, colored pencils, dice, scissors, string, paper clips, copies of graphs and figures (pages 157–160)
In-program tests	Tests 1–9 (tests follow every 10th regular lesson, i.e., Lesson 10, 20, 30, through 90) Final Test (follows Lesson 100)
Remedies	See page 28, Test Remedies

Connecting Math Concepts, Level F

Lessons

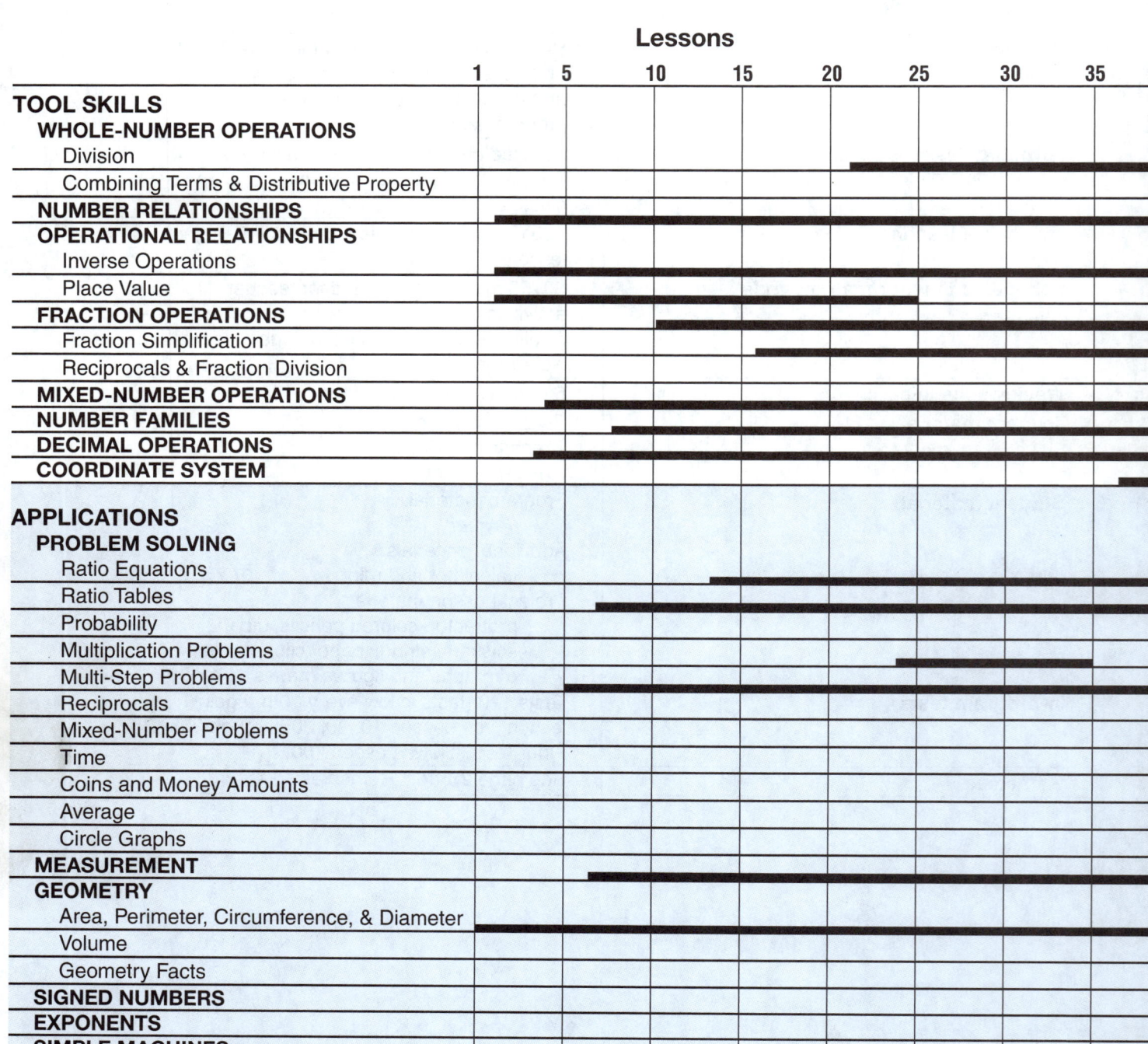

	1	5	10	15	20	25	30	35
TOOL SKILLS								
WHOLE-NUMBER OPERATIONS								
Division					▬▬▬▬▬▬▬▬▬			
Combining Terms & Distributive Property								
NUMBER RELATIONSHIPS	▬▬▬							
OPERATIONAL RELATIONSHIPS								
Inverse Operations	▬▬▬▬▬▬▬▬▬▬▬▬▬▬▬▬▬▬▬▬▬▬▬▬▬▬▬							
Place Value	▬▬▬▬▬▬▬▬▬▬▬▬▬▬▬▬							
FRACTION OPERATIONS								
Fraction Simplification			▬▬▬▬▬▬▬▬▬▬▬▬▬▬▬▬▬▬					
Reciprocals & Fraction Division				▬▬▬▬▬▬▬▬▬▬▬▬▬▬▬				
MIXED-NUMBER OPERATIONS		▬▬▬▬▬▬▬▬▬▬▬▬▬▬▬▬▬▬▬▬▬▬						
NUMBER FAMILIES		▬▬▬▬▬▬▬▬▬▬▬▬▬▬▬▬▬▬▬▬▬▬						
DECIMAL OPERATIONS	▬▬▬▬▬▬▬▬▬▬▬▬▬▬▬▬▬▬▬▬▬▬▬▬▬							
COORDINATE SYSTEM								▬
APPLICATIONS								
PROBLEM SOLVING								
Ratio Equations					▬▬▬▬▬▬▬▬▬▬▬▬▬▬▬▬▬			
Ratio Tables		▬▬▬▬▬▬▬▬▬▬▬▬▬▬▬▬▬▬▬▬▬▬▬▬▬▬▬						
Probability								
Multiplication Problems						▬▬▬▬▬▬		
Multi-Step Problems		▬▬▬▬▬▬▬▬▬▬▬▬▬▬▬▬▬▬▬▬▬▬▬▬▬▬▬▬▬						
Reciprocals								
Mixed-Number Problems								
Time								
Coins and Money Amounts								
Average								
Circle Graphs								
MEASUREMENT		▬▬▬▬▬▬▬▬▬▬▬▬▬▬▬▬▬▬▬▬▬▬▬▬▬						
GEOMETRY								
Area, Perimeter, Circumference, & Diameter	▬▬▬▬▬▬▬▬▬							
Volume								
Geometry Facts								
SIGNED NUMBERS								
EXPONENTS								
SIMPLE MACHINES								
PROJECTS								

The Scope and Sequence Chart shows where each track or major topic begins and where it ends. The chart does not show various lessons on which activities are presented. For more details on the lessons in which particular skills are taught, see pages 145–153.

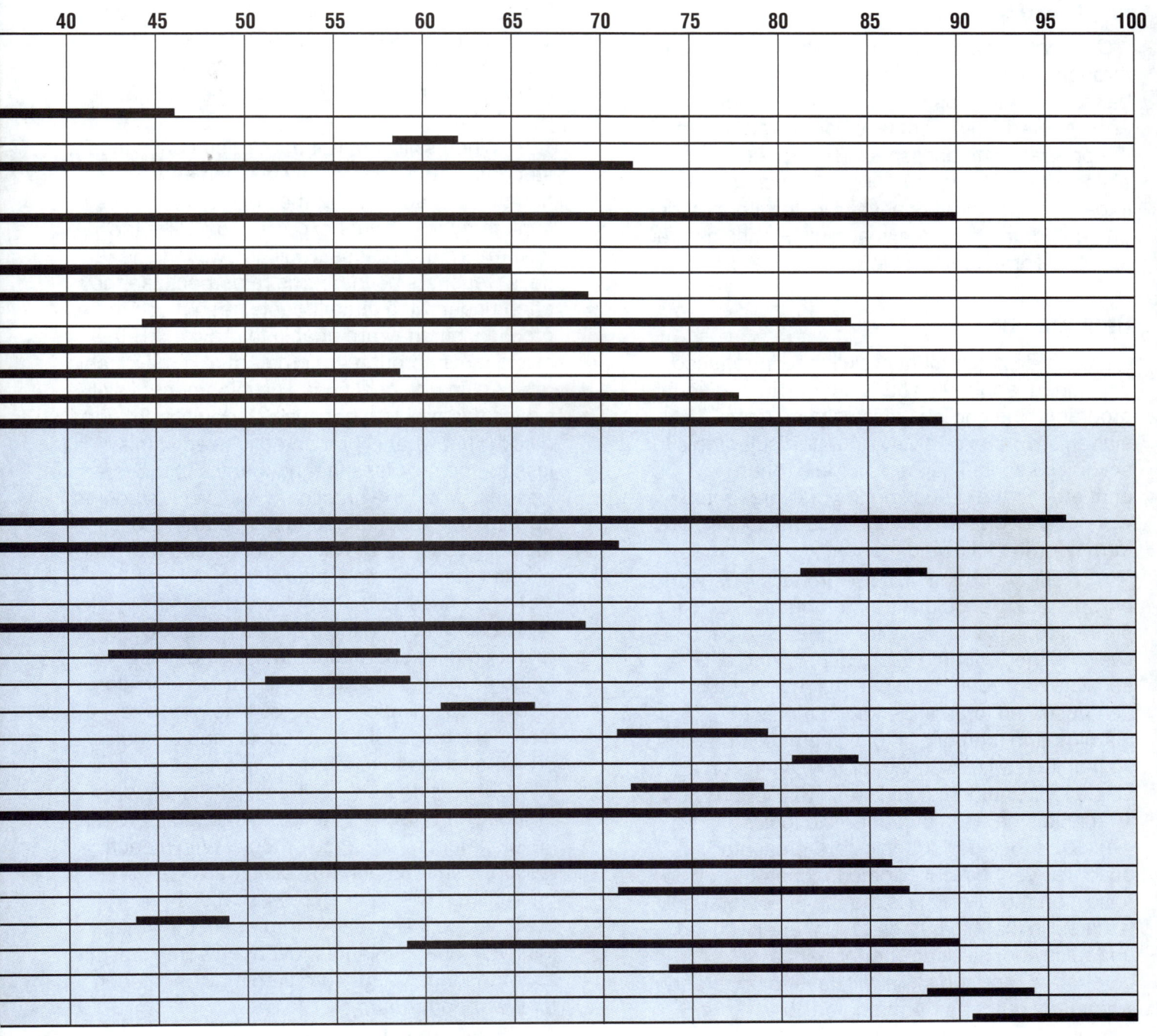

How the Program Is Different

Connecting Math Concepts differs from traditional approaches in the following ways:

Field Tested

Connecting Math Concepts has been shaped through extensive field testing and revision based on difficulties students and teachers encountered. This work was completed before the program was published. The field-test philosophy of *Connecting Math Concepts* is that if teachers or students have trouble with material presented, the program is at fault. Revisions are made to correct the problems.

Organization

The organization of how skills are introduced, developed, and reviewed is unique. In traditional programs, the curriculum is called a spiral. The students work exclusively on a particular topic for several lessons. Then a new topic (often unrelated to the preceding topic) is presented. *Connecting Math Concepts* does not follow this format for the following reasons:

a) During a period, it is not productive to work only on a single topic. If new information is being presented, it is very easy for students to become overwhelmed with the information. A more sensible procedure, and one that has been demonstrated to be superior in studies of learning and memory, is to distribute the practice, so that instead of working for 50 minutes on a single topic, students work each day for possibly 10 minutes on each of four or five topics.

b) When full-period topics are presented, it becomes very difficult for the teacher to provide review on the latest skills that have been taught. If the skills that have been taught are not used and reviewed, students' performance will deteriorate, and the skills will have to be retaught when they reappear. A more sensible organization is to present work on skills continuously (not discontinuously), so that students work on a particular topic (such as division) for part of 40 lessons, not for 5 or 6 entire lessons at a time. In this context of continuous development of skills, review becomes automatic, and reteaching becomes unnecessary because students use the skills in every lesson.

c) When skills are not developed continuously, students are required to learn a lot of new concepts during a short period and are also expected to become "automatic" in applying the new concepts and skills. For most students, adequate learning will not occur. A better method is to develop skills and concepts in small steps, so that students are not required to learn as much new material at a time, and so they receive a sufficient amount of practice to become facile or automatic in applying it.

d) When skills are not developed continuously, students and teachers may develop very negative attitudes about mastery. Students may think that they are not expected to "learn" the new material, because it will go away in a few days. Teachers become frustrated because they often understand that students need much more practice, but they are unable to provide it if they are to move through the program at a reasonable rate. Again, the continuous development of skills solves this problem because students learn very quickly that what is presented is used in this lesson, the next lesson, and many subsequent lessons. When the practice is sufficient, students develop the mindset needed for learning to mastery because the skill is something they will need in the immediate future.

e) When lessons are not clearly related to periods of time, the teacher has no precise way to gauge the performance of the students or to judge how long to spend on a particular lesson. A more reasonable procedure is to organize material into lessons that require approximately 50–55 minutes to teach.

In *Connecting Math Concepts*, skills are organized in **tracks.** A track is an ongoing development of a particular topic. Within each lesson, work from four to seven tracks is presented. The teaching presentations are designed so it is possible to present the entire lesson in 50–55 minutes (although some lessons may run longer, and more time may be needed for lower performers).

From lesson to lesson, the work on new skills develops a small step at a time, so that students are not overwhelmed with new information and receive enough practice both to master skills and to become facile with them. Students, therefore, learn quickly about learning new concepts and realize that what they are learning has value because they will use it.

Connections

The teaching and the design of the tracks in Level F permit all students to learn connections that are typically presented but not mastered by students in traditional programs.

For the teacher and the student, the track design and the development of problem-solving skills means that anything introduced in one lesson will appear in later lessons. It will be further developed and integrated into a full range of problem types. It will later become a component skill in sophisticated applications.

An example of the connections and applications is the work with related units. The chart below shows the connections that are made between topics.

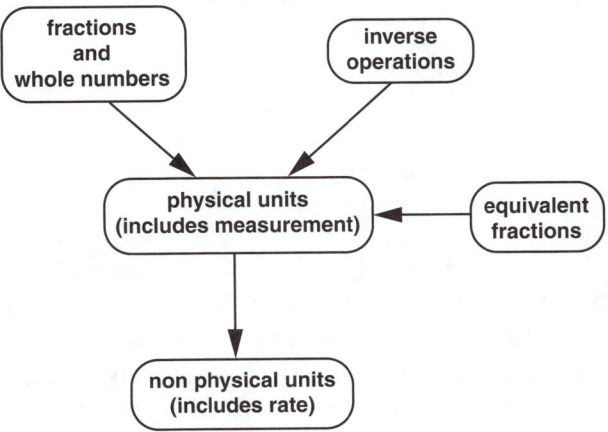

The work begins with fractions that equal whole numbers or mixed numbers. This equation shows the basic relationship:

$$\text{whole units} = \frac{\text{parts}}{\text{parts per unit}}$$

The basic analysis that students apply is to start with the denominator of the fraction. That number tells the number of parts in each whole unit. Therefore, when the number of parts is the same as the number of parts per unit, the fraction equals 1:

$$1 = \frac{8}{8}$$

The basic analysis suggests how students work problems that have the missing number in different positions. For all problems, students start with the denominator of the fraction:

$$18 = \frac{\square}{3}$$

For this problem, students start with the denominator of the fraction and work the problem: $3 \times 18 = \square$.

$$\square = \frac{27}{3}$$

For this problem, students start with the denominator and work the problem: $3 \times \square = 27$.

$$2 = \frac{6}{\square}$$

For this problem, students start with the denominator and work the problem: $\square \times 2 = 6$.

Note: The calculations that are required for the full range of related-unit problems are taught on an ongoing basis and practiced extensively before being applied to a problem-solving context.

Instead of the words **units** and **parts,** we'll use the words **boards** and **feet.** *Boards* is the whole unit. The parts are *feet.* Here's the equation:

$$\text{boards} = \frac{\text{feet}}{\text{feet per board}}$$

The key is the denominator because it gives both names and it suggests where the names go.

The same analysis can be applied to measurement units. The first name in the denominator indicates the parts:

$$\frac{\text{inches}}{\text{inches per yard}}$$

The second name indicates the whole unit:

$$\text{yards} = \frac{\text{inches}}{\text{inches per yard}}$$

Together, the names in the denominator describe what one whole must be. The name for the numerator must be the name for the parts—in this case, inches—and the number must be the same for both the numerator and denominator.

$$1 \text{ yard} = \frac{36 \text{ inches}}{36 \text{ inches per yard}}$$

Students are able to generate an equation of this form, given a fact about the parts in a whole. For example, given the fact that there are 220 yards per furlong, students can write the equation that shows the names:

$$\text{furlongs} = \frac{\text{yards}}{\text{yards per furlong}}$$

The larger unit is on the left. The smaller unit is the numerator. Given information about either the larger or the smaller unit, students can solve problems that ask about a missing value.

Example:

A furlong is 220 yards. How many yards are in 5.2 furlongs?

Students put in the number for the yards per furlong and the number for furlongs:

$$5.2 \ \text{furlongs} = \frac{\square \ \text{yards}}{220 \ \text{yards per furlong}}$$

To solve the problem, students multiply 220 by 5.2. The answer is 1144 yards.

Using the same analysis, students are able to solve similar problems.

Example:

How many furlongs are in 770 yards?

Students write the equation:

$$\square \ \text{furlongs} = \frac{770 \ \text{yards}}{220 \ \text{yards per furlong}}$$

To solve this problem, students work the problem: $220 \times \square = 770.$ They divide to figure out the missing value: $770 \div 220 = 3.5.$

Similarly, students would be able to figure out what a furlong equals by working a problem such as:

8 furlongs are 1760 yards. How many yards are in each furlong?

Students write:

$$8 \ \text{furlongs} = \frac{1760 \ \text{yards}}{\square \ \text{yards per furlong}}$$

They work the problem: $\square \times 8 = 1{,}760.$ The missing value is found by working the problem: $1760 \div 8.$ The answer is 220 yards per furlong.

Students use the same analysis to work problems that involve nonstandard units and rate. The difference between nonstandard problems and rate problems is that nonstandard problems indicate a physical relationship, or one that can be shown physically. That means that the larger unit and the smaller unit are clearly implied by the wording.

For example:

There were 46 apples in each box . . . The school had 26 students in each classroom . . . Each building had 88 windows.

For all of these applications, the denominator of the fraction is clearly determined, and there is only one possible relationship for the denominator and the numerator:

$$\frac{\text{students}}{\text{students per classroom}}$$

$$\frac{\text{apples}}{\text{apples per box}}$$

$$\frac{\text{windows}}{\text{windows per building}}$$

For rate relationships, there is no assumed physical relationship between the parts. We can say miles per hour or hours per mile. No contradiction occurs either way. Students work these problems after they have worked with convertible units (e.g., feet and inches) and nonconvertible units (e.g., apples per box). The problems are generally structured in a way that prompts the rate term (the term that refers to two units). The rate term may be in the problem or in the question:

If an insect moves at the rate of 3 inches per hour, how long does it take for the insect to move 16 inches?

If an insect moves 15 centimeters in 2 minutes, how many centimeters per minute does the insect move?

The work with related units permits students to work with problems that involve mixed numbers and answers with more than one unit name.

For example:

The fish moved at the rate of 4 fathoms per minute. How long would it take the fish to go 5 fathoms?

Students work the problem:

$$\square \text{ minutes} = \frac{5 \text{ fathoms}}{4 \text{ fathoms per minute}}$$

$$\tfrac{5}{4} \text{ minutes} = \boxed{1\tfrac{1}{4} \text{ minutes}}$$

The answer shows the fraction of a minute. Students can express this value as seconds by applying what they know about the number of seconds per minute. There are 60 seconds per minute. The mixed number 1 and 1/4 has a fraction with a denominator of 4. To convert this fraction to one that tells about seconds, the denominator must be changed to 60:

$$\frac{1}{4}\left(\frac{15}{15}\right) = \frac{15 \text{ seconds}}{60 \text{ seconds per minute}}$$

Students multiply 1/4 by 15/15 to create the fraction 15/60. The denominator of this fraction tells the number of seconds in each minute; therefore, the numerator tells the number of seconds. The answer to the problem, expressed as minutes and seconds, is 1minute and 15 seconds.

Students are able to apply this sort of conversion to any convertible units. Given the mixed number 2 and 1/4 years, the students could express the fraction as years and months, years and seasons, years and days, or years and weeks. For each conversion, students create an equivalent fraction with the appropriate denominator. The numerator of the fraction tells the number for the smaller unit

$$\frac{1}{4} = \frac{1 \text{ season}}{4 \text{ seasons per year}}$$

$$\frac{1}{4} = \frac{13 \text{ weeks}}{52 \text{ weeks per year}}$$

$$\frac{1}{4} = \frac{3 \text{ months}}{12 \text{ months per year}}$$

$$\frac{1}{4} = \frac{91\tfrac{1}{4} \text{ days}}{365 \text{ days per year}}$$

The numerators show that 1/4 of a year equals 1 season, 13 weeks, 3 months, and 91 and 1/4 days.

The work with related units incorporates calculation procedures that apply inverse operations. For example, this equation

$$19 = \frac{114}{\square}$$

implies that the students work this problem: $\square \times 19 = 114$. To work the problem, students use the logic of inverse operations. They start with the last number in the problem and undo the operation shown in the problem. The last number is 114.

What operation led to the answer of 114? *Multiplication.*
What operation undoes multiplication? *Division.*
What's the division problem? *114 divided by 19.*
The answer is 6.

Note: Students do a lot of work with inverse operations before they are introduced to related-unit problems that require applying this strategy.

Another strategy sets the stage for work with problems of this type: **How many days are in 72 hours?** Students work this problem: $24 \times \square = 72$. The problem can be solved by division.

Students also do a lot of work with equivalent fractions before working with related units.

Example:

$$\frac{5}{3} = \frac{20}{\square}$$

The fractions are equivalent, so it is possible to multiply the first fraction by 1 to get the other fraction. Students figure the fraction that equals 1 by starting on top and working the problem: $5 \times \square = 20$. The missing value is 4. So the fraction that equals 1 is 4/4.

$$\frac{5}{3} \times \frac{4}{4} = \frac{20}{\square}$$

Students can now multiply to figure out the missing value (12).

SUMMARY

Connections within Level F ensure that what students learn in one track, they will use in other tracks. The calculation procedures and the conventions that are used in the work with related units are also used in work with ratios, probability, and geometry.

Cumulative Tests

CMC Level F has cumulative tests following Lessons 30, 60, and 100. The tests sample the various key skills and discriminations taught in the previous 30-lesson or 40-lesson period, as well as important skills taught since the beginning of the level.

The tests appear in Appendix A, *Cumulative Tests*.

Each test has between 22 and 142 items. The cumulative tests require about 55 minutes to one hour and 15 minutes to complete. The final cumulative test requires about two hours to complete. The teacher presentation for each test appears first, followed by the Percent Summary, Scoring Chart, and Test Remedy Chart.

The reproducible blackline masters are presented after the teacher presentation in Appendix A. The answer key and Remedy Summaries for the cumulative tests follow the blackline masters. The Scoring Chart, answer key, Test Remedy Chart, and Remedy Summaries for the cumulative tests function like the corresponding elements of the 10-lesson mastery tests. (See 10-lesson tests, page 25.)

Scoring

Here is the Percent Summary and Scoring Chart for Cumulative Test 1. (Cumulative Test 1 follows Lesson 30, Test 3.)

CUMULATIVE TEST 1 PERCENT SUMMARY

SCORE	%	SCORE	%	SCORE	%
71	100	63	89	56	79
70	99	62	87	55	77
69	97	61	86	54	76
68	96	60	85	53	75
67	94	59	83	52	73
66	93	58	82	51	72
65	92	57	80	50	70
64	90				

CUMULATIVE TEST 1 SCORING CHART

PART	SCORE			POSSIBLE SCORE	PASSING SCORE
1	2 for each item			6	Parts 1, 2 combined 8
2	2 for each item			4	
3	EACH ITEM			6	6
	Answer 2	Unit Name 1	Total 3		
4	2 for each item			4	Parts 4, 5, 6 combined 13
5	3 for each item			6	
6	3 for each item			6	
7	1 for each item			4	4
8	3 for each item			6	Parts 8, 9, 10 combined 12
9	3 for each item			3	
10	3 for each item			6	
11	2 for each item			8	6
12	3 for each item			6	Parts 12, 13 combined 9
13	2 for each item			6	
	TOTAL			71	

The scoring chart shows how to score each item, the possible score for the part, and passing score for the part. This test has thirteen parts and a total possible score of 71.

Remedies

Remedies are to be provided for each part that is not passed. Students do not pass a part if they score less than the number of points indicated in the column "Passing Score." See 10-lesson tests, page 28, for more information about remedy procedures.

A summary table provides information on the exercises in the program that are to be presented to students who do not pass a particular part. Following is the remedies summary that appears with Cumulative Test 1.

Note: Bracketed exercises teach preskills for boldface remedies. For students who fail a part of the test but have mastered the preskills, present only the boldface remedies for that part.

CUMULATIVE TEST 1 REMEDIES	
PART	**LESSON and (EXERCISE)**
1	**1 (5), 2 (5), 3 (5), 5 (1), 6 (1)**
2	[9 (3), 10 (3), 13 (3)] **14 (2), 15 (3), 16 (3), 17 (5), 18 (7, part 9)**
3	**1 (7), 2 (7), 3 (7), 14 (7), 15 (6)**
4	[6 (2), 7 (4)] **27 (6), 28 (5), 29 (5)**
5	[11 (4)] **12 (4), 13 (4), 14 (6), 15 (2), 18 (6)**
6	[7 (2), 8 (1), 9 (1)] **25 (5), 26 (4), 27 (5)**
7	**24 (3), 25 (2)**
8	[1 (4), 2 (2)] **3 (4), 4 (4), 9 (4, steps a-c), 18 (2), 19 (2)**
9	[5 (3), 6 (4, 5)] **7 (5), 8 (3)**
10	[6 (3)] **13 (1), 14 (4)**
11 a, d	**2 (6), 3 (2), 4 (2), 5 (4)**
11 b, c	**8 (2), 10 (2), 11 (5), 18 (5)**
12	[16 (2), 17 (3)] **18 (4)**
13	**24 (5), 25 (3), 26 (2), 27 (3), 28 (4)**

For each part of the test that some students don't pass, you would present some or all of the exercises listed. (Present the exercises in the order they are listed. Present them only to the students who did not pass the part. Try to present the remedies at a time other than the regularly scheduled math period.) If students perform perfectly on a remedy, skip to the next new type of remedy exercise for that part. The lesson objective for that exercise will be boldfaced.

The goal of each remedy is to teach students well enough so they can work items of that type in the context presented in the CMC program.

Placing students who fail three or more parts of the test:

As a rule of thumb, if a student fails three or more parts of the test, the student is not placed properly in the program, which means that they will continue to have difficulty with the material. The ideal remedy would be to place students at a lesson in which they would be successful on about 90% of the tasks in each exercise.

Placing mid-year students:

The cumulative tests may be used to place students who come in after the school term has started. Here are the steps:

1) Present the Final Cumulative Test for CMC Level F.

2) Use the scoring chart to determine which of the parts the students passed.

3) Place students or provide further testing:

If the student passed no more than six parts, place the student at the beginning of Level F or test the student for placement in CMC Level E or Level Bridge. If the student passes 20–24 parts, place students so they need remedies for no more than two skills.

If the student passed seven to nine parts, give the student another cumulative test:

Cumulative Test 1, if student passed seven to fourteen parts

Cumulative Test 2, if student passed fifteen to nineteen parts

If the student passed 24 to 27 parts of the Final Cumulative Test, the student places out of CMC.

4) If you give the student another cumulative test, use the scoring chart for that test to determine which of the parts the student passed and which parts the student failed.

5) Place students so they need remedies for no more than two skills.

Here's an example:

A teacher gave a student the Final Cumulative Test (step 1).

The test was graded and the student passed thirteen parts of it (step 2).

Then, the teacher gave the student the Lesson 30 Cumulative Test 1 (per step 3).

According to the scoring chart for Cumulative Test 1 (presented earlier), the student failed parts 2, 3, 7, 12, and 13.

According to the remedies table for Cumulative Test 1 (presented earlier), the remedies for part 2 begin on Lesson 9; Part 3 begin on Lesson 1; Part 7 begin on Lesson 24; Part 12 begin on Lesson 16; and Part 13 begin on Lesson 24.

Placing the student on or before the beginning of Lesson 16 would be an acceptable placement because the student would need remedies for no more than two parts of the Cumulative Test (step 5). The student would only need remedies for Part 2 and Part 3. The other "remedies" would be included in the upcoming instruction.

Placing the student beyond Lesson 16 wouldn't be acceptable because the student would need remedies for at least three parts—Part 2, Part 3, and Part 12.

Test Preparation Materials

Level F contains six Test Preparation lessons that acquaint students with some of the formats and contents of standardized achievement tests. The material appears at the end of the *Presentation Book.*

Reproducible blackline masters for all six Test Preparation lessons follow the teacher presentation for the Test Preparation lessons.

For each of the six Test Preparation lessons, students need (1) a copy of the Multiple-Choice Response Sheet and (2) specific pages from the test preparation student booklet.

The blackline master for the Multiple-Choice Response Sheet appears immediately following the teacher presentations for the Test Preparation lessons (page 463).

Connecting Math Concepts, Level F

Multiple-Choice Response Sheet

TEST PREPARATION LESSON [ ]   NAME _____

1. A○	B○	C○	D○	E○	29. A○	B○	C○	D○	E○
2. F○	G○	H○	I○	J○	30. F○	G○	H○	I○	J○
3. A○	B○	C○	D○	E○	31. A○	B○	C○	D○	E○
4. F○	G○	H○	I○	J○	32. F○	G○	H○	I○	J○
5. A○	B○	C○	D○	E○	33. A○	B○	C○	D○	E○
6. F○	G○	H○	I○	J○	34. F○	G○	H○	I○	J○
7. A○	B○	C○	D○	E○	35. A○	B○	C○	D○	E○
8. F○	G○	H○	I○	J○	36. F○	G○	H○	I○	J○
9. A○	B○	C○	D○	E○	37. A○	B○	C○	D○	E○
10. F○	G○	H○	I○	J○	38. F○	G○	H○	I○	J○
11. A○	B○	C○	D○	E○	39. A○	B○	C○	D○	E○
12. F○	G○	H○	I○	J○	40. F○	G○	H○	I○	J○
13. A○	B○	C○	D○	E○	41. A○	B○	C○	D○	E○
14. F○	G○	H○	I○	J○	42. F○	G○	H○	I○	J○
15. A○	B○	C○	D○	E○	43. A○	B○	C○	D○	E○
16. F○	G○	H○	I○	J○	44. F○	G○	H○	I○	J○
17. A○	B○	C○	D○	E○	45. A○	B○	C○	D○	E○
18. F○	G○	H○	I○	J○	46. F○	G○	H○	I○	J○
19. A○	B○	C○	D○	E○	47. A○	B○	C○	D○	E○
20. F○	G○	H○	I○	J○	48. F○	G○	H○	I○	J○
21. A○	B○	C○	D○	E○	49. A○	B○	C○	D○	E○
22. F○	G○	H○	I○	J○	50. F○	G○	H○	I○	J○
23. A○	B○	C○	D○	E○	51. A○	B○	C○	D○	E○
24. F○	G○	H○	I○	J○	52. F○	G○	H○	I○	J○
25. A○	B○	C○	D○	E○	53. A○	B○	C○	D○	E○
26. F○	G○	H○	I○	J○	54. F○	G○	H○	I○	J○
27. A○	B○	C○	D○	E○	55. A○	B○	C○	D○	E○
28. F○	G○	H○	I○	J○	56. F○	G○	H○	I○	J○

The blackline masters pages for the student booklet corresponding to each Test Preparation lesson appear on pages 435–462 of the *Presentation Book.* This material presents the items to which students respond. They respond by filling in the appropriate bubble on their Multiple-Choice Response Sheet. Students should not write on the pages of the test-taking booklet.

The pages for each student's test-taking material may be assembled into a reusable booklet that contains the items for all 6 lessons.

Each Test Preparation lesson has teacher-directed activities. In the last exercise of each lesson, students learn test-taking strategies. These exercises present the test-taking strategies and provide students practice applying them.

Sample Lesson

Here is the teacher and student material for Lesson 3.

Test Preparation

LESSON 3

> *Note:* This exercise involves exponents. Exponents are taught in lessons 74–87 of Level F, and in the test-preparation lessons of the Bridge and Level E. If students have not yet received instruction in exponents, skip this exercise.

> *Materials Note:*
>
> Each student will need:
> - lined paper
> - test booklet and Multiple-Choice Response Sheet

EXERCISE 1
Least Common Multiple

a. (Write on the board:)

$$\frac{5}{12} + \frac{1}{8}$$

- Here's another term that you haven't learned: **least common multiple.**
- What term? (Signal.) *Least common multiple.*
- You already know how to find the least common multiple. When you find the lowest common denominator, you find the smallest multiple that is common to the denominators. That's the least common multiple.
- Read the problem. (Signal.) *5-twelfths plus one-eighth.*
- What's the denominator of the first fraction? (Signal.) *12.*
- What's the denominator of the second fraction? (Signal.) *8.*

- Get ready to tell me the first common number you would reach if you counted by 12 and by 8. (Pause.) What's the first common number? (Signal.) *24.*
  Yes, 24 is the lowest common denominator for 5-twelfths plus one-eighth. It's also the least common multiple for 12 and 8.
b. Your turn: Copy the problem in a column. Figure out the answer. After the equation, write the least common multiple in a box.
- (Observe students and give feedback.)
- (Write on the board:)

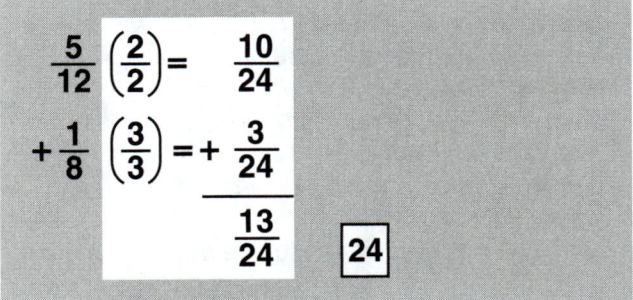

- What does 5-twelfths plus one-eighth equal? (Signal.) *13 twenty-fourths.*
- What is the least common multiple of 12 and 8? (Signal.) *24.*
c. (Direct students to write their name and indicate lesson 3 on their answer sheets and find lesson 3 in their test booklet.)
- Find item 1. √
- Items 1 and 2 are items that ask about the problem you just worked. Remember, read all the choices for each item before you mark the answer.
- Raise your hand when you've marked the answers to items 1 and 2.
- (Observe students and give feedback.)
d. Check your work.
e. Item 1. What letter did you mark? (Signal.) *C.*
f. Item 2. What letter did you mark? (Signal.) *I.*
- Yes, the least common multiple is 24.
g. Find the problem for items 3 and 4. √
- Your turn: Copy the problem. Figure out the answer. After the equation, write the least common multiple in a box.
- (Observe students and give feedback.)
- (Write on the board:)

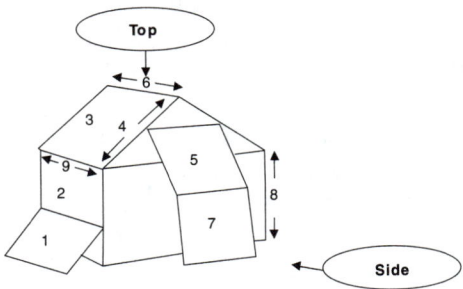

- Here's what you should have.

- Item 3. What's the answer to 10-ninths minus 8-fifteenths? (Signal.) *26 forty-fifths.*
- Item 4. What's the least common multiple of 9 and 15? (Signal.) *45.*
h. Find the problem for items 5 and 6. √
- Copy the problem. Figure out the answer. After the equation, write the least common multiple in a box.
- (Write on the board:)

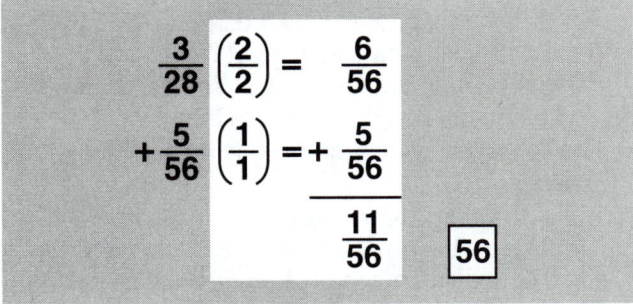

- Here's what you should have.
- Item 5. What's the answer to 3 twenty-eighths plus 5 fifty-sixths? (Signal.) *11 fifty-sixths.*
- Item 6. What's the least common multiple of twenty-eight and fifty-six? (Signal.) *56.*
i. Go back and mark the answers for items 3 through 6.
- Raise your hand when you're finished.
- (Observe students and give feedback.)
j. Check your work.
k. Item 3: What letter did you mark? (Signal.) *A.*
l. Item 4. What letter did you mark? (Signal.) *I.*
m. Item 5. What letter did you mark? (Signal.) *E.*
  The answer to 3 twenty-eighths plus 5 fifty-sixths is 11 fifty-sixths. That was not one of the choices so the answer is: None of these.
n. Item 6. What letter did you mark? (Signal.) *G.*

EXERCISE 2 DIMENSIONS AND VIEWS

a. Find the barn above item 7 in your test booklet and touch it. √
- (Teacher reference:)

- This object looks like a barn. The roof has two rectangular parts. The roofline, where the parts of the roof come together, is labeled number 6. Touch it. √

- The rectangular part of the roof you can see is labeled number 3. Touch it. √
- The edge of the roof is labeled number 4. Touch it. √
- The walls are rectangles. The front wall is labeled number 2. Touch it. √
- The line where the front wall and the roof meet is labeled number 9. Touch it. √
- A rectangular wall is leaning diagonally on the front wall. It is labeled number 1. Touch it. √
- A slanted wall is leaning against the side of the barn, resting on another wall. Those parts are labeled numbers 5 and 7. Touch them. √
- The line where two walls meet is labeled number 8. Touch it. √

b. Touch the word **top,** above the object. √
   If you follow the arrow pointing from the word **top,** you'd be looking at the object from which view? (Signal.) *The top view.*
- Touch the drawing of the top view of the object. √
   That's what the object looks like from the top view.
- Go back to the barn and touch the word **side.** √
   If you follow the arrow from the word **side,** you'd be looking at the object from which view? (Signal.) *The side view.*
- Touch the drawing of the side view. √
   That's what the object looks like from the side view.

c. (Repeat step b until firm.)

d. Back to the barn. Touch number 1. √
   Number 1 labels the lean-to in front of the barn.

e. Raise your hand when you know the letter of the lean-to in the **top** view. √
- Everybody, what's the letter of the lean-to in the **top** view? (Signal.) *P.*
   Yes, P represents number 1.

f. Raise your hand when you know the letter of the lean-to in the **side** view. √
- Everybody, what's the letter of the lean-to in the **side** view? (Signal.) *S.*

g. Touch the part of the barn labeled number 6.
   Number 6 is the roof line.
- Raise your hand when you know the letter of the roof line in the **side** view. √
- Everybody, what's the letter of the roof line in the side view? (Signal.) *Z.*
   Yes, point Z represents number 6.

h. Raise your hand when you know the letter of the roof line in the **top** view. √
- Everybody, what's the letter of the roof line in the **top** view? (Signal.) *L.*
   Yes, line L represents number 6.

i. Touch number 7.
- Raise your hand when you know the letter for number 7 in the **side** view. √
- Everybody, what's the letter for 7 in the side view? (Signal.) *U.*

j. Raise your hand when you know the letter for 7 in the **top** view. √
- Everybody, what's the letter for number 7 in the top view? (Signal.) *Q.*
   Yes, line Q represents number 7.

k. Touch number 8. √
- Raise your hand when you know the letter for number 8 in the **top** view. √
- Everybody, what's the letter for number 8 in the top view? (Signal.) *K.*
   Yes, point K represents number 8.

l. Raise your hand when you know the letter for number 8 in the **side** view. √
- Everybody, what's the letter? (Signal.) *X.*
   Yes, line X represents number 8.

m. (Repeat steps d through l until firm.)

n. Your turn: Work items 7 through 16. Pencils down when you're finished.
- (Observe students and give feedback.)

o. Check your work.

p. Item 7: Which letter in the top view represents the roof?
- What letter did you mark? (Signal.) *A.*
   Yes, choice A is part M.

q. Item 8: Which letter in the side view represents the roof line?
- What letter did you mark? (Signal.) *I.*
   Yes, choice I is point Z.

r. Item 9: Which letter in the side view represents number 2?
- What letter did you mark? (Signal.) *C.*
   Yes, choice C is line T.

s. Item 10: Which letter in the top view represents number 8?
- What letter did you mark? (Signal.) *I.*
   Yes, choice I is point K.

t. Item 11: Which letter in the side view represents the lean-to?
- What letter did you mark? (Signal.) *A.*
   Yes, choice A is line S.

u. Item 12: Which letter in the top view represents number 7?
- What letter did you mark? (Signal.) *G.*
   Yes, choice G is line Q.

v. Item 13: The line for the letter X in the side view represents one of the numbered parts of the object.
- Everybody, what letter did you mark? (Signal.) *E.*
   Yes, letter X represents number 8. Eight was not one of the choices, so you should have marked: None of the above.

w. Item 14: What letter did you mark? (Signal.) *H.*
   Yes, point Y represents line number 9.

Item 15: What letter did you mark? (Signal.) *B.*
Yes, line W, in the side views could represent the roof of the barn or the edge of the roof. The roof of the barn was the only choice listed, so that's the best description.
y. Item 16: What letter did you mark? (Signal.) *F.*
Yes, the best description for line L is the roofline.

EXERCISE 3 DISTRIBUTION

a. (Write on the board:)

> 1. $6 \times (L + R + 3)$
> 2. $(15 + H + 4H) \times 8$

b. Read problem 1. (Signal.) *6 times L plus R plus 3.*
• Say the problem with the product distributed. Get ready. (Signal.) *6 times L plus 6 times R plus 6 times 3.*
c. (Repeat step b until firm.)
• Read item 2. (Signal.) *15 plus H plus 4 H times 8.*
• Say the problem with the product distributed. (Signal.) *15 times 8 plus H times 8 plus 4 H times 8.*
d. Copy these problems. Below, distribute the product. Below the distributed products, write what each part equals.
• (Observe students and give feedback.)
• (Write to show:)

> 1. $6 \times (L + R + 3)$ =
> $(6 \times L) + (6 \times R) + (6 \times 3)$ =
> $6L + 6R + 18$ =
>
> 2. $(15 + H + 4H) \times 8$ =
> $(15 \times 8) + (H \times 8) + (4H \times 8)$ =
> $120 + 8H + 32H$ =

e. Check your work. Here's what you should have.
• Item 1. What does 6 times L plus R plus 3 equal? (Signal.) *6 L plus 6 R plus 18.*
• Item 2. What does 15 plus H plus 4 H **times** 8 equal? (Signal.) *120 plus 8 H plus 32 H.*
f. You've worked item 1 as far as you can work it. But you can work more on item 2. To finish working item 2, you combine like terms.
• Listen: Numbers without letters are like terms.
• 2 and 5 are like items. They are both whole numbers. So, you can add or subtract them.
• 2 and 5 T are not like terms. So, you can't add or subtract them.
• You can add 2 T and 5 T because they are like terms.
• You can add 2 cups and 5 cups because they are like terms.

• You can add 2 V and 5 V because they are like terms.
• But you can't add 2 V and 5 cups.
g. Can you add 2 T and 5 V? (Signal.) *No.*
• Can you add 2 cups and 5 V? (Signal.) *No.*
• Can you add 2 cups and 5? (Signal.) *No.*
• Can you add 2 cups and 5 cups? (Signal.) *Yes.*
h. You've distributed the product. Now you combine the Hs. They are like terms.
• What does 8 H plus 32 H equal? (Signal.) *40 H.*
i. Combine the like terms below.
• (Observe students and give feedback.)
• (Write to show:)

> 2. $(15 + H + 4H) \times 8$ =
> $(15 \times 8) + (H \times 8) + (4H \times 8)$ =
> $120 + 8H + 32H$ =
> $120 + 40H$ =

j. Find item 19 in your test booklet. √
• (Teacher reference:)

19 $(3T - R + 71) \times 6 =$
  A $9T - 6R + 77$
  B $18T - 6R + 77$
  C $9T - 6R + 77$
  D $18T - 6R + 426$
  E   None of the above

20 $5 \times (800 + 40 + 3) =$
  F $4000 + 200 + 15$
  G $(5 \times 800) + (5 \times 40) + (5 \times 3)$
  H 5×843
  I 4215
  J   All of the above

21 $(4T + Z - 2T) \times 12 =$
  A $12T + 12Z - 24T$
  B $24T + 12Z$
  C $38T + 12Z$
  D $(4T + Z) - 24T$
  E $24TZ$

22 $(9000 + 200 + 50 + 6) \times 10 =$
  F 9266
  G $90,000 \times 2000 \times 500 \times 60$
  H $90,205,600$
  I $92,560$
  J   None of the above

23 $20 \times (6R + 11 - R) =$
  A $100R + 31$
  B $119R + 220$
  C $100R + 220$
  D $25R + 31$
  E $6R + 220$

• Some of the answers for items 19 through 23 show the distributed products. For items 21 and 23, you'll have to combine like terms. Copy each item. Write the distributed products below. Write what each part equals. Then mark the answer for each item.
• Raise your hand when you've marked answers through item 23. Don't mark answers for items 17 and 18.
• (Observe students and give feedback.)
k. Check your work.
l. Item 19. What letter did you mark? (Signal.) *D.*
• Yes, D. It equals 18 T minus 6 R plus 426.

m. Item 20. What letter did you mark? (Signal.) *J.*
- Yes, J. 5 **times** 8 hundred plus 40 plus 3 equals 4 thousand plus 2 hundred plus 15.
- It also equals 5 times 8 hundred plus 5 times 40 plus 5 times 3.
- And it also equals 5 times 8 hundred 43 and it equals 4 thousand 2 hundred 15.
- So you should have marked: All of the above.
n. Item 21. What letter did you mark? (Signal.) *B.*
- Yes, B. 4 T plus Z minus 2 T **times** 12 equals 24 T plus 12 Z. You combined T terms.
o. Item 22. What letter did you mark? (Signal.) *I.*
- Yes, I. 9 thousand plus 2 hundred plus 50 plus 6 **times** 10 equals 92 thousand 5 hundred 60.
p. Item 23. What letter did you mark? (Signal.) *C.*
- Yes, C. 20 **times** 6 R plus 11 minus R equals 100R plus 220. You combined R terms.

EXERCISE 4 QUADRILATERALS

a. Find the figures above item 24 in your test booklet. √
- (Teacher reference:)

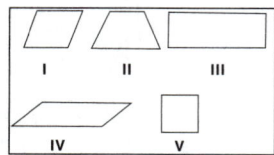

b. All of these figures have 4 sides. What's the name for any 4-sided figure? (Signal.) *Quadrilateral.*
c. (Repeat step b until firm.)
d. Use the figures numbered Roman numeral one through Roman numeral five to mark answers for items 24 through 28.
- Raise your hand when you've marked answers for items 24 through 28.
- (Observe students and give feedback.)
e. Check your work.
f. Item 24: Which figures show a rectangle?
- What letter did you mark? (Signal.) *I.*
  Yes, figures 3 and 5 are both rectangles.
g. Item 25: Which figure shows a trapezoid?
- What letter did you mark? (Signal.) *B.*
  Yes, figure 2 is a trapezoid.
h. Item 26: Which figure shows a parallelogram?
- What letter did you mark? (Signal.) *J.*
  Yes, figures 1, 3, 4, and 5 all show parallelograms, so the answer is: All of the above. That's choice J.
i. Item 27: Which figures show a rhombus?
- What letter did you mark? (Signal.) *C.*
  Yes, figures 1 and 5 show rhombuses.
j. Item 28: Which figure shows a square?
- What letter did you mark? (Signal.) *I.*
  Yes, figure 5 shows a square.

EXERCISE 5 EXPONENTS

a. Find item 31 in your test booklet. √
- (Teacher reference:)

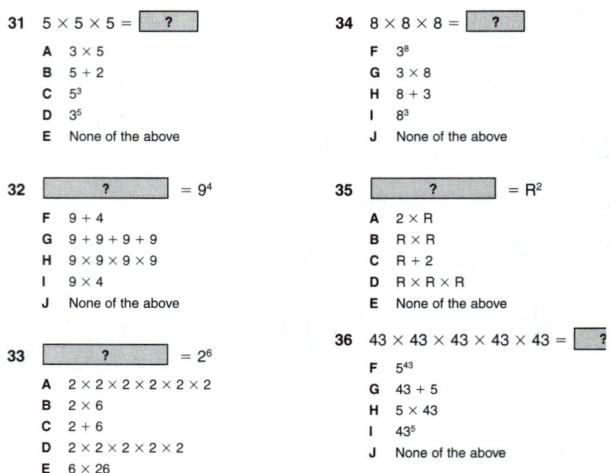

31 $5 \times 5 \times 5 =$ ☐?
- A 3×5
- B $5 + 2$
- C 5^3
- D 3^5
- E None of the above

32 ☐? $= 9^4$
- F $9 + 4$
- G $9 + 9 + 9 + 9$
- H $9 \times 9 \times 9 \times 9$
- I 9×4
- J None of the above

33 ☐? $= 2^6$
- A $2 \times 2 \times 2 \times 2 \times 2 \times 2$
- B 2×6
- C $2 + 6$
- D $2 \times 2 \times 2 \times 2 \times 2$
- E 6×26

34 $8 \times 8 \times 8 =$ ☐?
- F 3^8
- G 3×8
- H $8 + 3$
- I 8^3
- J None of the above

35 ☐? $= R^2$
- A $2 \times R$
- B $R \times R$
- C $R + 2$
- D $R \times R \times R$
- E None of the above

36 $43 \times 43 \times 43 \times 43 \times 43 =$ ☐?
- F 5^{43}
- G $43 + 5$
- H 5×43
- I 43^5
- J None of the above

- For items 31 through 36, you're going to figure out the complete equation with the multiplication, the base number, and the exponent it equals.
b. Item 31. What's the base number? (Signal.) *5.*
- Yes, 5 times 5 times 5 equals **5** to what power? (Signal.) *3.*
- Say the complete equation for item 31. (Signal.) *5 times 5 times 5 equals 5 to the third.* Yes, 5 to the third. That's 5 cubed.
c. Item 32 shows: 9 to the fourth.
- Say the complete equation for item 32. (Signal.) *9 times 9 times 9 times 9 equals 9 to the fourth.*
d. Item 33 shows: 2 to the sixth.
- Say the complete equation for item 33. (Signal.) *2 times 2 times 2 times 2 times 2 times 2 equals 2 to the sixth.*
e. Item 34. Say the complete equation. (Signal.) *8 times 8 times 8 equals 8 to the third.*
f. Your turn: Work items 31 through 36.
- Raise your hand when you've marked the answers for items 31 through 36. Don't mark answers for items 29 and 30.
- (Observe students and give feedback.)
g. Check your work.
h. Item 31. What letter did you mark? (Signal.) *C.* Yes, the answer is: 5 cubed.
i. Item 32. What letter did you mark? (Signal.) *H.*
j. Item 33. What letter did you mark? (Signal.) *A.*
k. Item 34. What letter did you mark? (Signal.) *I.* Yes, the answer is: 8 cubed.
l. Item 35. What letter did you mark? (Signal.) *B.* Yes, R times R equals R to the second. That's R squared.
m. Item 36. What letter did you mark? (Signal.) *I.* Yes, the answer is: 43 to the fifth.

EXERCISE 6   TEST-TAKING RULES
What to Do When You're Running Out of Time

a. There are three rules that help you do well when you're taking a test.

b. Rule 1: Work the problems that you can work.
- What's rule 1? (Signal.) *Work the problems that you can work.*

c. Rule 2: If you don't know how to work a problem, skip it and come back to it.
- What's rule 2? (Signal.) *If you don't know how to work a problem, skip it and come back to it.*

d. Rule 3: Make sure that each problem has one and only one answer.
- What's rule 3? (Signal.) *Make sure that each problem has one and only one answer.*

e. (Repeat steps b through d until firm.)

f. When do you start marking the items that don't have answers? (Signal.) *When there's one minute left.*

g. Look at your answer sheet and find the first item you'd mark if there was only one minute left.
- Everybody, what's the number of the first item you'd mark? (Signal.) *17.*
- Find the next item you'd mark. What's the number of the next item? (Signal.) *18.*
- What's the number of the next item you'd mark? (Signal.) *29.*
- What's the number of the next item you'd mark? (Signal.) *30.*
- What's the number of the next item you'd mark? (Signal.) *37.*
- What's the number of the **last** item you'd mark? (Signal.) *56.*

h. (Repeat step g until firm.)

i. We're going to pretend you're taking a test, and there's not much time left. You haven't answered items 17, 18, 29, 30, and 37 through 56. So when I tell you there's only one minute left, you'll mark one and only one answer for each of those items. There really aren't any problems; you're just guessing. But if this were a real test, you wouldn't have time to work the problems, so you would have to guess.

j. Get ready to mark the answers. After you're finished, we'll find out how many more points you scored by following the rules for doing well on tests.

k. Here we go. There is only one minute left. Finish up your paper.

l. (Reinforce students who quickly fill in one and only one answer for items 17, 18, 29, 30, and 37 through 56 on the answer sheet.)
- (Prompt students who don't fill answers in quickly to start marking answers more quickly.)
- (Alert students who have more than one answer filled in on any item to make sure that there's only one answer per item.)

m. (After one minute, say:) Stop working.
- Item 17. The answer is **B.** Make an X by item 17 if you didn't mark B. Make a C by item 17 if you marked B. Raise your hand if you got it right. √

n. For the for the rest of the items, I'll tell you the make-believe answer. Mark it with a C if you marked the correct answer and an X if you got it wrong. Raise your hand after I say each answer if you guessed the right one.
- Item 18. The answer is **I.** (Acknowledge students who raise their hands.)
- Item 29. The answer is **A.** (Acknowledge students who raise their hands.)
- Item 30. The answer is **F.** (Acknowledge students who raise their hands.)
- Item 37. The answer is **C.** (Acknowledge students who raise their hands.)
- (Repeat for items: 38, F; 39, A; 40, G; 41, D; 42, H; 43, B; 44, G; 45, A; 46, I; 47, C; 48, F; 49, E; 50, G; 51, C; 52, I; 53, B; 54, H; 55, A; 56, F.)

o. Count the C's you wrote next to the numbers.
- Raise your hand if you got seven or more of them correct. (Students respond.)
- Raise your hand if you got six of them correct. (Students respond.)
- Raise your hand if you got five of them correct. (Students respond.)

p. (Repeat for four, three, two, one, and zero of them correct.)
- Most of you got three to five of the items correct. You wouldn't have gotten any of these problems correct if you hadn't filled answers in for those items.

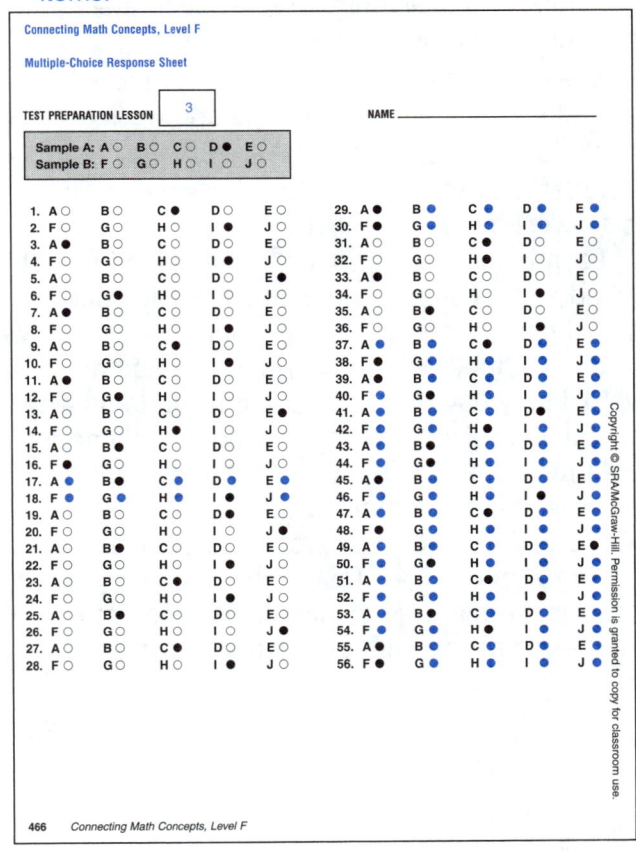

Test-Taking Strategies

The Test Preparation material teaches three critical test-taking strategies in addition to acquainting students with some of the formats and content of standardized achievement tests. In Lesson 1, Exercise 6, the three strategies are introduced:

(1) Work the problems that you can work.

(2) If you don't know how to work a problem, skip it and come back to it.

(3) Make sure that each problem has one and only one answer.

Students are taught what each rule means, and they are taught to apply the rules. The first rule, "Work the problems that you can work," means that students should write down the problems that they can't work in their head to figure out the answer. Exercises 1 and 3 of Test Preparation Lesson 3 (shown previously) show examples of problem types students are trained to work on paper. In Exercise 1, students are directed to copy each item and figure out the least common multiple before working the problem and marking the answer.

Students who are not taught this strategy often perform poorly on standardized tests because they incorrectly answer problems that they know how to work. These students don't write down and work those problems because the test directions don't tell them to, and consequently they get the wrong answer.

Throughout the remaining lessons, students are trained to apply this strategy and work various types of problems.

Students are taught that the second rule, "If you don't know how to work a problem, skip it and come back to it," means that they should not spend a lot of time on problems that they don't know how to work. Students should skip problems that they can't work and come back to them if they have time. Sometimes students who take standardized tests spend too much time on one problem and don't have time to answer many problems that they are capable of answering correctly. The practice students receive in the CMC F Test Preparation program teaches them how to avoid spending too much time on problems they can't work quickly.

The last rule, "Make sure that each item has one and only one answer," means that when there is only one minute remaining in the test, students should guess on the items that aren't filled in and mark one answer for each of them. Exercise 7 of Lesson 1 teaches students to look over their answer sheet and identify the items that are not filled in. Earlier in Test Preparation Lesson 1, students were directed to skip items 16, 27, 28, and 34. These items were omitted to provide students practice in identifying items on their Multiple-Choice Response Sheets that are not filled in.

In Lessons 2 through 6, students are directed to skip a few items on their Multiple-Choice Response Sheets. On the last exercise of these lessons, the teacher tells students to pretend that there is only one minute left and they are to mark answers for all items that don't have answers. Students mark an answer for each item. At the end of the exercise, the teacher indicates the correct answers for items that students did not mark. Students mark the correct answers and tally the number of correct guesses for those items to see how much their score improved by guessing.

Teaching the Program

Level F is designed to be presented to the entire class. You should generally be able to teach one lesson during a 50–55 minute period. Students' independent work requires another 20–30 minutes. The independent work is usually scheduled as homework.

Level F may be used as the only program presented during the school year, or it may follow the completion of the Bridge (which is a 70-lesson program). If Level F is the only program presented during the year, further math instruction may be needed following Level F. You may choose to extend the projects that are presented during the last ten lessons of the program.

If Level F is presented during the same school year as the Bridge, you will have to teach a total of 170 lessons during the year. If students have been taught well in the Bridge, they should be able to move through Level F at an accelerated rate—particularly during the first twenty lessons. You will be able to identify skills that do not require the amount of structured teaching the teacher presentation book specifies, and you should be able to complete the early lessons at a rate of more than one lesson during a period. Later lessons will probably require a full period.

Organization

Arrange seating so you can receive very quick information on high performers and lower performers. A good plan is to organize the students something like this:

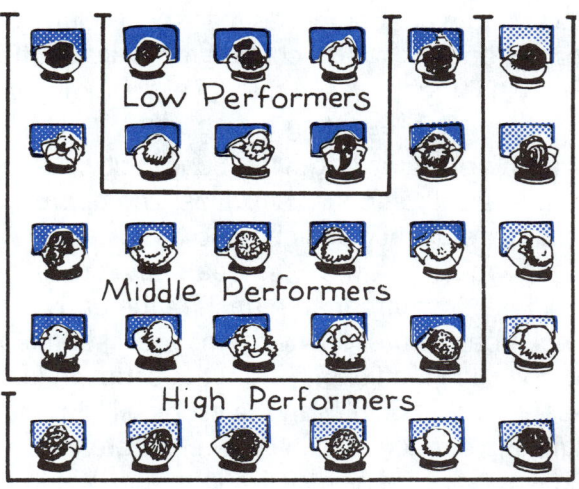

Front of Classroom

Low Performers

Middle Performers

High Performers

The lowest performers are closest to the front of the classroom. Middle performers are arranged around the lowest performers. Highest performers are arranged around the periphery. With this arrangement, you can position yourself so that, by taking a few steps during the time that students are working problems, you can sample low, average, and high performers.

Although different variations of this arrangement are possible, be careful not to seat low performers far from the front-center of the room. The highest performers, understandably, can be farthest from the center because they attend better, learn faster, and need less observation and feedback.

Teaching

When you teach the program, a basic rule is that **you should not present from the front of the room unless you are showing something on the board.**

For most of the activities, you direct students to work specified problems. For these activities, you should present from somewhere in the middle of the room (in no set place) and, as students work each problem, observe an adequate sample of students. Although you won't be able to observe every child working every problem, you can observe at least half a dozen students in approximately 30 seconds.

Rehearse the lesson before presenting it to the class. Each lesson has a script that you will follow. Don't simply read the script, but act it out. Attend to the shaded boxes that show board displays and how you'll change the displays. If you keep the changes in mind, you'll be much more fluent in presenting the activity.

Watch your wording. Non-board activities are much easier than board activities. The board formats are usually designed so they are manageable if you have an idea of the steps you'll take. If you rehearse each of the early lessons before presenting them, you'll soon learn how to present efficiently from the script. In later lessons, you should scan the list of skills at the beginning of each lesson. New skills are in boldface type. If a new skill is introduced in that lesson, rehearse it. Most of what occurs in the lesson will not be new, but a variation of what you've presented earlier, so you may not need to rehearse these activities.

Remind students about the two important rules for doing well in this program: Always work problems the way they are shown, and no shortcuts are permitted.

Remember that everything introduced will be used later. Reinforce students who apply what they learn. Always require students to rework incorrect problems.

Using the Teacher Presentation Scripts

The script for each lesson indicates precisely how to present each structured activity. The script shows what you say, what you do, and what the students' responses should be.

What you say appears in **blue** type:

You say this.

What you do appears in parentheses:

(You do this.)

The responses of the students are in italics:

Students say this.

Follow the specified wording in the script. While wording variations from the specified script are not always dangerous, you will be assured of communicating clearly with the students if you follow the script exactly. The wording is controlled, and the tasks are arranged so that they focus clearly on important aspects of what the students are to do. Although you may feel uncomfortable "reading" a script (and you may feel that the students will not pay attention), try to

present the exercises as if you're saying something important to the students. If you do, you'll find that working from a script is not difficult and that students respond well to what you say.

A sample script appears on page 14. The arrows show five different things you'll do in addition to delivering the wording in the script.

- You'll **signal** to make sure that group responses involve all the students. (arrow 1)
- You'll **"firm"** critical parts of the exercises. (arrow 2)
- You'll **pace** your presentation based on what the students are doing. You'll judge whether to proceed quickly or to wait a few more seconds before moving on with the presentation. (arrow 3)
- For some exercises, you'll **write** things on the board, and you'll often **change** the board display. (arrow 4)
- You'll **check** students' written work to ensure mastery of the content. (arrow 5)

ARROW 1: GROUP RESPONSES (SIGNAL)

Some of the tasks call for group responses. If students respond together with brisk unison responses, you receive good information about whether most of the students are performing correctly. The simplest way to **signal** students to respond together is to adopt a timing practice— just like the timing in a musical piece.

A signal follows a question, a direction (as shown by arrow 1), or the words, "Get ready."

You can signal by nodding, clapping one time, snapping your fingers, or tapping your foot. After initially establishing the timing for signals, you can signal through voice inflection only.

Students will not be able to initiate responses together at the appropriate rate unless you follow these rules:

a) Talk first. Pause a standard length of time (possibly 1 second), then signal. Never signal when you talk. Don't change the timing for your signal. Students are to respond on your signal— not after it or before it.

b) Model responses that are paced reasonably. Don't permit students to produce slow, droning responses. These are dangerous because they rob you of the information that can be derived from appropriate group responses. When students make droning responses, many of them are copying responses of others. If students are required to respond at a reasonable speaking rate, all students must initiate

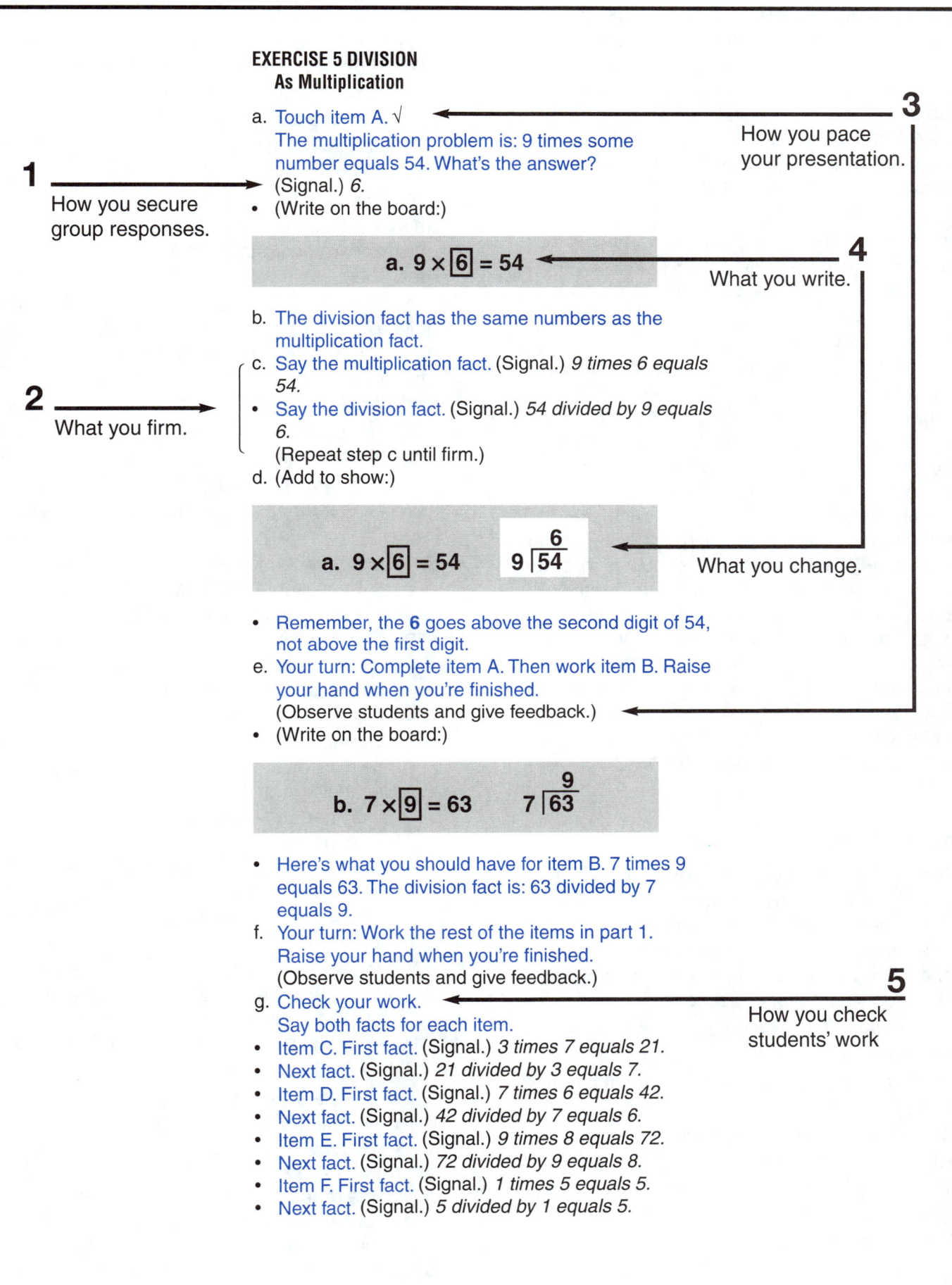

EXERCISE 5 DIVISION
As Multiplication

1 How you secure group responses.

a. Touch item A. √
The multiplication problem is: 9 times some number equals 54. What's the answer? (Signal.) *6.*
• (Write on the board:)

a. 9 × [6] = 54

3 How you pace your presentation.

4 What you write.

b. The division fact has the same numbers as the multiplication fact.
c. Say the multiplication fact. (Signal.) *9 times 6 equals 54.*
• Say the division fact. (Signal.) *54 divided by 9 equals 6.*
(Repeat step c until firm.)
d. (Add to show:)

2 What you firm.

a. 9 × [6] = 54   9)‾5‾4‾ (with 6 above)

What you change.

• Remember, the **6** goes above the second digit of 54, not above the first digit.
e. Your turn: Complete item A. Then work item B. Raise your hand when you're finished.
(Observe students and give feedback.)
• (Write on the board:)

b. 7 × [9] = 63   7)‾6‾3‾ (with 9 above)

• Here's what you should have for item B. 7 times 9 equals 63. The division fact is: 63 divided by 7 equals 9.
f. Your turn: Work the rest of the items in part 1. Raise your hand when you're finished.
(Observe students and give feedback.)
g. Check your work.
Say both facts for each item.

5 How you check students' work

• Item C. First fact. (Signal.) *3 times 7 equals 21.*
• Next fact. (Signal.) *21 divided by 3 equals 7.*
• Item D. First fact. (Signal.) *7 times 6 equals 42.*
• Next fact. (Signal.) *42 divided by 7 equals 6.*
• Item E. First fact. (Signal.) *9 times 8 equals 72.*
• Next fact. (Signal.) *72 divided by 9 equals 8.*
• Item F. First fact. (Signal.) *1 times 5 equals 5.*
• Next fact. (Signal.) *5 divided by 1 equals 5.*

responses; therefore, it is relatively easy to determine which students are not responding and which are saying the wrong response. Also, don't permit students to respond at a very fast rate or to "jump" your signal. Listen very carefully to the **first** part of the response.

To correct oral responses that are too fast or too slow, show students exactly what you want them to do. For example:

• My turn to read the equation: 14 plus some number equals 96.

• Your turn: Read the equation. *14 plus some number equals 96.*

• Good reading it the right way.

c) Do not respond with the students unless you are trying to work with them on a difficult response. You present only what is in blue. You do not say the answers with the students, and you should not move your lips or give other spurious clues about the answer.

Think of signals this way: If you use them correctly, they provide you with much diagnostic information. A weak response suggests that you should repeat a task and provides information about which students may need more help. Signals are, therefore, important early in the program. After students have learned the routine, the students will be able to respond on cue with no signal. That will happen, however, only if you always give your signals at the end of a consistent time interval after you complete what you say.

ARROW 2: FIRMING

When students make mistakes, you correct them. A correction may occur during any part of the teacher presentation that calls for the students to respond. It may also occur in connection with what the students are writing. Here are the rules for corrections:

You correct a mistake on an oral task as soon as you hear it.

A mistake is either saying the wrong thing or not responding.

To correct: Say the correct answer. Repeat the task the students missed.

For example: The multiplication problem is: 9 times some number equals 54. What's the answer? (Signal.)

If some students do not respond, respond late, or say anything but 6, there's a mistake. As soon as you hear the mistake, correct it.

Say the correct answer: It's 6.

(Repeat the task.)

Listen again: 9 times some number equals 54. What's the answer? (Signal.) *6.*

Remember that wherever there's a signal, there's a place where students may make mistakes. You correct mistakes as soon as you hear them.

A special correction is needed when correcting mistakes on tasks that teach a relationship. This type of correction is marked with a bracket in the margin and with the note **(Repeat step ____ until firm).**

The note **(Repeat step ____ until firm)** usually occurs when students must produce a series of related responses (as in step c).

When you repeat-until-firm, you follow these steps:

1) Correct the mistake. (Tell the answer and repeat the task that was missed.)

2) Return to the beginning of the specified step and present the entire step.

For example, students make a mistake in step c; when you say, Say the division fact, some students don't respond.

1) Correct the mistake:

• The division fact is 54 divided by 9 equals 6. Say the division fact. (Signal.) *54 divided by 9 equals 6.*

2) Repeat step c.

• Listen: Say the multiplication fact. (Signal.) *9 times 6 equals 54.*

• Say the division fact. (Signal.) *54 divided by 9 equals 6.*

When you repeat-until-firm, you present the context in which the mistake occurred, and the students show you through their responses whether or not the correction worked, whether or not they are firm.

The repeat-until-firm direction appears only in the most critical parts of new teaching exercises. It usually focuses on knowledge that is very important for later work. As a general procedure, follow the repeat-until-firm directions. However, if you're quite sure that the mistake was a "glitch" and does not mean that the students lack understanding, you need not follow the repeat-until-firm direction.

ARROW 3: PACING YOUR PRESENTATION AND INTERACTING WITH STUDENTS AS THEY WORK (OBSERVE STUDENTS AND GIVE FEEDBACK *AND* √.)

You should pace your verbal presentation at a normal speaking rate—as if you were telling somebody something important.

The arrows for number 3 on page 19 show two ways to pace your presentation for activities in which students write or touch or find parts of their workbook or textbook page. The first is a √. The second is a note to **(Observe students and give feedback).** Both indicate that you will interact with students. Some interactions will serve to correct mistakes. Others reinforce desired behaviors. In other words, √ and **(Observe students and give feedback)** are signals for managing students and giving feedback that helps the students perform better.

A √ is a note to check what the students are doing. It requires only a second or two. If you are positioned close to several average-performing students, check whether they are responding appropriately. If they are, proceed with the presentation.

The **(Observe students and give feedback)** direction implies a more elaborate response. You sample more students and you give feedback, not only to individual students, but to the group. Here are the basic rules for what to do and what not to do when you observe and give feedback:

a) Move from the front of the room to a place where you can quickly sample the performance of low, middle, and high performers.

b) As soon as students start to work, start observing. As you observe, make comments to the whole class. Focus these comments on students who are following directions, working quickly, and working accurately: Wow, a couple of students are almost finished. I haven't seen one mistake so far.

c) Students raise their hands to indicate that they are finished. (Alternatively, you may have them put their pencils down when they are finished. They are not to work ahead.) Acknowledge students who have finished.

d) If you observe mistakes, do **not** provide a great deal of individual help. Point out any mistakes, but do not work the problems for the students. For instance, if a student gets one of the problems wrong, point to it and say: You made a mistake. If students don't line their numerals up correctly, say: You'd better erase

that and try again. Your numerals are not lined up. If students are not following instructions that you gave, tell them: You didn't follow my directions. You have to listen very carefully.

e) Do not wait for the slowest students to complete the problems before presenting the workcheck during which students correct their work and fix any mistakes. Allow students a **reasonable** amount of time. You can usually use the middle performers as a gauge for what is reasonable. As you observe that they are completing their work, announce: Okay, you have about 10 seconds more to finish up. At the end of that time, continue with the exercise.

f) During the workcheck, continue to circulate among the students and make sure that they are checking their work. They should fix any mistakes. Praise students who are following the procedure. Allow a reasonable amount of time for them to check each problem. Do not wait for the slowest students to finish their check. Try to keep the workcheck moving as quickly as possible.

g) If you observe a serious problem that is not unique to the lowest performers, tell the class, Stop. We seem to have a serious problem. Repeat the part of the exercise that gives them information about what they are to do. ***Note:*** Do not provide new teaching or new problems. Simply repeat the part of the exercise that gives students the information they need and reassign the work. Say, for example, let's see who can get it this time.

h) While higher-performing students do their independent work, you might want to go over any parts of the lesson with the students who had trouble with the structured work (made mistakes or didn't finish). Make sure that you check all the problems worked by the lower performers and give them feedback. Show them what they have done wrong. Keep your explanations simple. The lengthier your explanations, the more they'll probably get confused. If there are serious problems, repeat the exercise that presented difficulties for the lower performers.

If you follow the procedures for observing students and giving feedback, your students will work faster and more accurately. They will also become facile at following your directions.

If you don't follow these guidelines, you may think that you are helping students, but you will actually be reinforcing undesirable behaviors.

• If you wait far beyond a reasonable time period before presenting the workcheck, you punish those who worked quickly and accurately. Soon, they will learn that there is no payoff for doing well—no praise, no recognition—but instead a long wait while you give attention to those who are slow.

• If you don't make announcements about students who are doing well and working quickly, the class will not understand what's expected. Students will probably not improve much.

• If you provide extensive individual help on independent work, you will actually reinforce students for not listening to your directions, for being dependent on your help. Furthermore, this dependency becomes contagious. If you provide extensive individual guidance, it doesn't take other students in the class long to discover that they don't have to listen to your directions, that they can raise their hand and receive help, and that students who have the most serious problems receive the most teacher attention. These expectations are the opposite of the ones you want to induce. You want students to be self-reliant and to have **reasons** for learning and remembering what you say when you instruct them. The simplest reasons are that they will use what they have just been shown and that they will receive reinforcement for performing well.

• If you provide lengthy explanations and extensive reteaching to correct any problems you observe, you run a further risk of confusing the students. Their problem is that they didn't attend to or couldn't perform on some detail that you covered in your initial presentation. So tell them what they didn't attend to and repeat the activity (or the step) that gives them the information they need. This approach shows them how to process the information you already presented. A different demonstration or explanation, however, may not show them how to link what you said originally with the new demonstration.

Because Level F is carefully designed, it is possible to teach all the students the desired behaviors of self-reliance, following instructions, and working quickly and accurately. If you follow the management rules outlined above, by the time the students have reached Lesson 15, all students should be able to complete assigned work within a reasonable period of time and have reasons to feel good about their ability to do math. That's what you want to happen. Follow the rules, and it will happen. As they improve, you should tell them about it: What's this? Everybody's finished with that problem already? That's impressive. . . .

ARROW 4: BOARD WORK

What you **write** on the board and what you **change** is indicated with display boxes. In the sample exercise, you first write the problem in step a:

$$\text{a. } 9 \times \boxed{6} = 54$$

Then you write a second problem in step d:

$$9 \overline{\smash{)}54} \;\; ^6$$

What you present initially is shown in a gray box. Any changes in that display (additions or deletions) are shown in white:

$$\text{a. } 9 \times \boxed{6} = 54 \qquad 9 \overline{\smash{)}54} \;\; ^6$$

Scanning the boxes shows both what you'll write and how you'll change the display.

ARROW 5: WORKCHECKS (CHECK YOUR WORK)

It is important to observe students to make sure that they are both attending to workchecks and correcting their mistakes.

The simplest procedure is to use a colored pen for checking. Students should write their work in pencil so they can erase and make any corrections that are necessary as they work. When you indicate that it is time for them to check their work, they put down their pencil and pick up their marking pen. If their work or answer is correct, they mark a **C** for the problem. If their work is wrong, they mark an **X**. Students correct all mistakes before handing in their work.

If you establish the organizational procedures at the beginning of the program, students will learn more and learn faster because they will be far more likely to learn from their mistakes. They will not be as tempted to cheat. Instead they will be more likely to read what they have written on their paper, and they will more easily learn that they will use everything that is introduced in the program.

Independent Work

The goal of the independent work is to provide review of previously taught work, requiring about 20–30 minutes per lesson. The student answer key, which is at the end of the student textbook, shows the answer to every other item in the independent work. This key does not show the work. Students are to refer to this answer key and see if each answer corresponds. If not, students are to rework the problem and try to obtain the correct answer.

The independent work generally has four to seven parts, each dealing with a different set of skills that have been taught. Some of the skills have been recently taught in the program; others have been taught earlier and appear in the independent work to make sure that the students retain information about how to work these problems.

Starting with Lesson 91, the independent work presents problems that are more challenging than those presented earlier in the program. Students should be able to work these problems by applying what they have been taught; however, the problems are not in the same "format" as earlier problems.

Grading Papers—Feedback

The teacher material includes a separate book called *Answer Key.* This key shows the work for all problems presented during the lesson and as independent work. When students are taught a particular method for working problems, they should follow the steps specified in the key. You should indicate that the work for a problem is wrong if the procedure is not followed.

After completing each lesson and before presenting the next lesson, follow these steps:

1) Make sure that **all** errors marked by the students during workchecks have been corrected.

Here's how a corrected mistake should look:

$$
\begin{array}{r} 6\ 0^{1}0 \\ -1\ 2\ 7 \\ \hline 5\ 2\ 3 \end{array}\!\!\times \qquad \begin{array}{r} {\scriptstyle 5\ 9} \\ \cancel{6}\ \cancel{0}\ 0 \\ -1\ 2\ 7 \\ \hline 4\ 7\ 3 \end{array}
$$

The **X** indicates that it was originally wrong. The correct work is shown next to the original problem. This procedure is better than requiring students to erase mistakes. (After they have been erased, you don't know what type of error students made and therefore, what types of adjustments would be implied for the next lesson.)

2) Conduct a workcheck for the independent work. One procedure is to provide a structured workcheck of independent work at the beginning of the period. Do not attempt to provide students with complete information about each problem. Read the answers. Students are to mark any mistakes. The workcheck should take no more than 10 minutes. Students are to correct errors at a later time. You should have some method for checking off each student's name for every lesson. The check shows that the student made corrections and turned in a corrected paper.

3) Spot check each student's corrected paper. Attend to three aspects of the student's work:

a) Were all the mistakes corrected?

b) Is the appropriate work shown for each correction (not just the right answer)?

c) Did the student perform acceptably on tasks that tended to be missed by other students?

The answer to question c provides you with information on the student's performance on difficult tasks.

4) Award points for independent work performance. A good plan is to award one point for completing the independent work, one point for correcting all mistakes, and three points for making no more than four errors on the independent work. Students who do well can earn five points for each lesson. These points can be used as part of the basis for assigning grades. The independent work would be worth approximately one-third of the grade. The rest of the grade would be based on the 10-lesson tests. (The independent work would provide students with up to 45 points for a 10-lesson period; each 10-lesson test provides another possible 100 points—100 percent for a perfect test score.) The final test, presented after Lesson 100, should also contribute points toward a final grade.

Unacceptable Error Rates

During structured activities, firm the students to make sure that they can perform on each activity quickly and accurately (if not on the first attempt, after the firming has been provided).

Students' independent work should also be monitored. Specifically, no more than 30 percent of the students should make mistakes on any independent activity. On the first lesson that a recently taught skill is perfectly "independent," error rates may exceed the ideal (more than 30 percent of the students making mistakes).

However, if an excessive error rate continues, there is a problem that should be corrected.

Consider whether the preceding steps you've taken are adequate. High error rates on independent practice may be the result of the following:

a) The students may not be placed appropriately in the program.

b) The initial presentation may not have provided adequate firming. (The students made mistakes that were not corrected. The parts of the teacher presentation in which errors occurred were not repeated until firm.)

c) Students may have received inappropriate help. (When they worked structured problems earlier, they received too much help and became dependent on the help.)

d) Students may not have been required to follow directions carefully. (If students do not learn early in the program that they are to follow directions precisely, serious problems may result later.)

Consider these possibilities if students tend to have many problems with independent work. If you look at their work as feedback about the way you are presenting material, the mistakes can be a source of information that is useful to you in showing you how to teach more effectively. Also make sure that you do not permit high error rates to continue. The simplest procedure is to show the students the types of mistakes they are making and give them information about what they should be doing. Then award bonus points (or some other form of reward) for doing well on independent work.

Inducing Appropriate Learning Behaviors

Some students may enter Level F of *Connecting Math Concepts* with notions about learning math that are highly inappropriate. For example, they may not follow directions. They may tend to copy what neighbors are doing, work ahead, and not use the specific solution strategies that have been taught. Their work may be characterized by being careless—missing signs in equations, using inappropriate shortcuts, writing answers without showing the work, and failing to write answers to word problems with the unit name. What preempts these students most from learning is their failure to attend to what the teacher says when presenting exercises. The paradox is that the more the teacher tries to

explain and to stress important points, the slower the exercise moves; the less students attend; and the less information they remember.

Exercises that are the most difficult for these students to attend to (and the most difficult for the teacher to present effectively) are those that have long explanations. The great temptation is to make these explanations seem more enticing, to dramatize and stress important parts. A far more effective procedure is to move fast enough to keep the students attentive.

The general rule is to **go fast** on parts that do not require responses from the students; **go more slowly** and be more emphatic when presenting directions for what the students are to do.

Here's an example, from Lesson 4:

a. Find part 6.
• This table should show fractions, decimal values and mixed numbers.
• You know how to write the decimal value for the fraction: The numerator of the fraction shows the digits you'll write; the denominator of the fraction shows the number of decimal places you need.
b. Write the headings for the table. Then complete row A. Raise your hand when you've done that much. (Observe students and give feedback.)
• (Write on the board:)

	Fraction	Decimal	Mixed number
a.	$\frac{789}{10}$	78.9	$78\frac{9}{10}$

• Here's the first row.
c. Your turn: Complete row B. Raise your hand when you're finished.
(Observe students and give feedback.)
• (Write to show:)

	Fraction	Decimal	Mixed number
a.	$\frac{789}{10}$	78.9	$78\frac{9}{10}$
b.	$\frac{105}{100}$	1.05	$1\frac{5}{100}$

• Here's what you should have for row B. The decimal value and the mixed number are 1 and 5-hundredths.

Step a consists of teacher talk with no student responses. Present this part of the script very quickly. Don't try to stress the points. Treat the entire step as something the students know, and therefore, something that you're summarizing in a perfunctory manner.

When you provide the instructions in step b, use a different tone of voice—one that is louder and that makes the directions very clear.

If you follow the general guideline of going fast on parts that require no student responses and of providing greater emphasis on parts that tell students what they are to do, students will attend better to what you say. They'll learn to listen because they'll learn the link between your explanations and what they'll do.

When observing students and giving feedback, make sure that you refer to the directions you gave. You indicated that the students are to write the headings and complete row A. Typically, some students will not follow these directions. They'll either fail to write the headings, or they'll complete more than row A. Treat either type of behavior as a mistake. Demonstrate early to students that they are to follow directions precisely. Students who become facile in following directions become facile in learning new material.

Use the first ten lessons of the program to establish the ground rules that you expect them to follow. You expect them to go fast, follow directions, and apply what they have learned. Use Test 1 (following Lesson 10) as the primary checkpoint for evaluating whether students should repeat some of the earlier exercises or lessons before proceeding in the program. If students perform poorly on Test 1, provide the specified remedies (see **In-program Tests,** which follow); then repeat Lessons 6 through 10. Tell students, "We're going to do these lessons again. This time, we'll do them perfectly." Be positive. Reinforce students for following directions and not making the kinds of mistakes they had been making.

Once students have completed several lessons perfectly, they will understand your criteria for what they should do to perform acceptably. For some students the relearning required to perform well is substantial, so be patient, but persistent.

10-Lesson Tests and Cumulative Tests

Level F has a series of nine criterion-referenced mastery tests that permit you to monitor the performance of students on the program material that is presented. Following every tenth lesson, a test assesses the most important skills taught in the previous ten lessons. Each 10-lesson test, therefore, provides you with information about how well prepared students are to proceed in the program.

The 10-lesson tests are presented in the student textbook.

The 10-lesson tests can also be used to help place students who are new to *Connecting Math Concepts,* Level F. (See **Cumulative Tests,** Placing mid-year students, page 9.) Several of the 10-lesson tests include content unique to CMC. Holding students accountable who haven't received instruction on content unique to CMC isn't appropriate. To alert teachers and students to material that is unique, parts of the test are gray-screened. Students new to the program should ignore material that is gray-screened in their textbooks or workbooks on the 10-lesson tests.

Part 2 of Test 2 (following) tests the solving of multiple equations to find a "mystery number." The configuration of equations used in Part 2 is unique to CMC, so the entire part is gray-screened. Part 2 of the Scoring Chart is also gray-screened to remind teachers that students new to CMC should not be held accountable for the material tested in that part. The gray screen indicates that Part 2 should not be presented to or completed by students who have not received instruction in CMC F from Lesson 10 to 20. Part 7 of the student material for Test 2 contains a segment of the directions that is gray-screened because the direction refers to a number family and a ratio table. These terms are also unique to CMC. The gray screen indicates to students who have not received instruction in CMC F from Lessons 10 to 20 that they should ignore that segment of the directions. Students are expected to complete the word problems for Part 7, however.

Sometimes, students copy from their neighbors. A good method for discovering who is copying is to spread out students during the test if it's physically possible to do so. Discrepancies in the test performance and daily performance of some students pinpoint which students may be copying.

If copying is occurring, reassign seating so that the students who tend to copy are either separated from those who know the answers or seated near the front-center of the room where it is easier for you to monitor them.

Here's Test 2, which is presented after Lesson 20:

Test 2

Part 1 | Work each item.

a. What is $\frac{60}{24}$ days?

b. What is $\frac{3}{4}$ of a year?

c. What fraction of a pound is 15 ounces?

d. What fraction of a year is 200 days?

e. What fraction of a yard is 9 inches?

f. What fraction of a foot is 9 inches?

Part 2 | Copy and complete each item.

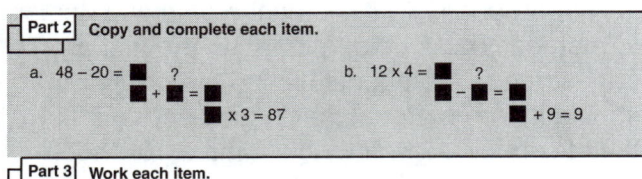

a. $48 - 20 = \blacksquare$?
$\blacksquare + \blacksquare = \blacksquare$
$\blacksquare \times 3 = 87$

b. $12 \times 4 = \blacksquare$?
$\blacksquare - \blacksquare = \blacksquare$
$\blacksquare + 9 = 9$

Part 3 | Work each item.

a. 4 identical tiles weigh 11 ounces. How much do 7 tiles weigh?

b. It takes a machine 16 seconds to make 3 holders. How long does it take the machine to make 15 holders?

Part 4 | Work each item.

a. Ginger had $145. She spent $25. Then she bought something for $42. Then she received some money for her birthday. She ended up with $300. How much money did she receive for her birthday?

b. A tank of water was full. Then 45 gallons of water were removed from the tank. Then the amount of water remaining in the tank was doubled. There were 66 gallons in the tank. How much is in a full tank?

Part 5 | Write each item in columns and work it.

a. $56 - 3.18$

b. $20.5 + 2.05 + .205$

c. $.23 \times .06$

d. $50.35 \times .2$

Part 6 | Copy and work each item. Cross out zeros if you can.

a. $2 \times \frac{280}{30} = \blacksquare$

b. $100 \times \frac{50}{3000} = \blacksquare$

c. $20 \times \frac{506}{100} = \blacksquare$

Part 7 | For each item, make a fraction number family and a ratio table. Answer the questions.

a. 26% of the crop was ripe. The entire crop weighed 160 tons. How much of the crop was ripe? How much of the crop was not ripe?

b. .7 of the soup was water. The soup contained 5 quarts of water. How much soup was there? How much of the soup was not water?

Part 8 | Work each probem. Show the answer as a proper mixed number.

a. 56
$- 6\frac{5}{8}$
$\blacksquare$

b. 2
$12\frac{9}{10}$
$+ 3\frac{5}{10}$
$\blacksquare$

c. 9
$- 7\frac{3}{20}$
$\blacksquare$

TEST ANSWER KEY

The teacher's *Answer Key* provides the correct answers for each lesson and 10-lesson test. The answer key for each test shows the correct work for each item, and a table for assigning percent grades based on the number of points earned.

Here's the answer key for Test 2:

TEST 2 PERCENT SUMMARY

SCORE	%	SCORE	%	SCORE	%
56	100	50	89	44	79
55	98	49	88	43	77
54	96	48	86	42	75
53	95	47	84	41	73
52	93	46	82	40	71
51	91	45	80	39	70

TEST 2 SCORING CHART

PART	SCORE				POSSIBLE SCORE	PASSING SCORE
1	2 for each item				12	10
2	2 for each item				4	4
3	3 for each item				6	Parts 3, 4 combined
4	3 for each item				6	9
5	2 for each item				8	6
6	2 for each item				6	6
7	EACH ITEM				8	6
	Fraction number family	Ratio table	Answer	Total		
	1	1	2	4		
8	2 for each item				6	6
	TOTAL				56	

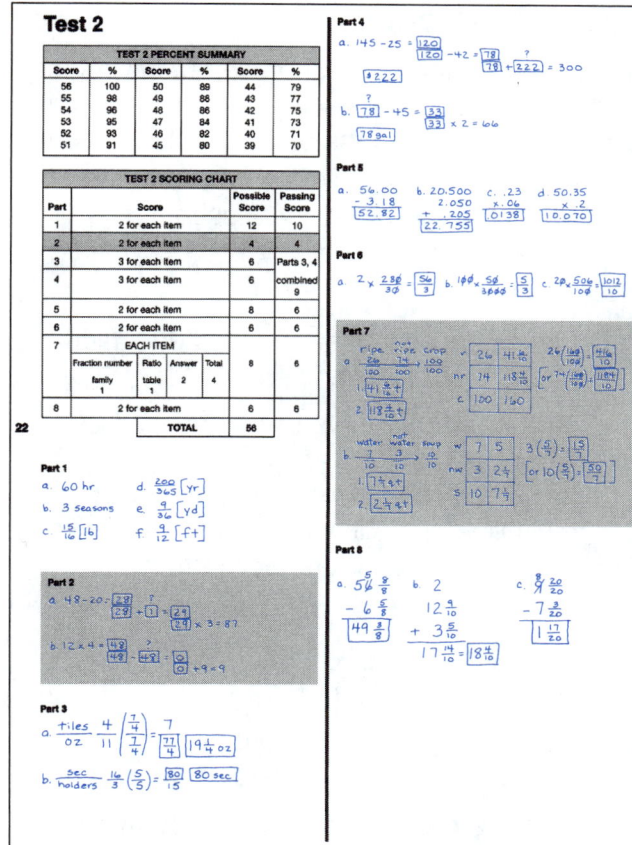

The percent-conversion table shows the percentage grade you'd award for students who have a perfect score of 56, a score of 55, and so forth.

The answers for each part of the test indicate the possible points for each item, the possible points for the part, and the passing criterion.

Students fail a part of the test if they score fewer than the specified number of passing points.

The Test 2 Scoring Chart indicates that the passing score for Parts 3 and 4 combined is 9 points. If a student earns fewer than 9 points for those parts, the student fails the part(s) in which the student made errors. If the student missed one problem in each of the parts, the student fails both parts. If a student missed two problems in Part 3, and didn't make any errors in Part 4, the student fails only Part 3.

Note that points are sometimes awarded for working different parts of the problem. For example, for Part 7, students earn 1 point for the fraction number family, 1 point for the ratio table, and 2 points for the answer.

MARKING IN-PROGRAM TESTS

Use the criteria in the *Answer Key* for marking each student's test. Record the results on the **Group Summary of Test Performance** (provided on page 154 of the *Teacher's Guide*).

Here's how the results could be summarized following Test 2:

Group Summary of Test Performance

Note: Test remedies are specified in the Answer Key. Percent Summary is also specified in the

	Test 2								
	Check parts not passed								Total %
Name	1	2	3	4	5	6	7	8	
1. Amanda Adams		✓							97%
2. William Alberts		✓			✓		✓		88%
3. Henry Bowman									100%
4. Phillip Caswell	✓			✓		✓	✓	✓	78%
19. Zoë Fowler				✓					97%
20. Chan Won Lee	✓	✓			✓			✓	84%
Number of students Not Passed = NP	6	5	3	3	7	4	4	3	
Total number of students = T	20	20	20	20	20	20	20	20	
Remedy needed if NP/T = 25% or more	R	R			R				

The summary sheet provides you with a cumulative record of each student's performance on the 10-lesson tests. Summarize each student's performance.

• Make a check in the appropriate columns to indicate any part of the test that was failed.

• At the bottom of each column, write the total number of failures for that part and the total number of students in the class. Then divide the number of failures by the number of students to determine the failure rate for each part.

• Provide a group remedy for each part that has a failure rate of 25 percent (.25) or more.

The *Answer Key* specifies remedies for each test. Any necessary remedies should be presented before the next lesson (Lesson 21).

Here are the remedies for Mastery Test 2:

Note: Provide any remedies for Test 2 before beginning Lesson 21. If more than 1/4 of the students did not pass a test part, present a remedy for that part. You are granted permission to reproduce the Remedy Summary Sheet at the back of the Teacher's Guide.

TEST 2 REMEDIES			
TEST 2	**LESSON**	**EXERCISE**	**TEXTBOOK PART**
Part 1	13	2	1
	17	—	10 (IW)
	19	—	7 (IW)
Part 2	18	2	2
	19	2	2
Part 3	14	4	4
	15	—	12 (IW)
Part 4	16	1	1
	17	1	1
Part 5	11	5	8
	18	5	5
Part 6	18	4	4
	19	—	6 (IW)
Part 7	15	2	2
	18	6	6
Part 8	15	3	3
	17	5	7
	18	—	9 (IW)

If the same students predictably fail parts of the test, it may be possible to provide remedies for those students as the others do a manageable extension activity. The program is designed so that students use everything that has been taught. If individual students are weak on a particular skill, they will have trouble later in the program when that particular skill becomes a component in a larger operation or more complex application.

If students consistently fail tests, they are probably not placed appropriately in CMC F.

On the completed Group Test Summary for Mastery Test 2 (shown earlier), .25 or more of the students failed parts 1, 2, and 5. After the teacher provides group remedies, William Alberts, Phillip Caswell, Zoë Fowler, and Chan Won Lee need individual remedies. Phillip Caswell failed several parts. If Phillip receives individual remedies for parts 4, 6, 7, and 8, he should pass the retest for Test 2. If he is unable to pass the retest or later fails Mastery Test 3, he should probably be placed in a less challenging group.

Lesson Objectives

Each lesson in the *Presentation Book* begins with objectives that show the various skills that are being taught and the order of activities in the lesson.

Here are the objectives for Lesson 8:

Objectives

- Make fractions that are based on a fact about related units. (Exercise 1)

- **Multiply decimal values.** (Exercise 2)
  Note: Students determine the number of decimal places in the values that are multiplied and show the same number of places in the answer. For example:

$$\begin{array}{r} 2.6 \\ \times\ .05 \\ \hline .130 \end{array}$$

- Work a word problem that requires inverse operations. (Exercise 3)

- **Complete a fraction number family that has names.** (Exercise 5)
  Note: Problems are of the form:

green   other   bottles
$$\xrightarrow{\ \ \frac{3}{11}\ \ }$$

What's the fraction for the other bottles? Students make the complete number family and box the fraction that answers the question:

green other   bottles
$$\frac{3}{11}\quad \boxed{\frac{8}{11}} \longrightarrow \frac{11}{11}$$

Some of the objectives are in regular type:
- Work a word problem that requires inverse operations. (Exercise 3)

These are objectives for exercises that are versions of exercises from a preceding lesson.

Some of the objectives are in bold type:
- **Multiply decimal values.** (Exercise 2)

These objectives signal a new activity or a variation that is more difficult than earlier examples. It's a good idea to rehearse exercises signaled by bold type before presenting them to the students.

Tracks

The various **tracks** in Level F move toward problem-solving applications. To master any type of advanced problem, the students must have knowledge about how to translate the problem into an equation or into a form that permits calculation. Once the problem has been appropriately translated, the students must have the tool skills needed to perform the calculations. Level F teaches the tool skills first, then presents problem-solving applications that use the tool skills. The tracks are divided accordingly into **tool skills** and **applications.**

TOOL SKILLS

The tool skills are presented first in this guide. They include all the calculation skills, basic relationships (e.g., between multiplication and division and between division and fractions), and the component representations (such as number families) that will be used later in the more elaborate applications. Level F assumes that the students have the following tool skills: solving addition, subtraction, multiplication, and division problems with a calculator. Tool skills taught in Level F include whole-number operations, number relationships, operational relationships, fractions, mixed-number operations, number families, decimal operations, and measurement/geometry facts.

Whole-Number Operations

DIVISION

From the beginning of Level F, students work division problems that divide by a single digit. Students express the answer as a whole number or a mixed number. This convention has been established in the Bridge or in Level E. Students are not taught how to work these problems in Level F. Students write the answer like this:

$$92\frac{1}{5}$$
$$5\overline{)461}$$

Not like this:

$$92 \text{ r } 1$$
$$5\overline{)461}$$

The reason for this convention is that division is the inverse operation of multiplication. This relationship is maintained only if the answer is shown as a mixed number. The mixed number answer times the divisor gives the dividend. Note that students may solve these problems in different ways. Students who have been through the Bridge may solve the problems by "long division." Students who have been through Level E solve the problems by "short division," which does not involve showing work in columns below the dividend.

Long Division

In Level F, starting with Lesson 21, students learn to work some problems using a long-division algorithm. These problems divide by a two-digit value and have a two-digit answer:

$$25\frac{48}{49}$$
$$49\overline{)1273}$$
$$\underline{-\ 98}$$
$$293$$
$$\underline{-245}$$
$$48$$

The program assumes that students are able to work problems that divide by a two-digit value and have a one-digit answer:

$$2\frac{29}{49}$$
$$49\overline{)127}$$
$$\underline{-\ 98}$$
$$29$$

Here's part of the introduction for Lesson 21:
- (Write on the board:)

$$52\overline{)4764}$$

- To get the first digit of the answer, you work the problem: 476 divided by 52.
- The estimation problem is 47 divided by 5. What's the answer? (Signal.) *9.*
- (Write to show:)

$$9$$
$$52\overline{)4764}$$

- Copy the problem. Do the multiplication for 9 times 52. Make sure you write the answer under the underlined part. Don't write it under the 4. Raise your hand when you've written what 9 times 52 equals. √
- (Write to show:)

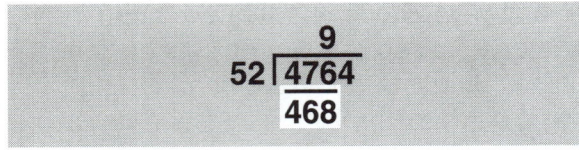

$$52\overline{)4764} \quad {}^9$$
$$468$$

- Here's what you should have. Now you subtract 468 from 476 and write the answer. Do it. √
- (Write to show:)

$$52\overline{)4764} \quad {}^9$$
$$-468$$
$$8$$

- You know that the problem is not completed because there's not a whole number in the answer above the 4.
- Complete the problem. Bring down the 4. Then work the division problem: 84 divided by 52. √ (Observe students and give feedback.)
- (Write to show:)

$$91\frac{32}{52}$$
$$52\overline{)4764}$$
$$-468$$
$$84$$
$$-52$$
$$32$$

- Here's what you should have. The answer is 91 and 32/52. Raise your hand if you got it right.

Teaching note: The most common mistakes students make are:
- They don't write the first digit of the answer where it belongs.
- They don't write the product of 52 times 9 directly below 476.
- They don't show the subtraction sign.
- They don't bring down the next digit.
- They don't write the answer as a mixed number or they "reverse" the numbers in the fraction part of the answer.

The underlined part gives the students information about where to write the first digit of the answer, and where to write the product of 52 times 9. The underlining appears for two lessons.

To correct mistakes of number placement (either in the answer or below 476) follow these steps:

Ask the students, "What's the last underlined digit? . . . You write the first digit of the answer directly above that digit. You write the answer to 52 times 9 directly below the underlined digits."

If students forget the subtraction sign, ask, "What operation are you doing with 476 and 468? . . . Show the sign."

If students don't bring down the 4, tell them, "Read the division problem you'll work for the last digit of the answer." *84 divided by 52.*

"You can't work that problem. Bring down the 4 and you'll have a problem you can work."

After students bring down the 4, say, "Tell me the problem you'll work for the last digit." *84 divided by 52.* "You can work that problem."

If students show the remainder as a whole number (r 32), point out that they must divide that remainder by 52. That's the fraction: 32/52.

If students write the remainder as 52/32, say, "Read the problem you started with . . . What are you dividing by? . . . That's what you divide the remainder by. Write the remainder and show it is divided by 52. That's 32 divided by 52. Remember, the remainder must be less than 1."

DISTRIBUTIVE PROPERTY

Starting in Lesson 58, students work problems that involve both multiplication and addition. These problems show that the same answer is obtained whether the addition is done first or the multiplication is done first.

Example:

$$4 + 6 + 1$$
$$\times \qquad 5$$

In Lesson 58, students do the multiplication for each part. They copy the plus signs in the answer then do the multiplication for each of the top numbers. The answer they get is: 20 + 30 + 5.

In later lessons, students work the same type of problems by first adding the values on top, then doing the multiplication. Students also use this technique to check the work they do when they work problems the longer way. For the problem above, students would add 4, 6, and 1. Then they multiply the sum (11) by 5. This work sets the stage for similar problems that have signed numbers.

COMBINING TERMS

Another skill that sets the stage for signed numbers is combining terms. In Lesson 59, this skill is introduced. Students follow the practice of combining all the numbers with the same sign, then working a simplified problem. In Lesson 59, for instance, students work the problem:

$$
\begin{array}{r}
14 \\
-4 \\
-2 \\
-6 \\
\hline
\end{array}
$$

Students first combine all the minus values (-12), then work the simplified problem: $14 - 12$.

In subsequent lessons, students work similar problems in which all the values are signed and values with the same sign may not be juxtaposed.

For example:

$$-11 + 31 + 6 - 17 + 5 - 12 = \square$$

Students first combine all the positive values and write the value with a sign (42), and do the same thing with the negative values (40). Students work the problem:

$$
\begin{array}{r}
+42 \\
-40 \\
\hline
\boxed{+2}
\end{array}
$$

Number Relationships

Beginning with Lesson 1, students convert fractions to decimals. The fractions are tenths, hundredths, and thousandths. Students write an equation to show the corresponding decimal values.

Examples:

$$\frac{5}{100} = .05 \qquad \frac{856}{1000} = .856 \qquad \frac{7}{10} = .7$$

The denominator tells the number of decimal places. For a fraction with a denominator of 10, students need one decimal place; for 100, students need two decimal places; for 1000, students need three decimal places. The fraction 24/100 requires two decimal places. The numerator shows the digits needed in the decimal value—24. The decimal value is .24.

To convert decimals into fractions, students use the digits in the decimal number as the numerator of the fraction. The number of decimal places indicates whether the fraction has a denominator of 10, 100, or 1000.

Examples:

$$1.24 = \frac{124}{100} \qquad .003 = \frac{3}{1000} \qquad \frac{55}{100} = .55$$

Students also convert mixed numbers or whole numbers into improper fractions. For example:

$$3\frac{5}{8} = \frac{29}{8} \qquad 7 = \frac{35}{5}$$

To convert a mixed number, students start with the denominator of the fraction, multiply by the whole number, then add the numerator of the mixed number. For 5 and 2/3, students multiply 3 by 5, then add 2. The improper fraction is 17/3:

$$5\frac{2}{3} = \frac{17}{3}$$

Note that this is a prototype of the equation that students will later use to do extensive conversions with measurement units. The fraction is on the right; the mixed number or whole number is on the left.

Students review the procedure of converting any improper fraction into a mixed number. They read the fraction as a division problem and work it. The fraction 17/3 is read as 17 divided by 3. When it is worked as a long division problem, the answer is 5 and 2/3.

Students also review percents, starting in Lesson 11. They show percents as fractions with a denominator of 100. 4% is 4/100.

Starting in Lesson 41, students learn relationships between simple fractions and percents. Here are the facts they learn:

$$1/2 = 50\%$$
$$1/4 = 25\%$$
$$1/5 = 20\%$$
$$1/10 = 10\%$$
$$1/20 = 5\%$$

Students also use these facts to convert fractions such as 6/10 or 2/5 into percents. (If 1/10 = 10%, 6/10 = 60%, if 1/5 = 20%, 2/5 = 40%.)

All of these conversions are extended to table formats.

	Mixed number	Fraction
a.		$\frac{26}{3}$
b.	$5\frac{1}{4}$	
c.		$\frac{19}{7}$
d.		$\frac{62}{9}$
e.	$10\frac{5}{6}$	

	Fraction	Decimal	%
a.	$\frac{789}{100}$		
b.		1.05	
c.	$\frac{1949}{100}$		
d.			201%
e.		.86	

Operational Relationships

INVERSE OPERATIONS

Students review basic operational relationships, starting with Lesson 1. They review inverse operations and how they interact. Addition and subtraction are inverse operations; multiplication and division are inverse operations. Any operation is undone by its inverse. Adding 11 is undone by subtracting 11. Multiplying by 34 is undone by dividing by 34. This relationship is initially applied to problems of the form:

$$\square \times 3 = 21$$

$$\square - 4 = 21$$

Students write the undoing problem. They start with the last number in the problem and use the inverse of the operation that is shown.

Here's part of the exercise from Lesson 1:

> **Sample problems**
>
> 1. ■ × 3 = 42   2. ■ − 10 = 85
>
> a. ■ + 14 = 100   b. ■ ÷ 2 = 51   c. ■ × 5 = 95
>
> d. ■ ÷ 7 = 49   e. ■ − 28 = 71

c. These are problems that have the first number missing.

- You can figure out that number by working backwards and undoing the operation.
d. Sample problem 1. First you identify the operation. Everybody, what's the operation? (Signal.) *Multiplication.*
- Which operation undoes multiplication? (Signal.) *Division.*
- Start with the last number in the problem and say the **division problem.** (Signal.) *42 divided by 3.*
- The answer is 14. If you start with 14 and multiply by 3, you end up with 42.
e. Sample problem 2. What's the operation? (Signal.) *Subtraction.*
- What's the operation that undoes subtraction? (Signal.) *Addition.*
- Start with the last number and say the addition problem. (Signal.) *85 plus 10.*
- Raise your hand when you know the answer. √
- Everybody, what's the answer? (Signal.) *95.*
- Yes, if you start with 95 and subtract 10, you end up with 85.
f. For each problem in part 5, you'll figure out the **first** number. You'll work the undoing problem that starts with the **last** number.
g. Item A. What's the operation? (Signal.) *Addition.*
- Write the undoing problem and the answer. Raise your hand when you're finished. (Observe students and give feedback.)
- (Write on the board:)

$$\begin{array}{r} 100 \\ \text{a.} \quad -\ 14 \\ \hline \boxed{86} \end{array}$$

- Here's what you should have. 100 minus 14 is 86.

> **Teaching note:** If students have trouble with any of these problems, ask the following questions:
> "What operation does the problem show? What operation will you use to undo _____?
> Say the problem you'll work."
> If students are weak on any step, give them practice with different problems that have the first number missing. Do not proceed in the program unless students are firm in working the problems.

In Lessons 3 and 4, students apply the inverse-operation logic to problems that have more than one equation.

Here's an example from Lesson 4:

$$\begin{array}{r} \overset{?}{\square} - 7 = \square \\ \square \times 2 = \square \\ \square + 10 = 16 \end{array}$$

Students start with the last equation and work backward. When they write a missing number for either the last equation or the middle equation, they write that answer in two places. The answer to 16 minus 10 is 6. They write it in two places:

$$\boxed{}^{?} - 7 = \boxed{}$$
$$\boxed{} \times 2 = \boxed{6}$$
$$\boxed{6} + 10 = 16$$

The answer to 6 divided by 2 is 3. They write it in two places:

$$\boxed{}^{?} - 7 = \boxed{3}$$
$$\boxed{3} \times 2 = \boxed{6}$$
$$\boxed{6} + 10 = 16$$

Now they figure out the first number in the problem by adding: 3 plus 7.

In Lesson 45, students use inverse operations to find the missing denominator in problems of the form:

$$3 = \frac{270}{\boxed{}}$$

Students first write the multiplication problems for finding the missing value:

$$\boxed{} \times 3 = 270$$

Students then express the missing factor as a division problem: $3\overline{)270}$. The missing factor is 90.

Here's part of the exercise from Lesson 45:

a. $8 = \dfrac{56}{\blacksquare}$ b. $7 = \dfrac{91}{\blacksquare}$

c. $17 = \dfrac{34}{\blacksquare}$ d. $5 = \dfrac{2}{\blacksquare}$

c. Problem A: 8 equals 56 over some number.
• Start with the box and write the multiplication equation. Then figure out the missing value and write it. Raise your hand when you're finished. (Observe students and give feedback.)
• (Write on the board:)

a. $\boxed{7} \times 8 = 56$

• Here's what you should have. Box times 8 equals 56. So the box is 56 divided by 8. That's 7.

d. Write the equation and the answer for problem B. Raise your hand when you're finished. (Observe students and give feedback.)
• (Write on the board:)

b. $\boxed{13} \times 7 = 91$ $7\overline{)91}^{\,13}$

• Here's what you should have. Box times 7 equals 91. The missing value is 91 divided by 7. That's 13.

This work sets the stage for some of the rate problems that students will solve (starting with Lesson 38). These problems involve units such as miles per hour or parts per gallon.

In Lessons 5 and 6, students use inverse-operation logic to work problems for which the missing factor is a fraction. For example:

$$\boxed{} \times 4 = 3$$

If the first factor in the problem is missing, students say a division problem: 3 divided by 4. That value can be expressed as the fraction 3/4. Students write the same fraction when the second factor in the problem is missing:

$$4 \times \boxed{\dfrac{3}{4}} = 3$$

In Lessons 5 and 6, students write the fraction for the division.

Here's part of the exercise from Lesson 6:

a. $10 \times \blacksquare = 6$ b. $5 \times \blacksquare = 4$ c. $\blacksquare \times 8 = 15$

d. $20 \times \blacksquare = 38$ e. $\blacksquare \times 11 = 52$

c. Problem A: 10 times some value equals 6.
• Say the division problem for the missing value. (Signal.) *6 divided by 10.*
• Write the complete equation. Show the missing value as a fraction. Raise your hand when you're finished. (Observe students and give feedback.)
• (Write on the board:)

a. $10 \times \boxed{\dfrac{6}{10}} = 6$

• Here's what you should have.
d. Your turn: Work the rest of the problems in part 4. Show the missing value as a fraction, even if it is more than 1. Remember, the value on the right side of the equals sign is always the numerator of the fraction. Raise your hand when you're finished. (Observe students and give feedback.)

e. (Write on the board:)

$$b. \quad 5 \times \boxed{\frac{4}{5}} = 4 \qquad c. \quad \boxed{\frac{15}{8}} \times 8 = 15$$

$$d. \quad 20 \times \boxed{\frac{38}{20}} = 38 \qquad e. \quad \boxed{\frac{52}{11}} \times 11 = 52$$

- Here's what you should have for problems B through E.
f. You're going to check the first three problems on your calculator.
g. Problem A. Listen: Say the division problem for the fraction. (Signal.) *6 divided by 10.*
- Start with 10 and say the whole problem you'll work on your calculator. (Signal.) *10 times 6 divided by 10 equals.*
- (Repeat step g until firm.)
h. Work the problem. You should end up with 6. Raise your hand when you're finished.
(Observe students and give feedback.)
i. Your turn: Check problems B and C. Raise your hand when you're finished.
(Observe students and give feedback.)

Teaching note: Students may write fractions that are upside down. For example, they may show the missing factor in problem A as 10/6. There are several ways to correct this error. The simplest is to compare the numbers that appear on either side of the equals sign. In this case, 10 is on the left and 6 is on the right.

"You're starting with 10 and multiplying to end up with 6. Are you going to a number that is less than 10 or more than 10? . . . So, is the missing value less than 1 or more than 1? . . . It's less than 1, so it can't be 10/6. What is it?"

If students continue to make mistakes, have them repeat all the missing-factor problems in Lessons 5 and 6 before continuing in the program.

Students apply inverse operations to find a missing value in the first column of a table.

For example:

Each value in the first column is multiplied by the same factor, yielding each value in the second column. Students first work a row with two numbers to figure out the missing factor:

$$12 \left(\frac{8}{12} \right) = 8$$

Now students can write a multiplication equation for each row. For the top row, students work the problem:

$$\blacksquare \times \frac{8}{12} = 10$$

Using inverse operations, students work the problem to figure out the missing value.

$$10 \div \frac{8}{12}$$

The same procedure may be applied to each row of the table.

PLACE VALUE

Students work problems that involve values that range from millions through less than 1. An assumption is that they can write these numbers, line them up appropriately in columns, and perform basic calculations. In Lessons 1 and 2, students review simplifying decimals that end in zeros. For example, they rewrite .0700 as .07. They also use their calculator to confirm that the values are equivalent. (They enter the value .0700 and =. The calculator displays .07.)

Starting in Lesson 24, students review rounding. In Level F, students round to hundredths. They follow the procedure of looking at the third digit after the decimal point. If that digit is 5 or more, they round the hundredths digit up. If the third digit after the decimal point is less than 5, students copy that digit.

Example:

9.235 rounds to 9.24
9.234 rounds to 9.23

Teaching note: Students should be firm on the conventions for this rounding. If they have difficulty, have them follow these steps: "Make a line under the second digit after the decimal point. That's the digit you'll round. Circle the next digit if it is 5 or more.

Fraction Operations

Level F assumes that students are able to add and subtract fractions with like denominators, work basic equivalent-fraction problems, and work multiplication problems that involve two fractions or a fraction and a whole number. Level F reviews these problem types and also provides work with lowest common denominators and complex equivalent fractions.

Here's part of the work with complex equivalent fractions from Lesson 11:

a. $\dfrac{3}{5} \left(\blacksquare\right) = \dfrac{\blacksquare}{7}$ b. $\dfrac{7}{9} \left(\blacksquare\right) = \dfrac{3}{\blacksquare}\ \blacksquare$

c. Problem A. Can you work the problem for the numerators or for the denominators? (Signal.) *Denominators.*
- Say that problem. (Signal.) *5 times some value equals 7.*
- What's the missing value? (Signal.) *7-fifths.*
- Copy the equation. Show the missing fraction that equals 1. Raise your hand when you've done that much. √
- (Write on the board:)

a. $\quad \dfrac{3}{5} \left(\dfrac{\frac{7}{5}}{\frac{7}{5}}\right) = \dfrac{\square}{7}$

- Here's what you should have so far.
- Now multiply on top. Write the fraction. Then figure out the whole number or the mixed number you end up with. Raise you hand when you're finished. (Observe students and give feedback.)
- (Write to show:)

a. $\quad \dfrac{3}{5} \left(\dfrac{\frac{7}{5}}{\frac{7}{5}}\right) = \dfrac{\frac{21}{5}}{7}\quad \boxed{4\ \frac{1}{5}}$

- Here's what you should have. You end up with 21/5. That's 4 and 1/5. Raise your hand if you got everything right.

The strategy for working common-denominator problems presented in Level F is different from that shown in Level E. This strategy is introduced in Lesson 61. It involves counting by each of the denominators, then identifying the first common number.

The conventions for setting up the problem are the same as those used in Level E. Students show the original problem in a column. Then they work an equivalent-fraction problem for each of the fractions, which gives them a new column problem with a common denominator.

Here's part of the introduction from Lesson 61:

a. $\dfrac{1}{6}$ b. $\dfrac{5}{3}$ c. $\dfrac{3}{4}$
$+\dfrac{5}{8}$ $-\dfrac{2}{5}$ $+\dfrac{1}{12}$

b. You'll work these problems by finding the first common number for the denominators.
c. Problem A. The denominators are 6 and 8.
- Write the numbers for counting by 6 and counting by 8. Circle the first common number. Raise your hand when you've done that much. (Observe students and give feedback.)
- Everybody, what's the first common number? (Signal.) *24.*
- (Write on the board:)

a. $\quad \dfrac{1}{6} \left(-\right) = \dfrac{}{24}$

$+\ \dfrac{5}{8} \left(-\right) = +\dfrac{}{24}$

- Copy what's on the board and figure out the fraction that equals 1/6. Then figure out the fraction that equals 5/8. Raise your hand when you've completed both the fractions that have a denominator of 24.
(Observe students and give feedback.)
- (Write to show:)

$$\text{a.} \quad \frac{1}{6}\left(\frac{4}{4}\right) = \frac{4}{24}$$
$$+ \frac{5}{8}\left(\frac{3}{3}\right) = +\frac{15}{24}$$

- 1/6 equals 4/24. 5/8 equals 15/24.
- Now add those values and write the answer. Raise your hand when you're finished.
(Observe students and give feedback.)
- Everybody, what does 4/24 plus 15/24 equal?
(Signal.) *19-twenty-fourths.*

Teaching note: Although the procedure involves several steps, all the component steps are familiar once students take the first step. When observing students and providing feedback, make sure students see that they are working a pair of equivalent-fraction problems. "Find the first common number for the denominators and write it. Then you have **two equivalent-fraction problems** that you know how to work."

Expect students to make the following mistakes:

1) Omitting equals signs. Remind students: "You're working two equivalent-fraction problems. Remember the equals signs."

2) Omitting the operational signs (+ or −). Remind students: "Don't write an answer to your column problem without a sign that tells you to add or subtract."

3) Attempting to write an answer below the original equation. If you stress that students must work two equivalent-fraction problems, it will be easier for students to set up the equations and, therefore, write the answer in the appropriate place.

FRACTION SIMPLIFICATION

As simplifying fractions is taught in both Level E and the Bridge, Level F assumes that students are proficient in this skill. Level F exercises do not specify that students simplify fractional answers. However, you may require students to simplify.

Students in Level F work multiplication problems that can be simplified by crossing out zeros in the numerator and the denominator (beginning with Lesson 16), or by crossing out fractions equal to 1 (beginning in Lesson 66).

Examples:

$$\frac{2}{1\cancel{00}} \times 80\cancel{00} = \boxed{160} \qquad \frac{\cancel{5}}{8} \times \frac{3}{\cancel{5}} = \frac{3}{8}$$

RECIPROCALS AND FRACTION DIVISION

The work with reciprocals begins in Lesson 44. Students learn that any nonzero value has a reciprocal and that the reciprocal times the original value equals 1. The first demonstrations show the relationship between expressing parts of a whole as fractions or as numbers. If a whole is divided into 7 parts, each part is 1/7 of the whole.

Here's part of the introduction from Lesson 44:

a. Each part is $\frac{1}{5}$ of the total. How many parts are there?

b. Each piece of the pie is $\frac{1}{6}$ of the total pie. How many pieces are in the pie?

c. A deck of playing cards has 52 cards. What's the fraction for each card?

b. For each problem you'll write the equation that shows the fraction for each part and the number of parts that make up the whole thing.

c. Problem A: Each part is 1/5 of the total. How many parts are there?

- If each part is 1/5, what's the **fraction** for the total? (Signal.) *5-fifths.*
- Start with 1/5 and show the number of times you multiply to get the total of 5/5. Box the value that answers the question. Raise your hand when you're finished. √
- (Write on the board:)

$$\text{a.} \quad \frac{1}{5} \times \boxed{5} = \frac{5}{5}$$

- Here's what you should have: 1/5 times 5 or 5 over 1 equals 5/5. There are 5 parts.

d. Problem B: Each piece of the pie is 1/6 of the total pie.

- The problem asks about the number of pieces in the pie. Write the equation that starts with the fraction. Box the value that answers the question. Raise your hand when you're finished. √

- (Write on the board:)

$$\text{b.} \quad \frac{1}{6} \times \boxed{6} = \frac{6}{6}$$

- Here's what you should have. There are 6 pieces of pie.
- e. Problem C says: A deck of playing cards has 52 cards. What is the fraction for **each card?**
- If the deck has 52 cards, what's the fraction for the whole deck? (Signal.) *52-fifty-seconds.*
- Write the equation that starts with the fraction for each card. Box the answer to the question. Raise your hand when you're finished.
  (Observe students and give feedback.)
- (Write on the board:)

$$\text{c.} \quad \boxed{\frac{1}{52}} \times 52 = \frac{52}{52}$$

- Here's what you should have. Each card is 1/52 of the total.

This relationship between the number of parts and the fraction for each part involves fractions that have a numerator of 1. It sets the stage for fractions with other numerators. Work with these fractions is introduced in Lesson 46, in which students also learn the term **reciprocal.**

In Lesson 47, students learn the rule that any value times its reciprocal equals 1. In Lesson 56, students work problems that show a whole divided into equal parts as division problems and as multiplication problems. For a rectangle divided into 6 parts, 1 of which is shaded, students work the problem: 1/6 times Area, and the problem: Area divided by 6.

In Lesson 81, students learn the general rule that they can rewrite any division problem or multiplication problem with the opposite sign.

Here are the problems from Lesson 81:

a. 3×4 b. $5 \times \frac{4}{5}$ c. $8 \div 2$

d. $5 \div \frac{1}{2}$ e. $3 \times \frac{5}{3}$ f. $6 \div \frac{2}{3}$

For problem A, students write: $3 \div 1/4$. They work the problem on their calculator. (Students first work the problem $1 \div 4$ and put the answer in the memory of their calculator. Then they work the problem: 3 divided by what's in the memory [memory recall].)

The work in Lesson 81 shows students the basic procedure for solving problems that divide by a fraction: Rewrite the problem as a

multiplication problem and work it. This strategy is applied to a set of problems in Lesson 82:

a. $4 \div \frac{2}{5} = \blacksquare$ b. $\frac{3}{2} \div \frac{4}{9} = \blacksquare$ c. $\frac{5}{3} \div \frac{1}{3} = \blacksquare$

- b. These are division problems. To work them, you'll write the multiplication problem.
- c. Problem A. 4 divided by 2/5.
- Write the multiplication problem that gives the same answer and work it. Show your answer as a whole number or a mixed number. Raise your hand when you're finished.
  (Observe students and give feedback.)
- (Write on the board:)

$$\text{a.} \quad 4 \times \frac{5}{2} = \frac{20}{2} = \boxed{10}$$

- d. Problem B: 3/2 divided by 4/9.
- Write the multiplication problem and the answer. Raise your hand when you're finished.
  (Observe students and give feedback.)
- (Write on the board:)

$$\text{b.} \quad \frac{3}{2} \times \frac{9}{4} = \frac{27}{8} = \boxed{3\frac{3}{8}}$$

- Here's what you should have. 3/2 times 9/4 is 27/8. That's 3 and 3/8.

Mixed-Number Operations

Addition and subtraction of mixed numbers is introduced in Lesson 9.

Here are the problems that the students work in Lesson 9:

a. $11\frac{5}{8}$ b. $12\frac{5}{9}$ c. $\frac{2}{15}$ d. $28\frac{1}{5}$
   $-8\frac{4}{8}$ $-1\frac{2}{9}$ $+7\frac{9}{15}$ $+2\frac{3}{5}$
   $\blacksquare$ $\blacksquare$ $\blacksquare$ $\blacksquare$

Students first work with the fractions, then with the whole numbers.

In Lesson 14, students work problems that require borrowing. Students rewrite the whole number as a mixed number that has a fraction equal to 1. For 12 minus 3/7, they rewrite 12 as 11 and 7/7.

Here's part of the introduction from Lesson 14:

a. 17 b. 23 c. 10
   $-4\frac{3}{5}$ $-10\frac{1}{4}$ $-\frac{5}{11}$
   $\blacksquare$ $\blacksquare$ $\blacksquare$

c. Problem A. You can't work the problem the way it is written. You must borrow 1 from 17 and write 1 as a fraction with the same denominator as 3/5.
- What's the denominator of 3/5? (Signal.) *5.*
- How many fifths are in one whole? (Signal.) *5.*
- Borrow 5/5 from 17 and work the problem.
- Raise your hand when you're finished. (Observe students and give feedback.)
- (Write on the board:)

$$\begin{array}{r} \overset{6}{17}\,\dfrac{5}{5} \\ \text{a.} \quad -\ 4\,\dfrac{3}{5} \\ \hline \boxed{12\,\dfrac{2}{5}} \end{array}$$

- Here's what you should have.

> **Teaching note:** For students who went through Level E (not the Bridge), this work is a review. You should be able to go through it very quickly. For students who went through the Bridge, this work may be new and may require more careful monitoring.

In Lesson 16, students work addition problems that have a fraction in the answer that is more than 1. Students rewrite the answer as a proper mixed number.

Here's an example of a problem that has been worked:

$$\begin{array}{r} \text{a.} \quad 2\,\dfrac{8}{9} \\ 4\,\dfrac{7}{9} \\ +\ 5\,\dfrac{6}{9} \\ \hline 11\,\dfrac{21}{9} \end{array} \qquad 11+2\,\dfrac{3}{9}=\boxed{13\,\dfrac{3}{9}}$$

Students first convert the fraction 21/9 into a mixed number. They do that by working the problem 21 divided by 9. They add the answer (2 and 3/9) to the whole number in the answer. Expect some students to do this addition mentally. For later work with mixed numbers, you will not always show the conversion of the improper mixed number to a proper mixed number.

In Lesson 48, students work problems that involve multiplying mixed numbers. The strategy that students use is to rewrite the problem with the mixed numbers shown as improper fractions.

Here's part of the exercise from Lesson 48:

a. $3\frac{1}{4} \times 3\frac{1}{2} = \blacksquare$

b. $2\frac{3}{5} \times 1\frac{1}{4} = \blacksquare$

c. $1\frac{2}{3} \times 6 = \blacksquare$

c. Problem A: 3 and 1/4 times 3 and 1/2.
- Write the problem with both mixed numbers shown as fractions. Raise your hand when you've done that much. √
- (Write on the board:)

$$\text{a.} \quad \dfrac{13}{4} \times \dfrac{7}{2} =$$

- Here's what you should have so far: 13/4 times 7/2. Raise your hand if you got it right.
- Do the multiplication. Show the fraction you end up with. Show the mixed number or whole number that fraction equals. Raise your hand when you're finished. (Observe students and give feedback.)
- (Write to show:)

$$\text{a.} \quad \dfrac{13}{4} \times \dfrac{7}{2} = \dfrac{91}{8} = \boxed{11\,\dfrac{3}{8}}$$

- Here's what you should have. The answer is 9/18. That's 11 and 3/8.

In Lesson 67, students work mixed-number problems that have fractions with unlike denominators. This work is new for all students. The procedure for working the problem is to work the common-denominator problem for the fractions, then add the whole number to the fraction in the answer. If the fraction is more than 1, students rewrite the answer as a proper mixed number.

Here's part of the work from Lesson 67:

a. $\begin{array}{r} 3\frac{3}{5} \\ +\ 4\frac{2}{7} \\ \hline \blacksquare \end{array}$ b. $\begin{array}{r} 2\frac{3}{4} \\ +\ 4\frac{7}{8} \\ \hline \blacksquare \end{array}$ c. $\begin{array}{r} 1\frac{7}{9} \\ +\ 3\frac{5}{6} \\ \hline \blacksquare \end{array}$

e. Copy problem C and work it. If the fraction you end up with is more than 1 whole, rewrite the answer as a proper mixed number. Raise your hand when you're finished. (Observe students and give feedback.)

- (Write on the board:)

$$
\begin{array}{r}
\text{c.} \quad 1\,\dfrac{7}{9}\left(\dfrac{2}{2}\right) = 1\,\dfrac{14}{18} \\[2mm]
+\ 3\,\dfrac{5}{6}\left(\dfrac{3}{3}\right) = +\,3\,\dfrac{15}{18} \\[2mm]
\hline
3\,\dfrac{29}{18} = \boxed{5\,\dfrac{11}{18}}
\end{array}
$$

- Here's what you should have. The common denominator is 18. The fraction you end up with is 29/18. So you rewrote the answer as 5 and 11/18.

The final type of mixed-number problem is introduced in Lesson 80. This type involves subtraction and has fractions with unlike denominators. To solve the problem, students must borrow.

Here's part of the work from Lesson 80:

a. $8\frac{1}{6}$ b. $7\frac{3}{5}$ c. $4\frac{2}{7}$
   $-1\frac{3}{4}$ $-4\frac{7}{10}$ $-3\frac{4}{5}$

c. Copy problem A and find the common denominator. Raise your hand when you've written the two fractions with that denominator.
(Observe students and give feedback.)
- (Write on the board:)

$$
\begin{array}{r}
\text{a.} \quad 8\,\dfrac{1}{6}\left(\dfrac{2}{2}\right) = 8\,\dfrac{2}{12} \\[2mm]
-\ 1\,\dfrac{3}{4}\left(\dfrac{3}{3}\right) = -\,1\,\dfrac{9}{12}
\end{array}
$$

- Here's what you should have so far.
- You can't subtract 9 from 2. So you have to borrow. Remember, show the new whole number; show the new top fraction. Raise your hand when you've done that much.
(Observe students and give feedback.)
- (Write to show:)

$$
\begin{array}{r}
\text{a.} \quad 8\,\dfrac{1}{6}\left(\dfrac{2}{2}\right) = \overset{7}{\cancel{8}}\,\dfrac{\overset{14}{\cancel{2}}}{12} \\[2mm]
-\ 1\,\dfrac{3}{4}\left(\dfrac{3}{3}\right) = -\,1\,\dfrac{9}{12}
\end{array}
$$

- The new whole number is 7. The new fraction is 14/12. That's 12/12 plus 2/12.
- Now complete the problem. Raise your hand when you're finished

- (Write to show:)

$$
\begin{array}{r}
\text{a.} \quad 8\,\dfrac{1}{6}\left(\dfrac{2}{2}\right) = \overset{7}{\cancel{8}}\,\dfrac{\overset{14}{\cancel{2}}}{12} \\[2mm]
-\ 1\,\dfrac{3}{4}\left(\dfrac{3}{3}\right) = -\,1\,\dfrac{9}{12} \\[2mm]
\hline
\boxed{6\,\dfrac{5}{12}}
\end{array}
$$

- Here's what you should have. You end up with 6 and 5/12.

The mixed-number operations set the stage for a variety of multi-step problems and problems involving area.

Number Families

Level F requires students to do a lot of work with number families. This work is not new. The number families used in Level F involve three fractions that generate four statements—two addition statements and two subtraction statements. All number families have the largest fraction at the right end of the number family and the two other fractions to the left.

Here's a family that involves the fractions 3/7, 4/7, and 7/7:

$$\dfrac{3}{7} \qquad \dfrac{4}{7} \longrightarrow \dfrac{7}{7}$$

If one fraction is missing, it can be computed. If the big number (7/7) is missing, it is found by adding the two fractions that are shown:

$$\dfrac{3}{7} \qquad \dfrac{4}{7} \longrightarrow \blacksquare \qquad \dfrac{3}{7} + \dfrac{4}{7} = \boxed{\dfrac{7}{7}}$$

If one of the other fractions is missing, it can be computed by starting with the big number and subtracting the fraction that is shown:

$$\dfrac{3}{7} \qquad \blacksquare \longrightarrow \dfrac{7}{7} \qquad \dfrac{7}{7} - \dfrac{3}{7} = \boxed{\dfrac{4}{7}}$$

In Level F, students review fraction number families in lessons 7 through 9. For all the families they work with in these lessons, the big number is a fraction that equals 1. Therefore, if only one fraction is shown—one of the small numbers—students are able to make a complete number family.

Here's part of the activity from Lesson 7:

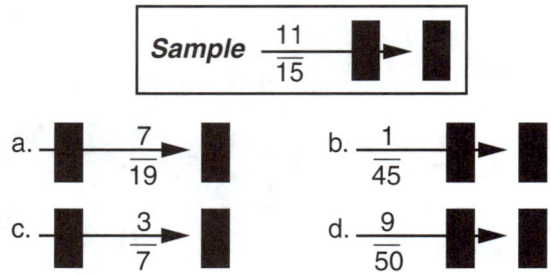

c. Sample problem: The fraction 11/15 is shown as the first fraction.
• The fraction at the end of the arrow will equal 1 and will have a denominator of 15. What fraction is that? (Signal.) *15-fifteenths.*
• To find the third fraction, you subtract 11/15 from 15/15. What's the fraction? (Signal.) *4-fifteenths.*
• (Write on the board:)

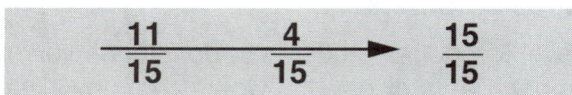

• Here's the family with all three fractions.
d. Problem A: The fraction for the second value is shown. Copy the family and write the missing fractions. Raise your hand when you're finished. (Observe students and give feedback.)
• (Write on the board:)

$$\text{a.} \quad \frac{12}{19} \quad \frac{7}{19} \longrightarrow \frac{19}{19}$$

• Here's what you should have. Raise your hand if you got everything right.
e. Your turn: Write fractions for the rest of the items in part 1. Remember, all the fractions have the same denominator. Raise your hand when you're finished. (Observe students and give feedback.)
f. (Write on the board:)

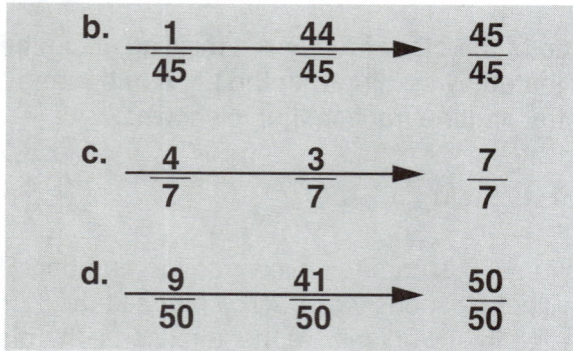

• Here are the families you should have for problems B through D.

In Lesson 8, students complete a number family that shows three names and one fraction. The names refer to parts and the whole (e.g., cracked plates, plates that are not cracked, and all plates).
Here's part of the introduction:

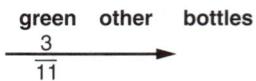

a. What's the fraction for the other bottles ?

$$\underset{\text{men}}{} \quad \underset{\text{women}}{\frac{62}{84}} \quad \underset{\text{employees}}{} \longrightarrow$$

b. What's the fraction for all the employees ?

b. Problem A. The fraction for green bottles is 3/11. The denominator is 11. So all the fractions will have that denominator.
• Make the complete number family. Write the names. Fill in the missing fractions and box the fraction that answers the question the problem asks. That question is: What's the fraction for the other bottles? Raise your hand when you're finished.
(Observe students and give feedback.)
• (Write on the board:)

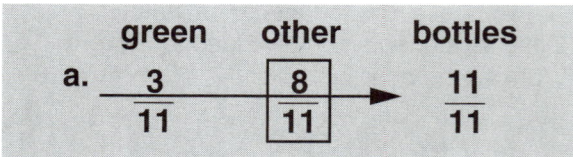

• Here's what you should have. The fraction for all the bottles is 11/11. The fraction for other bottles is **8/11.** That's the answer to the question.
c. Your turn: Make the number family for item B. Box the fraction that answers the question the problem asks. Raise your hand when you're finished. (Observe students and give feedback.)
• (Write on the board:)

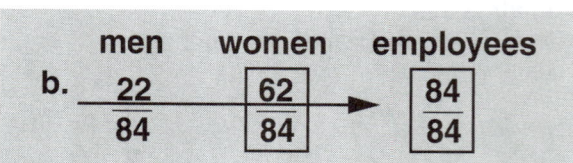

• Here's what you should have. The fraction for all the employees is **84/84.** That's the answer to the question the problem asks.

In Lesson 11 students make families for decimal and percent values. Students write these values as fractions. For .4, students write 4/10; for 80%, students write 80/100.

Here are the items the students work:

a. 3% of the adults owned sailboats.

b. .29 of the fish were bass.

c. 78% of the students graduated.

d. The bus was late on 30% of the days.

e. .02 of the products were defective.

For each item, students make the complete number family with three names and three fractions.

Here are some acceptable name options for item A:

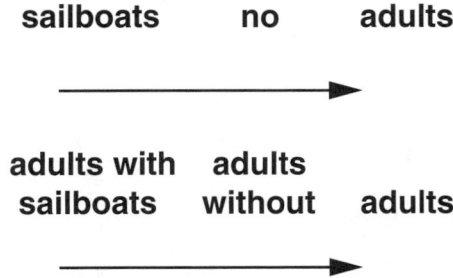

The name for the big number must refer to adults. The names for the small numbers must refer to sailboats and no sailboats.

Here are the complete number families with names for the different items:

	no		
	sailboats	sailboats	adults
a.	3/100	97/100 →	100/100

		not	
	bass	bass	fish
b.	29/100	71/100 →	100/100

| | graduated | didn't | students |
| c. | 87/100 | 22/100 → | 100/100 |

		not	
	late	late	days
d.	30/100	70/100 →	100/100

| | defective | okay | products |
| e. | 2/100 | 98/100 → | 100/100 |

Later, students will use these families to work problems that involve ratios. (See **Ratio Tables**.)

In Lesson 31, students make number families for statements that compare two values. Students make families that have two names and two fractions, one of which is equal to 1 whole. They first figure out which name is the big number. If the fraction is more than 1, the fraction is the big number. If the fraction is less than 1, the fraction is a small number.

Bill is 7/5 the age of his sister. Bill is 7/5. So Bill is the big number and his sister is a small number.

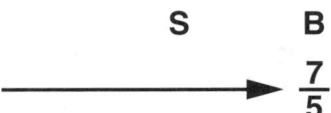

Bill is 6/7 the age of his sister. The fraction for Bill is less than 1. Bill is a small number. His sister is the big number.

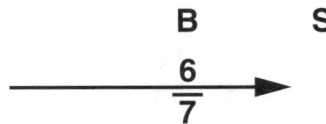

The next thing students do is figure out the value for the other name. They follow the rule that what something is compared to is always 1. In the Bill sentences, Bill is compared to his sister. So in both cases, the sister is 1.

The students should be facile with these steps. Make sure that you are firm on these conventions before presenting Lesson 31.

Here are the sentences and the correct families for Lesson 31:

a. **The sale price is 8/10 of the regular price.**

The regular price is the big number. The regular price is 1 because the sale price is compared to it.

b. The distance to the coast is 11/6 the distance to the river.

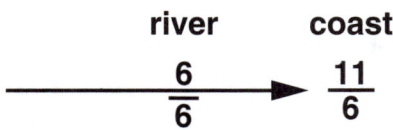

river   coast

$\dfrac{6}{6} \longrightarrow \dfrac{11}{6}$

Coast is the big number. **River** is 1 because the coast is compared to it.

c. Lunch costs 5/8 as much as dinner.

lunch   dinner

$\dfrac{5}{8} \longrightarrow \dfrac{8}{8}$

Dinner is the big number. Dinner is 1 because lunch is compared to it.

d. The man's age is 13/12 his wife's age.

wife   man

$\dfrac{12}{12} \longrightarrow \dfrac{13}{12}$

The man is the big number. His wife is 1 because his age is compared to hers.

In later lessons, students make families with three values. The third value is the **difference.**

Here are the complete families for items C and D above:

dif   lunch   dinner

c. $\dfrac{3}{8} \quad \dfrac{5}{8} \longrightarrow \dfrac{8}{8}$

dif   wife   man

d. $\dfrac{1}{12} \quad \dfrac{12}{12} \longrightarrow \dfrac{13}{12}$

In Lesson 52, students make two statements in connection with number families that show only two names and fractions for percents.

Examples:

dif   z   y   dif   y   z

$\dfrac{100}{100} \longrightarrow \dfrac{130}{100} \qquad \dfrac{80}{100} \longrightarrow \dfrac{100}{100}$

For the first family, one statement is: Y is 130% **of** Z. The other statement is: Y is 30% **more than** Z. For the second family, the statements are: Y is 80% **of** Z; Y is 20% **less than** Z.

In statements that refer to **more than** or **less than,** the number is the difference number. In statements that refer to **of,** the number is not the difference number but is the value for the name that precedes the percent number. Here are the statements and the complete family:

Y is 130% of Z.

dif   Z   Y

$\dfrac{30}{100} \quad \dfrac{100}{100} \longrightarrow \dfrac{130}{100}$

Y is 30% more than Z.

dif   Z   Y

$\dfrac{\mathbf{30}}{\mathbf{100}} \quad \dfrac{100}{100} \longrightarrow \dfrac{130}{100}$

Decimal Operations

The first five lessons of Level F review addition and subtraction of decimal values. When working decimal problems, students are to line up the decimal points, then make sure that all the values have the same number of decimal places. If decimal places are needed for some of the values, students add zeros. Students then carry out the specified operation and write the answer with a decimal point.

The review for multiplying decimal values begins in Lesson 8. Students follow these rules:

First multiply and write the digits in the answer.

Then count all the decimal places in the values that are multiplied.

Show the same number of decimal places in the answer.

The decimal places are always counted from the last digit of the number.

In Lessons 27 through 29, students confirm decimal multiplication by working the same problems as fraction multiplication and decimal multiplication. For example, students first work the problem .86 × .2 as a fraction problem:

$$\dfrac{86}{100} \times \dfrac{2}{10} = \dfrac{172}{1000}$$

Students then check their answer by working the original problem on their calculator.

In Lesson 53, students review dividing a decimal value by a whole number. They follow the procedure of first writing the decimal point in the answer (directly above the other decimal point), then doing the division. Students write a digit in the answer for every place after the decimal point, including the first digit after the decimal point. For the problem: $9\overline{)\,.450}$, the first digit of the answer is zero.

Beginning with Lesson 71, students work on more difficult decimal division problems.

Problems are of the form: $\dfrac{4}{.08}$. Students convert this fraction into one that has a whole-number denominator. They show the fraction that equals 1 to achieve this conversion.

$$\frac{4}{.08}\left(\frac{100}{100}\right) = \frac{400}{8}$$

Here's part of the introduction from Lesson 71:

a. $\dfrac{4}{.08}$ = ■ b. $\dfrac{11.52}{.6}$ = ■

c. $\dfrac{6}{.05}$ = ■ d. $\dfrac{.1075}{.025}$ = ■

b. You're going to change each denominator into a whole number that has the same digits.
c. Problem A. What's the denominator? (Signal.) *8-hundredths.*
• How many places do you have to move the decimal point to get a whole number? (Signal.) *Two.*
• Write the complete equivalent-fraction problem and show the fraction that has a denominator of 8. Raise your hand when you're finished. (Observe students and give feedback.)
• (Write on the board:)

a. $\dfrac{4}{.08}\left(\dfrac{100}{100}\right) = \boxed{\dfrac{400}{8}}$

• Here's what you should have. You multiply by 100/100. The equivalent fraction is 400/8. Raise your hand if you got it right
d. Copy and complete equation B so the denominator is a whole number. Raise your hand when you're finished. (Observe students and give feedback.)
• (Write on the board:)

b. $\dfrac{11.52}{.6}\left(\dfrac{10}{10}\right) = \boxed{\dfrac{115.2}{6}}$

• Here's what you should have. You multiply by 10/10. The equivalent fraction is 115 and 2-tenths over 6.

Teaching note: After students create the fractions with whole-number denominators, they do the division for these problems. For problem A, they work the fraction 400/8 as the division problem:

$$8\overline{)\,400}$$

Students then use their calculator to work the original problem and check their answer.

In Lesson 73, students work with the same range of decimal fractions; however, students write abbreviated equations. These do not show the fraction that equals 1. For example:

$$\frac{1.8}{.09} = \frac{180}{9}$$

Students figure out the number of places the decimal point must move to make the denominator a whole number; they move the decimal point in the numerator the same number of places. As they did with the earlier problems, students work the division problems for the second fraction: $9\overline{)\,180}$.

In Lesson 74, students work with division problems that have a decimal divisor.

Here's part of the work from that lesson:

• You've worked problems that have decimal denominators. You move the decimal point enough places to make the denominator a whole number.	$\dfrac{4}{.2\,5}$
• Then you do the same thing in the numerator.	$\dfrac{4.0\,0}{.2\,5}$
• You take the same steps when a fraction is written as a division problem:	$.2\overline{)\,.6\,8}$
• The denominator is .2. You move the decimal point one place, and move the other decimal point one place.	$.2\overline{)\,.6.8}$
• Remember, the number you **divide by** is the **denominator**. You move the decimal point for that number. Then you move the decimal point the same number of places for the other number.	

a. I'll read what it says. Follow along: You've worked problems that have decimal denominators. You move the decimal point enough places to make the denominator a whole number. Then you do the same thing in the numerator.
• You take the same steps when a fraction is written as a division problem. The denominator is 2-tenths. You move the decimal point one place and move the other decimal point one place.

- Remember, the number you **divide by** is the **denominator.** You move the decimal point for that number. Then you move the decimal point the same number of places for the other number.

a. .8⟌2.56   b. .48⟌24   c. .92⟌32.2

b. Problem A. Read the problem. (Signal.) *2 and 56-hundredth divided by 8-tenths.*
- You're dividing by tenths. You have to move the decimal points one place.
- Here's how to do that.
- (Write on the board:)

$$a. \quad .8 \overline{\smash{\big)}\,2.5.6}$$

- Your turn: Show the decimal points and the arrows for the new decimal points. Raise your hand when you've done that much. √
c. Your turn: Fix up problem B. You're dividing by a hundredth number. So you'll have to move both decimal points two places. You'll need two zeros after the 24.
- Copy the problem and fix it up. Raise your hand when you've done that much. √
- (Write on the board:)

$$b. \quad .48 \overline{\smash{\big)}\,24.00.}$$

- Here's what you should have.

> **Teaching note:** For problem B, students must move both decimal points two places. To do that, they must add two zeros to 24.
> Remind students: "You're doing the same thing that you do when the division problems are written as fractions. First change the number you divide by so it's a whole number. Then make the same change with the number under the division sign."

Coordinate System

   Starting in Lesson 87, students work with points on the coordinate system. They make points from information about the X and Y values; they use lines to answer questions about ratio relationships.

Here's part of the introduction from Lesson 87:

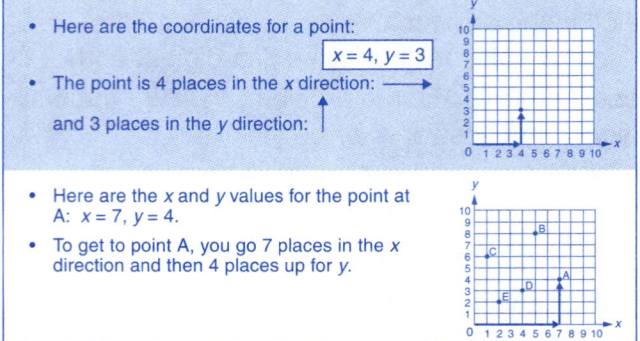

a. The two arrows on the grid show how to get to the point: **X equals 4, Y equals 3.** The point is 4 places to the right of zero and 3 places up.
- Touch the point. √
- The bottom coordinate system shows different letters. The two arrows show the X and Y values for the point at A.
- Touch A on the coordinate system.
- Here are the values for that point: X equals 7, Y equals 4.
b. (Write on the board:)

$$x = \quad , \ y =$$

c. Your turn: Write the X value and Y value for point B. Raise your hand when you're finished.
   (Observe students and give feedback.)
- (Write to show:)

$$B \quad x = 5, \ y = 8$$

- Here's what you should have for point B. X equals 5. Y equals 8.
d. Write the X and Y values for C. Raise your hand when you're finished.
   (Observe students and give feedback.)
- (Write on the board:)

$$C \quad x = 1, \ y = 6$$

- Here's what you should have. X equals 1. Y equals 6.
e. Write the X and Y values for D and E. Raise your hand when you're finished.
f. (Write on the board:)

$$D \quad x = 4, \ y = 3$$
$$E \quad x = 2, \ y = 2$$

- Here's what you should have.
g. Raise your hand if you got everything right.

The coordinate system is also used for earlier work with complex areas (Lessons 36 through 49). For those problems, the complex figures are shown on the coordinate grid. During the last ten lessons of the program, students also use the coordinate system to solve more advanced area problems and to construct forms that are symmetrical.

APPLICATIONS

In Level F, applications encompass a range of problems that involve words, tables, the coordinate system, and geometric figures. Some problems require students to construct tables or interpret graphs. For problems that involve measurement units, students refer to the table of weights and measures at the back of their textbooks:

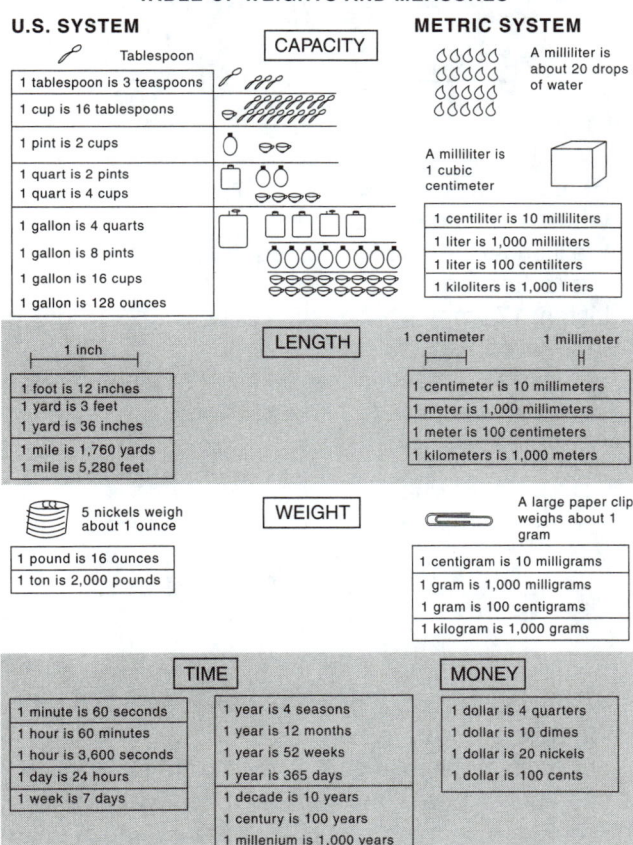

As a general rule, for every tool skill that students learn in Level F, there are corresponding problem-solving applications. After students work with equivalent fractions, they solve ratio and proportion problems that apply the same steps. Similarly, students apply their knowledge of fraction number families to a variety of complex word problems. After students learn about decimal operations, they work word problems that require the operational steps they have learned.

This point is important for the students and also for you. Skills that students work on are not ends. These skills will be used in more complex applications. If students are not well practiced in component skills, they will lack the tools they need to be successful with the problem-solving extensions.

The major categories of applications that students work in Level F are problem solving (ratios and proportions, rate, probability, multi-step problems), measurement, and geometry.

Problem Solving

RATIO EQUATIONS

The first work with ratios occurs in Lesson 2. Students review the basic procedures and setup for working problems.

Here's part of the review from Lesson 2:

a. If it takes a runner 11 seconds to run 30 feet, how many feet would the runner travel in 55 seconds?

b. 4 tires cost $200. How much do 12 tires cost?

c. If 9 identical drapes weigh 99 ounces, how much do 54 drapes weigh?

a. These are ratio problems. Let's review how to set up the problems: You make a ratio equation with equivalent fractions. You write two names and three numbers. You figure out the missing number.

b. Problem A: If it takes a runner 11 seconds to run 30 feet, how many feet would the runner travel in 55 seconds?

• First the names. What are they? (Signal.) *Seconds and feet.*

• (Write on the board:)

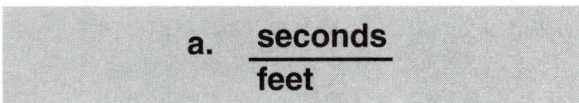

c. Now the numbers for the first fraction. What's the number for seconds? (Signal.) *11.*

• What's the number for feet? (Signal.) *30.*

• (Write to show:)

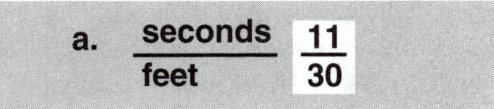

d. Now one number for the second fraction. What's the number? (Signal.) *55.*
- Is that the number for seconds or for feet? (Signal.) *Seconds.*
- (Write to show:)

$$\text{a.}\quad \frac{\text{seconds}}{\text{feet}}\quad \frac{11}{30}\left(\underline{}\right)=\frac{55}{}$$

e. Now you just figure out the missing number for feet. Copy the problem. You'll work it as part of your independent work.

> **Teaching note:** These problems should present no difficulties for the students. Make sure, however, that they follow the conventions for setting up the problem. The names go into the equation according to their order in the problem: the first mentioned name goes on top; the other name goes on the bottom. The numbers for the last fraction go next to the corresponding name. (In problem A, the number for seconds goes on top; the number for feet goes on the bottom.)
> The placement of the third number in the problem depends on the name. If the number is for seconds, it goes on top. If the number is for feet, it goes on the bottom.
> In problem A, you show the fraction that equals 1 (5/5). Expect many students not to show the fraction because it is simple. Do not require them to show it for problems that can be worked mentally. If students have difficulties, however, require them to show the fraction that equals 1.

In Lesson 13, students work problems that involve complex fractions that equal 1. Students have already reviewed the equation skills (starting with Lesson 11). The procedure is basically the same as the work with simpler ratio problems. The names and numbers for the first fraction go into the equation according to the order of their occurrence in the problem. The only difference is that students express the fraction that equals 1 as a fraction over a fraction. This convention is needed because the problem either presents numbers that are not multiples the student would be expected to know, or they are not multiples at all.

Here's part of the review from Lesson 13:

Sample	The ratio of whales to seals was 7 to 17. There were 102 seals. How many whales were there?

a. In a mixture, there were 7 parts of sand for every 4 parts of gravel. There were 200 parts of sand. How many parts of gravel were there?

b. A tractor used 3 gallons of fuel every 2 hours it worked. The tractor worked 11 hours. How many gallons of fuel did it use?

c. A soup recipe called for 3 onions for every 8 pints of water. The cook used 5 onions. How many pints of water did the cook use?

b. Sample problem: The ratio of whales to seals was 7 to 17. There were 102 seals. How many whales were there?
- Write the equation with names and three numbers. Raise your hand when you've done that much. (Observe students and give feedback.)
- (Write on the board:)

$$\frac{\text{whales}}{\text{seals}}\quad \frac{7}{17}\left(\underline{}\right)=\frac{\square}{102}$$

- Here's what you should have. The names are **whales** and **seals.**
- We'll show the fraction that equals 1 as a fraction over a fraction.
- Listen: 17 times what fraction equals 102? (Signal.) *102-seventeenths.*
- So what's the fraction that equals 1? (Signal.) *102-seventeenths over 102-seventeenths.*
- (Write to show:)

$$\frac{\text{whales}}{\text{seals}}\quad \frac{7}{17}\left(\dfrac{\frac{102}{17}}{\frac{102}{17}}\right)=\frac{\square}{102}$$

- When you multiply 7 times 102/17 you end up with 42. So there were 42 whales.

c. For each problem in part 1, you'll write the fraction that equals 1 as a fraction over a fraction.

d. Problem A: In a mixture, there were 7 parts of sand for every 4 parts of gravel. There were 200 parts of sand. How many parts of gravel were there?
- Make the ratio equation with two names and three numbers. Raise your hand when you've done that much.
(Observe students and give feedback.)

- (Write on the board:)

$$\underset{\text{gravel}}{\text{a. sand}} \quad \frac{7}{4} \left(\right) = \frac{102}{\square}$$

- The names are **sand** and **gravel.** The number after the equals sign is for parts of sand.
- Figure out the number of parts of gravel. Write the answer as a mixed number and a unit name. Raise your hand when you're finished.
  (Observe students and give feedback.)
- (Write to show:)

$$\underset{\text{gravel}}{\text{a. sand}} \quad \frac{7}{4} \left(\frac{\frac{200}{7}}{\frac{200}{7}} \right) = \frac{200}{\frac{800}{7}} \quad 114\frac{2}{7} \text{ parts of gravel}$$

- Here's what you should have. The unit name is **parts of gravel.** It's okay if you just wrote **parts.**

> **Teaching note:** Make sure that students follow all the conventions for showing the fraction that equals 1 and for writing the answer with the unit name. Expect some students to be lax about writing the answer. Accept unit names in the answer that differ from the ones you show. For problem A, the answer could be expressed as 114 and 2/7 parts. The answer 114 and 2/7 gravel is not acceptable.

RATIO TABLES

In Lesson 9, students work problems that require ratio tables. These tables have two columns of numbers. The total for each column is at the bottom. If a column has two numbers, the third can be computed by addition or subtraction. The numbers in each row of the table are related by multiplication. Here are the problems students work in Lesson 9:

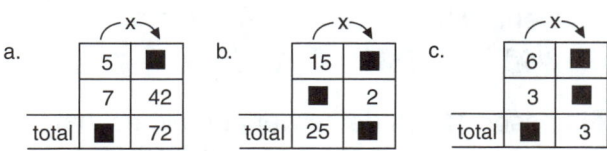

The times sign on the top of each table shows that the numbers in each row are related by multiplication.

To complete table A, students add in the first column and subtract in the second. The missing numbers are 12 and 30.

To complete table B, students subtract in the first column. The missing number is 10.

They then figure out the factor for the table. They work with the row that has two numbers—10 and 2. They figure out the missing factor: 2/10. Students are not required to make an equation to figure out this factor. If they have trouble, tell them to write the equation: 10 ( ) = 2, and show the missing factor as a fraction—2/10.

They multiply either 15 or 25 by 2/10 to obtain a second number in the second column. Then they add or subtract (or multiply again) to complete the table. Note that students are not required to make a ratio equation for finding the numbers in the second column. They just follow the rule that everything in the first column is multiplied by the same value. Expect some students to multiply both values in the first column by 2/10. This procedure is acceptable. If students who have been through Level E make the ratio equation for finding the second number, tell them that they can do it the fast way by just multiplying.

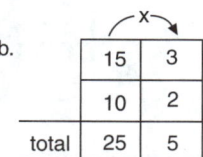

Make sure that you are familiar with the conventions for working with these tables before presenting Lesson 9.

In Lesson 10, students are given a partially completed number family and a table that has one number in the second column.

Here's a problem from Lesson 10:

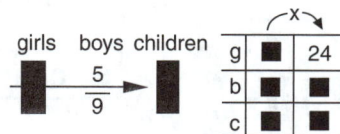

Students complete the number family, then put the numerators in the first column of the table along with letters for each name. The number family shows the order of the names for the table. The big number is the total.

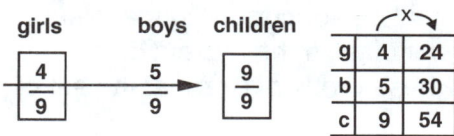

Students complete the table by finding the factor (6) that converts numbers in the first column to corresponding numbers in the second column (4 to 24, 5 to 30, 9 to 54).

In Lesson 11, students construct a number family and a table from a word problem.

Here's part of the review from Lesson 11:

b. Problem A: 2/5 of the children were hungry. There were 33 children who were not hungry. How many children were hungry? How many children were there in all?

• Make the family with three names and three fractions. Make a table with the numerators in the first column. Put 33 where it belongs in the second column. That's children who were not hungry. Raise your hand when you have a number family and a ratio table with names and four numbers in it.
(Observe students and give feedback.)

• (Write on the board:)

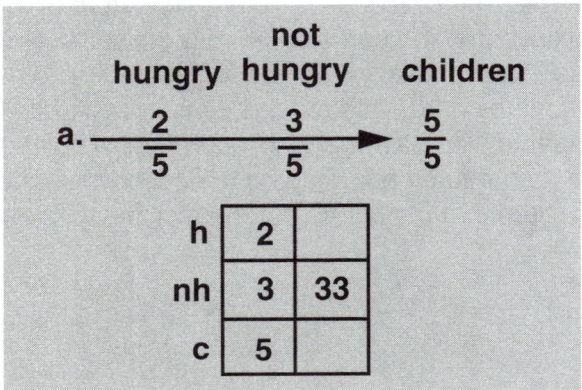

• Here's the number family and the table with four numbers.
• Complete the table and answer the questions. Each answer has a number and a unit name. Raise your hand when you're finished.
(Observe students and give feedback.)
• (Write to show:)

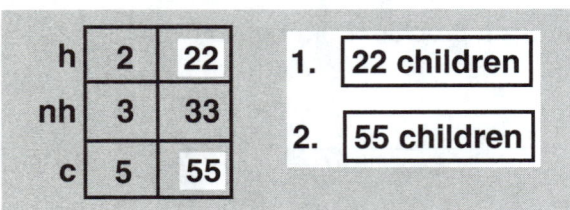

• Here's what you should have. There were 22 children who were hungry. There were 55 children in all.

Teaching note: Make sure that students do not take shortcuts. Also make sure that they work fast. If they take a lot of time to work these problems, repeat the set of

problems later. Tell them what you expect. "Show all the work. Show the number family with the names. Show the table. Show the answers to the questions. Make sure that you have the unit names in your answers." Students may use somewhat abbreviated names in their family, for instance:

hungry   not   children

These names are acceptable.

If the student who wrote the following names is very clear about what they mean, these are acceptable:

hung   not   ch

Tell students that you will show the full names when you put the work on the board. This avoids confusion. "You don't have to have exactly the same names that I have, but you should have a clear idea of what your headings stand for."

Also permit students to show answers in abbreviated ways. Students may just write the unit name after the number that appears in the table. This procedure is probably acceptable if students box the number and the name. They should show the unit for the boxed answer:

h	2	22	children
nh	3	33	
c	5	55	

The most telling difficulty that students will exhibit is completing problems at a slow rate. If they are very slow in solving these problems, they are not familiar with the steps. If they are not familiar with the steps, they are not in a good position to see what they are doing or why. For them, the work is mechanical and possibly void of much meaning. Give them additional practice. Set a time goal for working a problem. "See if you can do it in two minutes." Praise students who succeed. Permit the others to try again.

In Lesson 12, students work problems that refer to percent values or decimal values.

Example:

65% of the coins were pennies. There were 175 coins that were not pennies. How many coins were there in all? How many pennies were there?

Students follow the same steps used for working the other ratio-table problems. They make a fraction number family and a ratio table. They answer the questions with a number and a unit name. The number family shows the percents as fractions:

	pennies	not pennies	coins
	$\dfrac{65}{100}$	$\dfrac{35}{100}$ →	$\dfrac{100}{100}$

The names are shown in the same order as they appeared in the word problem. The table also shows the names in the same order:

p	65	
np	35	175
c	100	

The answers to the questions have numbers and unit names:

p	65	325
np	35	175
c	100	500

1. **500 coins**
2. **325 pennies**

For problems that involve decimal values (.7, for instance), students show corresponding fractions in the number family.

In Lesson 16, students work with tables that result in mixed-number answers.

Here's a problem from that lesson:

	5	■
	3	■
total	8	9

Students determine that the missing factor is 9/8. They work the problem: 3 times 9/8 equals 27/8. They write the answer as a mixed number: 3 and 3/8. To complete the table, they work the subtraction problem: 9 minus 3 and 3/8. The answer is 5 and 5/8.

Teaching note: The subtraction problem requires one of the tool skills taught in Lesson 14. Students must rewrite 9 as 8 and 8/8, then subtract.

In Lesson 19, students work word problems that require conversions to mixed numbers.

Here's a problem from that lesson:

80% of the corn was yellow. The rest was white. If there were 26 tons of corn in all, how many tons of white corn were there? How many tons of yellow corn were there?

Here are the number family and the ratio table with the numbers the problem gives:

	yellow	white	corn
	$\dfrac{80}{100}$	$\dfrac{20}{100}$ →	$\dfrac{100}{100}$

y	80	
w	20	
c	100	

Here's the completed table:

y	80	$20\frac{8}{10}$
w	20	$5\frac{2}{10}$
c	100	26

Teaching note: This problem shows why a variety of tool skills were reviewed earlier in the program. To work this problem, students convert percents to fractions. They use number family logic to show the related fractions and their classification (as part of a whole). Students express the missing factor as a fraction and work a multiplication problem. They translate the fractional answer into a division problem and express it as a mixed number. Finally, they work the mixed-number subtraction to complete the problem.

In Lesson 33, students work ratio-table problems that involve comparisons. Students have already practiced the component skill of making a number family for comparison statements (starting in Lesson 31). The problems presented in Lesson 33 have a difference number. Students follow the procedure of using the numerators of the fractions as ratio numbers in the first column of the table.

Here's part of the review from Lesson 33:

a. The regular price of a chair is $\frac{5}{4}$ the sale price of the chair. If you bought the chair on sale, you'd save $12. What's the regular price of the chair? What's the sale price of the chair?

b. The elephant weighs $\frac{3}{8}$ as much as the rock. The elephant weighs 6,000 pounds. How much does the rock weigh? How much more does the rock weigh than the elephant weighs?

c. The cost of the sewing machine is $\frac{7}{5}$ the cost of the TV set. The TV set costs $280. How much does the sewing machine cost? What's the difference between the cost of the sewing machine and the cost of the TV set?

b. You're going to make a number family and a ratio table for each problem.

c. Problem A: The regular price of a chair is 5/4 the sale price of the chair. If you bought the chair on sale, you'd save $12. What's the regular price of the chair? What's the sale price of the chair?

• The first sentence tells about the number family. Remember, figure out which is the big number. Write the names. Then put in the fractions. Raise your hand when you've finished your number family. (Observe students and give feedback.)

• (Write on the board:)

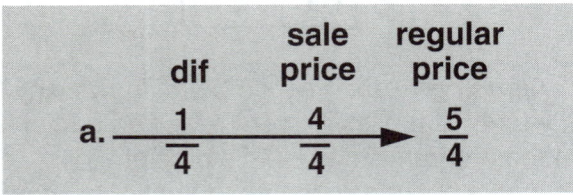

• Here's what you should have. The regular price is 5/4. That's more than 1, so it's the big number.

d. Now make the ratio table with the ratio numbers in the first column and the **dollar amount** the problem gives in the second column. The problem tells how much you'd save. **That's the difference number.**

• Raise your hand when you have the table with the names and four numbers. (Observe students and give feedback.)

• (Write on the board:)

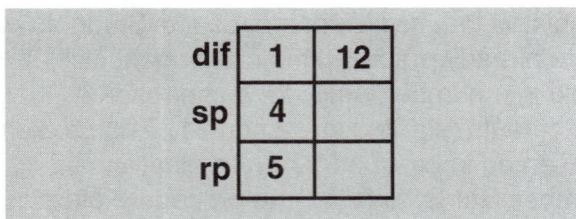

• Here's what you should have so far.

e. Now figure out the sale price and the regular price. Answer the questions the problem asks. Raise your hand when you're finished. (Observe students and give feedback.)

• (Write to show:)

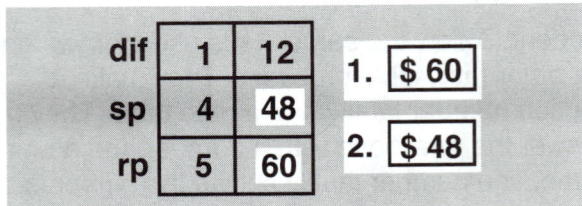

• Here's what you should have. The regular price is $60. The sale price is $48. Raise your hand if you got everything right.

> ***Teaching note:*** The problem-solving steps are not unique. The major difficulty that students have is setting up the table with the correct names. The first name is **difference** for all the comparison problems. Students have worked problems like these and should be able to work without much direction. Make sure that they are able to work quickly.

In Lesson 37, students apply the same problem-solving strategy to problems that refer to percents.

For example:

Fran's savings were 65% as much as Linda's savings. Fran's savings were $130. How much were Linda's savings? How much more were Linda's savings than Fran's savings?

Students make a number family with fractions for the percents:

	dif	Fran	Linda
	$\frac{35}{100}$	$\frac{65}{100}$	$\frac{100}{100}$

They put the percent numbers in the first column of the table and complete the table, then answer the questions (showing the answers boxed):

dif	35	70	1. $200
F	65	130	
L	100	200	2. $70

In Lesson 48, students work with comparison statements that will be used in later ratio-table problems. These statements sometimes present difficulties for some students.

Here are two statements:

The cost of the hat was 20% of the cost of the coat. The cost of the hat was 20% less than the cost of the coat.

The first sentence does not give the difference number; the second sentence does. As a rule, if the sentence tells about "a percent of" a value or "a percent as much as" a value, it does not tell about the difference number. If it tells about "a percent more" or "a percent less" than a value, it does tell about the difference number.

In Lesson 52, students do additional work with these statements. Students make both types of statements from a number family that shows the values for the two names (not the difference number). (See **Number Families.**)

In Lesson 56, students work a set of ratio-table problems that involve both types of statements.

Here's the entire exercise:

a. The crane was 40% lighter than the tractor. The crane weighed 24 tons. How much did the tractor weigh? How much more did the tractor weigh than the crane weighed?

b. The crane held 36% of the amount the truck held. The truck held 1500 pounds. How much did the crane hold? How much less did the crane hold than the truck?

c. The goose weighed 60% more than the hawk. The goose weighed 6 pounds more than the hawk. How much did the hawk weigh? How much did the goose weigh?

a. These are ratio-table problems. For each problem, you'll make the number family, then put the numbers in a ratio table. All the problems tell about percents. Some problems give a difference number.

b. Problem A. Read it carefully. Make the number family. Raise your hand when you've done that much.
(Observe students and give feedback.)

• (Write on the board:)

	dif	crane	tractor
a.	$\frac{40}{100}$	$\frac{60}{100}$ →	$\frac{100}{100}$

• Check your work. Problem A gives the difference number. It says: The crane was 40 percent lighter than the tractor. The difference number is 40-hundredths. The tractor is 100 percent.

c. Problem B. Read it carefully. Make the number family. Raise your hand when you've done that much.
(Observe students and give feedback.)

• (Write on the board:)

	dif	crane	tractor
b.	$\frac{64}{100}$	$\frac{36}{100}$ →	$\frac{100}{100}$

• Check your work. Problem B does not give a difference number. It says: The crane held 36 percent of the amount the truck held. The crane is 36-hundredths. The truck is 100-hundredths. The difference is 64-hundredths.

d. Problem C. Read it carefully. Make the number family. Raise your hand when you've done that much.
(Observe students and give feedback.)

• (Write on the board:)

	dif	hawk	goose
c.	$\frac{60}{100}$	$\frac{100}{100}$ →	$\frac{160}{100}$

• Check your work. Problem C gives a difference number. The goose weighed 60 percent more than the hawk. The difference is 60-hundredths. The hawk is 100-hundredths. And the goose is 160 hundredths.

e. Raise your hand if you got everything right.

f. As part of your independent work, you'll make the ratio tables for the problems in part 8. Use the information the problem gives and answer the questions.

Teaching note: Students may make the wrong number families for the problems. For problem A, students may show the cranes as 40/100, and the difference as 60/100. Point out: "The problem says that the crane is 40 percent **lighter than.** Does that tell about how much more or less the crane is?" *Yes.*

"So it tells about the difference."

For problem B, students may show 36/100 as the difference number. Point out:

"The problem says that the crane held 36 percent of the amount the truck held. Does that statement tell how much more or less the crane held?" *No.*

"So it does not tell about the difference."

For C, students may show 60/100 as the number for either the goose or the hawk.

Point out:

"The problem says that the goose weighed 60 percent **more than** the hawk. Does that statement tell how much more or less the goose weighed?" *Yes.*

"So it's the difference number."

If students have trouble with these statements, require them to rewrite statements that do not present a difference number. For example:

The rabbit weighed 70% as much as the fox.
The girl's age was 115% of the boy's age.
The girl ran 80% as fast as the dog.

For each sentence, students are to make the corresponding statement that refers to the difference number:

The rabbit was 30% lighter than the fox.
The girl was 15% older than the boy.
The girl ran 20% slower than the dog ran.

Students should be very quick at making these statements. If they are slow, present similar statements until students become facile. Remind them, "If the sentence tells about a percent more than or less than, it's a difference number. Otherwise, it's a number for the first value named in the sentence.

Starting in Lesson 47, students work a mixed set of problems that involve classification and comparison problems.

Here are the problems from Lesson 59:

a. 36% of the days were wet. The rest were dry. There were 150 days. How many wet days were there? How many dry days were there?

b. The new price is 120% of the old price. The new price is $30. What is the old price? What is the difference between the new price and the old price?

c. The time spent working is 25% more than the time spent sleeping. 8 hours are spent sleeping. How much time is spent working? How much less time is spent sleeping than working?

Problem A is a classification problem with **days** as the big number (100%). Problem B is a comparison problem with a **new price** (120%) as the big number. Problem C is a comparison problem with the difference number given (25%).

The final work with ratio-table problems occurs in Lessons 69 and 71. Students work problems that involve dollar-and-cents amounts. The work

with ratio tables is maintained for the remainder of Level F through independent-work exercises.

PROBABILITY

The work with probability extends the work with ratio tables. Students do not make number families for these applications, and the tables that they construct to show probability have more than three rows. However, the problems are a simple extension of what students learn about ratio tables.

The primary type of probability application students work with in Level F is a spinner on a circle graph. (See **Circle Graphs.**) The circle is divided into slices. The probability of a spinner stopping on a particular slice depends on the size of the slice. If the slice is half of the entire circle, the probability is 1/2 or .5.

The work that prepares students for these problems begins in Lesson 72, where students complete ratio tables that have more than three rows and create such tables from information given in a circle graph.

Here's a table that appears in Lesson 72:

%	#
20	■
25	■
40	■
5	4
10	■
total 100	■

The students can't add in the second column. They figure out the missing numbers by first working the problem for the completed row: 5 times some value equals 4. The missing value is 4/5. Therefore, all the numbers in the first column are multiplied by 4/5 to obtain the corresponding numbers in the second column.

Here's the completed table:

%	#
20	16
25	20
40	32
5	4
10	8
total 100	80

Problem C in Lesson 72 requires students to construct a ratio table from a circle graph:

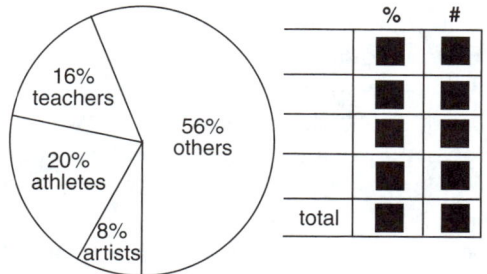

The conventions are:

1. The slices are ordered according to size, with the largest slice first and the smallest slice just above the total.

2. The information shown in the circle graph goes in the first column of the table. This graph gives percents; therefore, the percent numbers (without decimal points or percent signs) go in the first column. The total number of people is 350. That number goes in the second column.

	%	#
others	56	
athletes	20	
teachers	16	
artists	8	
total	100	350

3. Students complete the table by referring first to the row that has two numbers (100 and 350), figuring out the factor, then using their calculator to work multiplication problems for the rest of the rows.

Here's part of the introduction from Lesson 72:

d. Problem C. The circle graph shows percents for occupations of people at a meeting. The categories are **athletes, teachers, artists,** and **others.** The largest category is **others.**

• Your turn: Make a table. Show percents and the names in order of their size. Show **others** first, then **athletes,** then **teachers,** then **artists,** then **total.** The **total** is 100 percent because that's the whole circle. Raise your hand when your table has names and percents.

• (Write on the board:)

		%	#
c.	others	56	
	athletes	20	
	teachers	16	
	artists	8	
	total	100	

• Here's what you should have.
• The fact next to the circle graph tells about one of the numbers in the second column: There was a total of 350 people at the meeting.
• Write that number where it belongs and complete the table. Raise your hand when you're finished. (Observe students and give feedback.)
• (Write to show:)

		%	#
c.	others	56	196
	athletes	20	70
	teachers	16	56
	artists	8	28
	total	100	350

• Here's what you should have. You multiplied each row by the fraction 350/100 or the decimal 3 and 5-tenths. You could have simplified that into 35/10. Raise your hand if you got everything right.

For some problems that are presented in later lessons, students will make tables that have percents in the second column, not the first.

Here's an example from Lesson 74:

Make a complete table for the circle graph. Answer each question.

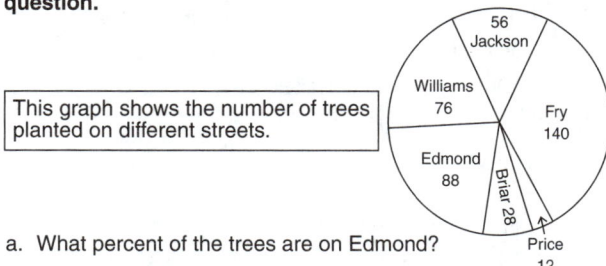

This graph shows the number of trees planted on different streets.

a. What percent of the trees are on Edmond?

b. What percent of the trees are on Briar?

c. What percent of the trees are on Fry?

d. What's the percent for the street that has the largest number of trees?

e. What's the percent for the street that has the fewest number of trees?

Starting in Lesson 79, students work similar problems that do not give a value for every category.

Here's a problem from Lesson 79:

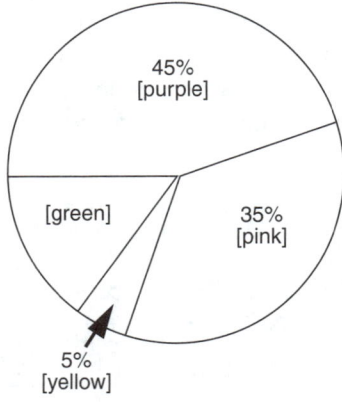

One part (green) is not given. To find it, students add the percents for the other slices and then subtract that total from 100. (In Lessons 76 through 78, students have already practiced the skill of combining values and subtracting.)

Variations of the problem type introduced in Lesson 79 require students to use information about fractions or percents to figure out the degrees for the various slices.

Probability problems are introduced in Lesson 81. The problems are simple extensions of the work with circle graphs. The only difference is the kind of information presented in the two columns of the table. The first column shows percents. The second shows expected numbers based on a total of so many trials.

Here's part of the introduction from Lesson 81:

A person spins the arrow 50 times.

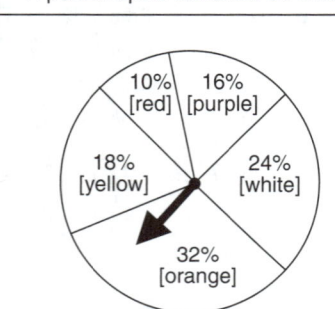

b. You're going to work a problem that asks how many times you would expect the spinner to land on different colors.
- You can work probability problems of this type just like other ratio-table problems.
- You'll show the percents in the first column of your table, and the second column will show the number of times you would expect the spinner to land on each color. The heading for that column is **trials.** 1 trial is 1 spin.
c. The circle shows the percents for the parts. The fact above the circle tells the total number of times somebody spins the spinner. That's the total for the second column.
- The most probable color is the color with the largest percent. What color is that? (Signal.) *Orange.*
- List the colors from **most probable** to **least probable.** Put percent numbers in the first column and one number in the second column. Raise your hand when you've done that much.
(Observe students and give feedback.)
- (Write on the board:)

	%	trials
orange	32	
white	24	
yellow	18	
purple	16	
red	10	
total	100	50

- Here's what you should have.
- Make sure your names are in the right order. Then figure out the number of times you would expect the spinner to land on different colors. Remember, you're spinning 50 times. Raise your hand when you've completed the table and answered the questions.
(Observe students and give feedback.)
- (Write to show:)

	%	trials
orange	32	16
white	24	12
yellow	18	9
purple	16	8
red	10	5
total	100	50

- Here's what you should have.
- If you take 50 trials, how many times would you expect the spinner to land on purple? (Signal.) *8.*
- If you take 50 trials, how many times would you expect the spinner to land on yellow? (Signal.) *9.*
- How many times would you expect the spinner to land on orange? (Signal.) *16.*
- How many times would you expect the spinner to land on white? (Signal.) *12.*
- How many times would you expect the spinner to land on red? (Signal.) *5.*

d. Raise your hand if you got everything right.

> **Teaching note:** Students should not have difficulties with this exercise if they are facile with the preceding work. The spinner problems are good applications for probability because they visually show the relationships rather than merely presenting numbers for the relationship. The larger slice would understandably have the larger probability. (If the circle were a single color, the probability would be 100 percent that the spinner would land on that color. If the circle had two colors in two slices of equal size, the probability would be 50 percent for each color, and so forth.) Students who have an understanding of spinner problems know that probabilities can be assigned for each of the slices (not just two of the slices) and that the probability relationships are simply ratio relationships.

More difficult probability problems are introduced in Lesson 83. These problems require a table with three columns—one for percents, one for expected numbers, and one for actual numbers. The problems give information about actual numbers, which are not the same as expected numbers. Students first figure out the expected numbers, then place the actual numbers in the table. Students follow the rule of finding the expected number that is closest to an actual number and placing the actual number in the same row as the corresponding expected number.

Here's the problem from Lesson 83:

Copy and complete the table.

This experiment involves 60 trials.

Facts
1. The spinner landed this color 14 times.
2. The spinner landed on this color 19 times.
3. The spinner landed on this color 23 times.
4. The spinner land on this color 4 times.

colors	%	expected	actual
■	■	■	■
■	■	■	■
■	■	■	■
■	■	■	■
total	■	60	60

Students complete the first two columns. They know that the total number of trials is 60, so they can work the problem: 100 times some value equals 60. Students work the problem on their calculator. The missing value is 6-tenths.

Students multiply the various rows by 6-tenths to complete the first two columns, showing the names for the different colors:

colors	%	expected	actual
blue	40	24	
yellow	30	18	
white	20	12	
red	10	6	
total	100	60	60

Next students compare the actual values with the expected values and put each actual value next to the value that is closest in size.

In subsequent lessons, students work different variations. For some, not all the percents are given. For some, the information about percents is presented through statements, not by a circle graph.

The final application is a project, presented in Lesson 93. Students first figure out the probabilities for different possible outcomes obtained by rolling two dice. Students make a table with the various possibilities in the first column and the expected outcomes for 72 trials in the second column. Finally, students make a circle graph that shows the various possibilities. (See **Projects**.)

MULTIPLICATION PROBLEMS

In some ratio activities, students learn to translate comparison statements into number families and ratio tables. (See **Ratio Tables.**) Students also learn a fast way to handle problems that give information about a fraction of a value and can be solved by multiplication.

Here's a problem of that type:

Milly was 3/4 as old as her brother. Her brother was 48 years old. How old was Milly?

The problem can be worked by figuring out what 3/4 of her brother's age equals. 3/4 **of** a value is 3/4 **times** that value. Since the problem gives the value for the brother, Milly's age is: 3/4 × 48.

Starting in Lesson 21, students work the simplest form of these problems, those that ask about a percent or a fraction of a number. For example: **What is 7/3 of 21?**

Here's part of the introduction from Lesson 21:

a. Listen: For some problems, you have to find a **fraction** of a value or a **percent** of a value. You may have to find 2/3 of 12. You may have to find 60 percent of 28.

b. You can figure out the answer to these problems a simple way. Listen: **To find a fraction of a value or a percent of a value, you multiply.** 2/5 **of** 20 is 2/5 **times** 20.

c. Listen: What's another way of saying: 1/9 of 80? (Signal.) *1-ninth **times** 80.*
- What's the fraction for 20 percent? (Signal.) *20/100.*
- So 20 percent of 90 is 20/100 **times** 90.
- What's the fraction for 40 percent? (Signal.) *40/100.*
- What's another way of saying: 40 percent **of** 60? (Signal.) *40-hundredths **times** 60.*
- What's the fraction for 8 percent? (Signal.) *8/100.*
- What's another way of saying: 8 percent **of** 12? (Signal.) *8-hundredths **times** 12.*
(Repeat step c until firm.)

d. (Write on the board:)

$$\frac{8}{100} \times 12$$

- Here's 8/100 times 12. On top, I multiply 8 times 12. That's 96.
- On the bottom, I have 100.
- (Write to show:)

$$\frac{8}{100} \times 12 = \frac{96}{100}$$

- I end up with 96/100.

a. What is $\frac{7}{3}$ of 21?

b. What's 8% of 300?

c. What is 2% of 15?

e. Open your textbook to Lesson 21 and find Part 1.
- For each of these problems, you'll write the multiplication problem and the answer.
f. Problem A: What is 7/3 of 21? Do the multiplication and figure out 7/3 of 21. Show the fraction you get when you multiply, then write an equal sign and show the simplified answer. Raise your hand when you're finished.
(Observe students and give feedback.)
- (Write on the board:)

$$\textbf{a.} \quad \frac{7}{3} \times 21 \; = \; \frac{147}{3} \; = \; 49$$

- Here's what you get when you multiply 7/3 times 21. 7/3 of 21 is 49. Raise your hand if you got it right.
g. Problem B: What is 8 percent of 300? Do the multiplication and figure out what 8 percent of 300 equals. Simplify the answer. Raise your hand when you're finished.
(Observe students and give feedback.)
- (Write on the board:)

$$\textbf{b.} \quad \frac{8}{1\cancel{00}} \times 3\cancel{00} = \frac{24}{1}$$

- Here's what you get when you multiply 8/100 times 300.
- You should have written **equals 24** after the last fraction. Raise your hand if you got it right.

> **Teaching note:** In step c, you ask a series of questions. Make sure that the students are firm in responding. If their responses are weak, repeat the questions.

Beginning with Lesson 24, students work problems that involve unit names. The answers to these problems consist of a number and the unit name.

Here are the problems from Lesson 24:

a. A car had traveled $\frac{3}{5}$ of the total distance. The total distance was 200 miles. How far had the car traveled?

b. There were 150 people. 40% of them wore glasses. How many people wore glasses?

c. .3 of the days were sunny. There were 50 days. How many days were sunny?

All the problems that students work through Lesson 25 refer to a fraction or percent **of** a value. In Lesson 26, new wording is introduced. This wording refers to **as** _____ **as** (as much as, as long as, as heavy as, etc.). The problems are solved the same way as previously presented problems. (A fraction **as much as** a value is the fraction **times** the value.)

Here are the problems that students work in Lesson 26:

a. The car weighs 40% as much as the truck weighs. The truck weighs 6 tons. What does the car weigh?

b. The economy battery lasts .6 as long as the premium battery. The premium battery lasts 4.8 years. How long does the economy battery last?

c. 25% of the animals were on leashes. There were 20 animals. How many animals were on leashes?

d. There is $\frac{7}{10}$ as much chicken soup as vegetable soup. there are 9 gallons of vegetable soup. How much chicken soup is there?

Students work the problems through either decimal multiplication or fraction multiplication.

For different problems, you give different instructions. This arbitrary switching from fractions to decimals assures that students learn that a given percent or decimal value can be expressed as a fraction or a decimal value.

In Lesson 28, students work a mixed set of problems. Some problems can be worked as fraction or decimal multiplication. Others can't. They are worked as ratio-table problems. The key to whether a problem can be worked as multiplication is whether the problem gives a number for the value something is compared to. In the statement **Milly was 3/4 as old as her brother,** something is compared to her brother. If the problem gives a number for her brother, therefore, the problem can be worked as a multiplication problem. If the problem gives information about Milly, however, the problem can't be worked as a multiplication problem.

The exercise in Lesson 28 requires students to write the multiplication problem for each item, using a fraction times the name. For **Dan weighs 7/5 as much as Mary,** students write: **7/5 × M.** If the problem gives a number for Mary, they circle the letter in the expression. If the problem does not give a number for Mary (but rather, for Dan), students cross out the expression. The problem can't be worked through simple multiplication.

Here's part of the work from Lesson 28:

a. Dan weighs $\frac{7}{5}$ as much as Mary. Dan weighs 80 pounds. How much does Mary weigh?

b. The train travels $\frac{3}{5}$ as far as the car. The car travels 60 miles. How far does the train travel?

c. The county is $\frac{1}{8}$ as large as the state. The county is 300 square miles. How large is the state?

d. The bug's weight is $\frac{8}{9}$ of the pebble's weight. The pebble weighs 20 grams. How much does the bug weigh?

e. The coast is $\frac{9}{5}$ as far away as the mountain. The mountain is 40 miles away. How far away is the coast?

d. Problem B. The first sentence says: The train travels 3/5 as far as the car.
• Write the problem with a fraction and a letter. Raise your hand when you're finished. √
• (Write on the board:)

> b. $\frac{3}{5}$ × c

• Here's what you should have. 3/5 as far as the car is 3/5 times the car.
• Read the rest of the problem. If it gives a number for car, circle **C.** If the problem doesn't give a number for car, cross out what you wrote. Raise your hand when you're finished. √
• You should have circled **C.** The problem gives a number for the car. So you can work it by multiplying. You'll do that later. Leave a space.

e. Problem C. Write the multiplication problem with a letter. Circle the letter or cross out what you wrote. Raise your hand when you're finished. (Observe students and give feedback.)
• (Write on the board:)

> c. $\frac{1}{8}$ × s (crossed out)

• Here's what you should have: 1/8 of the state is 1/8 times the state. The problem does not give a number for **state.** You can't work the problem by multiplying. You should have crossed it out.

f. Your turn: Write multiplication problems for the rest of the items in part 2. Circle or cross out. Raise your hand when you're finished. (Observe students and give feedback.)

g. (Write on the board:)

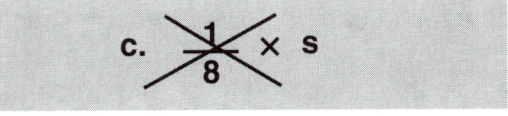

> d. $\frac{8}{9}$ × Ⓟ   e. $\frac{9}{5}$ × Ⓜ

- Here's what you should have for items D and E.
- For D, you wrote 8/9 times the pebble. The problem gives the pebble's weight. So you can work it by multiplying.
- For E, you wrote 9/5 times the mountain. The problem gives a number for mountain. So you can work that problem by multiplying.

> **Teaching note:** Students must be very firm on this discrimination. If they are not, present them with additional problems.
>
> Here is a mixed set that will help show the information the problem must give in order to be solved by multiplication:
>
> **Jan is 2/5 as old as the parrot. The parrot is 13 years old. How old is Jan?**
>
> **Tom is 7/5 the age of his brother. Tom is 13 years old. How old is his brother?**
>
> **Dan's weight is 4/5 the weight of Harry. If Harry weighs 200 pounds, how much does Dan weigh?**
>
> **Harry is 8/9 as tall as the fence. The fence is 76 inches tall. How tall is Harry?**
>
> **The cat is 3/7 the age of the dog. The cat is 7 years old. How old is the dog?**
>
> Present similar problems if students are not perfectly firm on the discrimination. Students are firm when they work these problems without a lot of assistance.

Problem sets similar to those above appear in Lessons 29 and 30. In Lesson 38, students work all the problems in a mixed set (rather than simply crossing out problems that can't be worked as multiplication). The work with these problems is important because it helps students see the difference between problem types. Typically, students learn to work the type of problem that can be solved through simple multiplication; however, they do not encounter the type that is worked as a ratio problem, and they often become confused about the difference between these problem types. The discrimination is actually fairly simple: "Does the problem ask about a fraction of a number?" If the problem gives the number, either directly or indirectly, it can be solved by multiplication.

MULTI-STEP PROBLEMS

A multi-step problem is one that requires more than one operation or calculation. A variety of these problems are introduced in Level F starting with Lesson 5 and continuing through Lesson 69.

These problems include those that are solved by inverse operations, those that require component calculations (e.g., money problems that involve tax) and area problems that involve complex or irregular figures (including figures that have "holes").

Inverse Operations

Students who went through Level E or the Bridge have solved problems by using inverse operations. The tool skills are reviewed in Level F starting with Lesson 1. (See **Operational Relationships**.)

The inverse-operation word problems give information for writing more than one equation. The first problem type requires students to figure out a mystery number. Here's a problem:

> **You start with some number and divide by 6. You add 9 and end up with 12. What's the number you start with?**

Here are the rules for writing equations: The reference to **some number** or **what number** calls for a box (or letter). The first sentence indicates that you start with some number and divide by 6. The equation for that sentence is:

$$\boxed{}^{?} \div 6 = \boxed{}$$

The next sentence indicates that you add 9 and end up with 12. The equation for that sentence is:

$$\boxed{}^{?} \div 6 = \boxed{}$$
$$\boxed{} + 9 = 12$$

Once the equations are set up, students find the missing values by starting at the end of the second equation and working backward until the mystery number is identified:

$$\boxed{18}^{?} \div 6 = \boxed{3}$$
$$\boxed{3} + 9 = 12$$

The mystery number is 18.

> **Teaching note:** The solution to these problems involves undoing operations. Ask students, "What operation was done?" and "How is that operation undone?"

For ending up with 12 in the second equation, ask, "What did we do to end up with 12?" *Added 9.*

"What undoes adding 9?" *Subtracting 9.*

"What's 12 minus 9?" *3.*

"So the first value in the second equation (and the value directly above it) is 3."

In Lesson 6, students make equations that refer to **doubling, tripling,** and **twice** as large. They translate these into the operations of: times 2, times 3, and times 2. In Lesson 7, students work problems that use these phrases.

Here are two problems presented in Lesson 7:

b. A train started out with some people in it. After the first stop, there were twice as many people in the train. After 38 people got off at the second stop, there were 120 people on the train. How many people were in the train at the start of the journey?

c. A delivery truck set out with some bicycles in it. In the morning it delivered 35 bicycles. After a visit to the warehouse, the number of bicycles in the truck tripled. There were now 60 bicycles in the truck. How many bicycles were in the truck to begin with?

The first problem refers to the number of people on a train. The equations are based on the idea that if people get on the train, the number is increased. In this case the operation is multiplication:

$$\overset{?}{\boxed{}} \times 2 = \boxed{}$$

If people get off the train, the number is decreased. In this case, the operation is subtraction:

$$\overset{?}{\boxed{}} \times 2 = \boxed{}$$
$$\boxed{} - 38 = 120$$

Beginning with Lesson 9, students work problems that have a missing number in the middle, not at the beginning of the first equation.

Beginning with Lesson 15, students work problems that involve three equations.

Here's a problem from that lesson:

c. A tank had 280 liters of water in it. The original amount was divided by 2. Then 50 liters were added to the tank. Then the tank sprung a leak. Water leaked out until the tank had only 5 liters in it. How many liters leaked out?

Here are the equations that students write:

$$280 \div 2 = \boxed{}$$
$$\boxed{} + 50 = \boxed{} \quad ?$$
$$\boxed{} - \boxed{} = 5$$

Teaching note: Students sometimes have trouble generating the different equations. Remind them: "For each operation, you write a new equation. The first sentence of the problem does not tell about the operation."

"The second sentence tells about an operation (dividing by 20). The equation has two numbers."

$$280 \div 2 = \boxed{}$$

"The next sentence tells about an operation—adding 50:"

$$\boxed{} + 50 = \boxed{}$$

"The next sentence tells about an operation but doesn't give a number." (*Then the tank sprung a leak.* The operation is subtraction, but no number is given.) "The next sentence gives the operation with a number." (Water leaked out until the tank had only 5 liters in it:)

$$\boxed{} - \boxed{} = 5$$

To solve the problem, students work forward, starting with the equation that has two numbers.

$$280 \div 2 = \boxed{140}$$
$$\boxed{140} + 50 = \boxed{} \quad ?$$
$$\boxed{} - \boxed{} = 5$$

Next, students complete the last equation:

$$280 \div 2 = \boxed{140}$$
$$\boxed{140} + 50 = \boxed{190} \quad ?$$
$$\boxed{190} - \boxed{} = 5$$

The missing number is 185. That's the answer to the question the problem asks.

The solution to the problems is not difficult once the problems are set up appropriately. If a missing number is at the end of an equation or the beginning of the equation, students write the number in two places. This generates equations that have two numbers. Those equations can be solved for the missing number.

The final type of inverse-operation problem is introduced in Lesson 21. These problems require students to make an equation with three boxes and an operational sign.

Example:

A garden had 42 plants in it. Then the number of plants was doubled. A storm destroyed some of the plants. 136 new plants were planted, and the garden ended up with 200 plants in it. How many plants were destroyed by the storm?

The equation for the highlighted sentence has three boxes:

$$42 \times 2 = \square$$
$$\square - \square = \square$$
$$\square + 136 = 200$$

Students work forward for the first equation, backward for the last equation. This work puts two numbers in the middle equation:

$$42 \times 2 = \boxed{84}$$
$$\boxed{84} - \square = \boxed{64}$$
$$\boxed{64} + 136 = 200$$

This missing number is 20.

Component Calculations

Some problems involve solving several component problems before a larger problem can be solved. Problems of this form are introduced in Level F, starting with Lesson 35.

Here's the set of problems from Lesson 35:

a. A farmer plants a field with wheat. The field is 240 feet long and 360 feet wide. The cost of wheat is $.03 per square foot. How much does it cost to plant the entire field?

b. A farmer wants to fence a square field that is 90 feet on each side. The cost of fencing is $2.58 per foot. What's the cost of fencing for the field?

c. A farmer gets $.90 per gallon of milk and $.55 for each dozen eggs. In April, the farmer sold 1,235 gallons of milk and 165 dozen eggs. How much money did the farmer receive?

d. A farmer receives $2.10 for each bushel of corn and $.50 for each dozen eggs. During one month, the farmer sold 1600 bushels of corn and 284 dozen eggs. How much did the farmer earn in all?

For problem A, students first figure the area of the field, then multiply by .03 to determine the cost of planting. For computing the area, students use the equation: base × height = Area, and then put in the numbers for base and height.

For problem B, students first find the perimeter of the field, then multiply by 2.58 to determine the cost of fencing. No equation is required for computing the perimeter. Some students will simply enter the numbers in their calculator and compute the distance. However, they must show a unit name in the answers to component problems. For B, the unit name is feet. For A, the unit name is square feet. Make sure that students use these names in their component answers. For both A and B, the answer to the final problem is a dollar amount and requires a dollar sign.

For problems C and D, students work a separate problem for each item of produce. They then add the amounts to find the total.

Teaching note: These problems are designed to discourage students from being "word bound" in problem solving (finding the key words in the problems and using those words as keys for the operations that are to be performed). The problems also provide extensive application of the skills that students are practicing, especially working addition and multiplication problems that involve decimals.

Students should not have difficulty with the strategies for solving these problems, but if they do, you can guide them: "Start out with the question the problem asks. That's your goal, to answer that question. Then see what you need to know to answer that question. If the problem doesn't give you all the numbers you need, it gives you information you can use to get those numbers. Find that information and work the problems."

You can ask questions to prompt students, particularly those students who tend to try to analyze word problems according to the words, not the ideas:

"What does the problem ask you to do?"

"What are the names of the things you need numbers for?"

"Does the problem give the numbers you need?"

"Which numbers will you have to figure out?"

Also remind students: "You have to think about what the problem asks. For problem D, does the problem ask about selling or earning?"

Students who work from word formulas may become confused. For selling, they want to subtract. For receiving and earning, they add. Point out that to work the problem, you can't just attend to these words. They don't tell you what to do to solve the problem.

In Lesson 36, students work multi-step problems that involve tax. The work on these problems dovetails with the work that students have done with problems that give information about a percent of a value or a fraction of a value. **Tax is a percent of a value.** To work the simplest tax problems, students first figure out the amount of the tax and then add it to the cost of the item.

Here's part of the work from Lesson 36:

a.   An item costs $36.15. The tax is 4%. How much would the person have to pay for the item?

b.   An item costs $18.49. That tax is 5%. How much would a person pay for the item?

b. These are tax problems.

c. Problem A: An item costs $36.15. The tax is 4 percent. How much would the person have to pay for the item?

• Figure out the tax. Remember, 4 percent is 4-hundredths. Round your answer to hundredths. Raise your hand when you've figured out the tax. (Observe students and give feedback.)

• (Write on the board:)

(**tax**)

a. $ 36.15
    × .04
    ‾‾‾‾‾‾‾
    1.446

    $1.45

• The answer you get when you multiply is 1 and 446-thousandths. You round that to 1 and 45-hundredths. That's $1.45. Now add that to the cost of the item. Raise your hand when you're finished.
(Observe students and give feedback.)

• (Write on the board:)

(**total cost**)

$ 36.15
+ 1.45
‾‾‾‾‾‾‾
$ 37.60

• The tax is $1.45. The item is $36.15. The total is $37.60. That's the amount a person would pay.

d. Problem B: An item costs $18.49. The tax is 5 percent. How much would a person pay for the item?

• Figure out the tax. Round the answer to hundredths. Then add the tax to the price of the item. Raise your hand when you're finished. (Observe students and give feedback.)

Teaching note: The procedure specified requires students to label the tax and the total amount. Although the problems in Lesson 36 are not confusing if they are worked without this specification, later problems are handled more easily if students label each part.

In Lesson 38, more involved problems are introduced. For these, students first total the items that are purchased, then compute the tax on the amount of the purchase, then compute the total cost.

Here's part of the work from Lesson 38:

b. Problem A: Fran purchases a radio for $44.60 and a pair of gloves for $9.80. The tax is 5 percent. What is the cost of both items? What is the tax? What is the total purchase price of the items including tax?

• Figure out the total cost of the items **without** tax. Remember to show your answer as hundredths. Raise your hand when you've done that much. (Observe students and give feedback.)

• (Write on the board:)

(**items**)

a. $ 44.60
    +   9.80
    ‾‾‾‾‾‾‾
    $ 54.40

• You added $44.60 and $9.80. The answer is $54.40.

- Now find the tax on $54.40 and add it to $54.40. Raise your hand when you've figured the total that Fran would pay for the items.
  (Observe students and give feedback.)
- (Write to show:)

items	tax	total cost
a. $\begin{array}{r} \$\ 44.60 \\ +\ \ 9.80 \\ \hline \boxed{\$\ 54.40} \end{array}$	$\begin{array}{r} \$\ 54.40 \\ \times\ \ .05 \\ \hline \boxed{\$\ 2.7200} \end{array}$	$\begin{array}{r} \$\ 54.40 \\ +\ \ 2.72 \\ \hline \boxed{\$\ 57.12} \end{array}$

- Here's what you should have. You added $2.72 to $54.40. The answer is $57.12.

> **Teaching note:** The problem is designed to guide the steps for solving the problem. For the problem above, there are three questions. The first refers to the cost of both items; the next to the tax; the last to the total cost.
>
> In later lessons, these guide questions will be dropped and students will operate only from the final question. If they organize the work as it is prompted in Lesson 38, they will tend to make fewer mistakes.

In later lessons, students work similar problems that have more steps and different patterns for combining values. In Lesson 43, students work problems that give information about multiples. (The number of watches a dealer sold was 6 times the number of clocks.) Students also work a variety of problems that involve geometry applications—painting a circular disk (which requires first determining the area of the disk), finding the circumference of a circle, working problems that involve circles cut out of the center of larger circles (a circular walkway around a garden), and other complex geometric figures (parallelograms connected to triangles, rectangles, semicircles, etc.). For problems that involve "holes" within larger geometric forms, subtraction is implied. (See **Geometry**.)

The variety of problem types and information presented for the various multi-step problems assures that students develop a variety of problem-solving strategies and receive practice in translating different types of information (descriptions, figures, etc.) into multi-step problems.

RECIPROCALS

Level F teaches students to use reciprocals to solve problems and to use the logic of reciprocals to understand how division by a fraction works.

In Lesson 44, students work problems that refer to equal-sized parts and that ask about the fraction for each part or ask about the number of parts. To work these problems, students use the basic equation of the fraction for each part times the number of parts equals 1 (the whole). For a pie that is divided into 7 equal parts, each part is 1/7 of the whole pie. Therefore:

$$\frac{1}{7} \times 7 = \frac{7}{7}$$

In Lesson 52, students work problems that refer to percents.

Example:

Each piece of the pie is 25%. How many pieces are there?

Students convert 25% to 1/4 and work the problem:

$$\frac{1}{4} \times \square = \frac{4}{4}$$

The missing value is 4. That's the number of pieces.

In Lesson 53, students work an elaborated version of the same problem.

Example:

Each slice of the pie is 1/6 of the pie. Each slice costs 95¢. How much does the whole pie cost?

To work this problem, students first find the number of slices (6), then multiply by the cost of each slice (95 cents).

In Lesson 55, students work similar problems that ask about the size of a part.

Example:

a. The field was divided into 9 parcels of equal size. The entire field was 720 acres. How many acres were in each parcel?

Students figure out that each parcel is 1/9 of the total. Then students figure out the acres in each parcel. They may do this by dividing (720 divided by 9) or by multiplying (720 times 1/9). The point of the exercise is to show that dividing by 9 is the same as multiplying by the reciprocal of 9.

Here's part of the exercise from Lesson 55:

c. Problem B: Each pile of gold dust weighs 1/5 of the total. The entire amount of gold dust weighs 260 ounces. How much does each pile weigh?

• Work the problem. Raise your hand when you're finished.

(Observe students and give feedback.)

• (Write on the board:)

$$b. \quad \frac{1}{5} \times \frac{260}{} = \frac{260}{5}$$

$$5 \overline{)260} \quad \boxed{52 \text{ oz}}$$

• You could divide by 5 or multiply by 1/5. The answer is 52 ounces.

> **Teaching note:** Most students will solve the problem by dividing. The reason is that when the problem is worked by multiplication, the answer is a fraction: 260/5. To express the fraction as a whole number or mixed number, students divide. Working the problem as a division problem requires fewer steps. You show the problem worked both ways, however, because it is very important for the students to see the relationship: Dividing by a number is the same as multiplying by the reciprocal of that number. This relationship is the basis for how students will later learn to divide by a fraction. Dividing by any fraction is the same as multiplying by the reciprocal of that fraction; therefore, students can rewrite a division problem as a multiplication problem (e.g., 2/5 ÷ 3/7 is the same as 2/5 × 7/3).

In Lesson 57, students apply this relationship to problems that ask about one part or more than one part of a whole. Here are two problems from that lesson:

a. The area of the circle is 100 square inches.

b. The area of the circle is 52 square miles.

The question mark indicates what the students are to compute. The instructions the students follow indicate that if the problem can be worked by either multiplication or division, they are to write both problems. If the problem can be solved only by multiplication, they work that problem only.

Item A asks about more than one part, so the problem is worked by multiplication: 3/8 × 100. (That's 3/8 of the total area.) Item B can be solved the same way as the first problem: 1/4 × 52. Because item B asks about only one part (the fraction has a numerator of 1), the problem can also be solved as a division problem: 52 ÷ 4. **Note:** This relationship is unique and applies only to problems that ask about one of the parts. This relationship is important, however, because it provides the basic rationale for how students will divide by fractions, which is introduced in Lesson 81. (See **Reciprocals and Fraction Division**.)

MIXED-NUMBER PROBLEMS

In Level F, students work mixed-number word problems that require either multiplication or addition/subtraction. For the addition/subtraction problems, students first work with the fraction in each mixed number, then with the whole numbers. For multiplication problems, students convert the mixed numbers into improper fractions and multiply.

In Lesson 51, students are introduced to problems that require multiplication. The tool skills have already been taught (see **Mixed Number Operations**.)

Here's one of the problems from Lesson 51:

Each load of sand weighs $3\frac{1}{5}$ tons. The worker used $7\frac{1}{2}$ loads. What was the weight of the sand they used?

Students write: 16/5 × 15/2 = 240/10. The answer is 24 tons.

In Lesson 57, students work a mixed set of problems, some of which involve multiplication, some of which involve either addition or subtraction.

Here are the problems from that lesson:

a. Each barrel holds $3\frac{1}{4}$ cubic feet of oil. Each jug holds $\frac{1}{4}$ cubic foot of oil. Somebody buys a barrel of oil and a jug of oil. How much oil does the person buy?

b. The container has 12 pounds of flour. The cook used $5\frac{3}{8}$ pounds. How much flour was left in the container?

c. Each barrel holds $3\frac{1}{4}$ cubic feet of oil. How much oil do $1\frac{2}{5}$ barrels hold?

d. Each block of wood weighs $5\frac{2}{7}$ pounds.

Each bag of wood chips weighs $1\frac{6}{7}$ pounds. What is the weight of one block and one bag?

> **Teaching note:** The rule that students use is: **If the problem tells about one or each and asks about more than one, you multiply. Otherwise, you add or subtract.**
>
> Note that this criterion has two parts. Problem D tells about each, but it doesn't ask about more than one. So D is not solved by multiplication.
>
> When giving students feedback on their work, ask them why they worked the problems the way they did. Ask, "Does the problem tell about one? . . . Does the problem ask about more than one?" If the answer to the last question is no, ask, "What does the problem ask?"

TIME

In Level F, students work a variety of time problems. They work problems that require converting an hour into 60 minutes; they work problems that go past 12 noon and therefore require converting P.M. times into the times on a 24-hour clock. They work problems that refer to clock time and problems that give clock time and ask about the difference.

In Lesson 61, the first time problems are introduced. To solve these problems, students add or subtract. Some problems require converting a value in the problem (either one of the times that was given in the problem or the answer).

Here are the introductory problems from Lesson 61:

Part 8

- Some problems refer to clock time. You can work those problems by showing the hours and minutes separated by a colon.
- Here's a problem:

  Jim worked from 7:30 a.m. until 11:10 a.m. How long did he work?

  $$\begin{array}{r} \overset{10}{\cancel{11}}\overset{70}{:}\overset{}{\cancel{10}} \\ -\ 7:30 \\ \hline 3:40 \end{array}$$

  - Jim worked for: | 3 hr | 40 min |

- Here's a different type of problem:

  Donna started work at 8:15 a.m. She worked for 2 hours and 45 minutes. When did she stop working?

- For this problem, you can show 2 hours and 45 minutes as 2:45.

  $$\begin{array}{r} 8:15 \\ +\ 2:45 \\ \hline 10:60 \end{array}$$

  - Donna stopped working at: | 11:00 a.m. |

Part 9 | **Work each item. Answer the question the problem asks.**

a. Hilda left home at 7:40 a.m. She returned home at 10:15 a.m. How long was she away from home?

b. Fred worked for 5 hours, 50 minutes. If he started work at 2:15 p.m., at what time did he finish work?

c. Andrew started work at 7:30 a.m. Sally started work 3 hours and 20 minutes later. At what time did Sally start work?

> **Teaching notes:** The first sample problem shows the conversion of 11:10 into 10:70.
>
> Here are the steps that students take:
>
> 1. They figure out that they can't subtract without borrowing.
>
> 2. They borrow 1 hour. When they do that, they reduce the number of hours from 11 to 10.
>
> 3. They convert the hour to 60 minutes.
>
> 4. They add 60 minutes to 10 minutes. The answer is 70 minutes.
>
> 5. They write the converted time of 10:70 above the original time.
>
> 6. They subtract.
>
> The key to the conversion is whether it's possible to subtract. If not, convert. If subtraction without borrowing is possible, don't convert.
>
> Expect some students to have trouble with the conversion. The most common mistake has to do with the number of hours. Students may either write the converted time as 11:70 or, in some cases, 12:70. Remind them: "You have only so much time. After you borrow, you have the same amount of time. It's just written differently. You started with 11 hours and 10 minutes. When you borrow, you'll still have 11 hours, but you'll show 1 of the hours as 60 minutes. How many hours will not be shown as minutes?" *10.*
>
> For the second problem, the conversion goes the other way. The answer is 10:60. That's not a proper expression. Students convert the 60 minutes into 1 hour and add it to the number of hours shown. The converted time is 11:00.
>
> Students may have trouble with this conversion. Point out that 10 hours and 60 minutes are shown in the answer. You're just going to write the answer differently. "How are you going to show the 60 minutes?" *As 1 hour.*
>
> "So how many hours will you have in all?" *11.*

Students practice problems that require conversion of hours to minutes and vice versa through Lesson 63. During this same lesson range, they also practice converting A.M. and P.M. time to time on a 24-hour clock. The rules they follow are: a) If it is a P.M. time, add 12 to the hours shown and write the time without the letters P.M.; b) If it is an A.M. time, write it without the letters A.M.

To go from time on the 24-hour clock to A.M. or P.M. time, students first note whether the time is more than 12 hours. If it is, they subtract 12 and write the difference as a P.M. time. If it is less than 12, they copy the time and write A.M.

In Lesson 64, students work word problems that require conversion to 24-hour time. Some of the problems involve subtraction. To work these, students convert the P.M. time into 24-hour time and subtract.

If addition problems result in a time that is more than 12 hours, students convert the answer into P.M. time by subtracting 12 from the hours in the answer.

Here's part of the introduction from Lesson 64:

c. Problem B: Millie leaves home at 7:10 A.M. She arrives at her aunt's house at 6:50 P.M. How long did the trip take?

• Convert the P.M. number to a 24-hour number and figure out the difference. Raise your hand when you're finished.
(Observe students and give feedback.)

• (Write on the board:)

$$
\begin{array}{r}
\text{b.} \quad 18:50 \\
-\ \ 7:10 \\
\hline
11:40 \\
\hline
\boxed{11\ \text{hr}\ \ 40\ \text{min}}
\end{array}
$$

• Here's the problem you worked: 18:50 minus 7:10. The difference is 11:40. That's the length of the trip: 11 hours and 40 minutes. Raise your hand if you got it right.

d. Problem C is a different kind of problem: Bill left Bradford at 11:20 A.M. His trip to Fairfax took 5 hours and 30 minutes. When did he arrive at Fairfax?

• For this problem, you add the time of the trip to the starting time. You'll get an hour number that is more than 12. You convert it to a P.M. hour.

• Do it. Raise your hand when you've worked the problem.
(Observe students and give feedback.)

• (Write on the board:)

$$
\begin{array}{r}
\text{c.} \quad 11:20 \\
+\ \ 5:30 \\
\hline
16:50 \\
\hline
\boxed{4:50\ \text{p.m.}}
\end{array}
$$

• Here's the problem you worked. You added: 11:20 and 5:30. You ended up with 16:50. To get the P.M. number, you subtracted 12. The answer is 4:50 P.M. That's when he arrived at Fairfax.

Teaching note: The questions these problems ask determine whether students write the answer as a clock time or as so many hours and minutes. If students have trouble, refer them to the question:

For item B, "What does the question ask?" *How long did the trip take?*

"Does that question ask about the time on a clock?" *No.*

"The question asks about the hours and minutes the trip took."

Require students to show the answer in hours and minutes. The answer 11:40 is not acceptable.

For item C, "The question asks, *When did he arrive at Fairfax? Does that question ask about the time on a clock?" Yes.*

"So you have to show it as an A.M. or P.M. time."

In later lessons, students work problems that result in P.M. time that must be converted twice.

Example:

Fran starts painting a wall at 10:50 A.M. She works for 5 hours and 30 minutes. At what time does she complete the wall?

Here's the work:

$$
\begin{array}{r}
10:50 \\
+\ \ 5:30 \\
\hline
15:80 \\
16:20 \\
\hline
\boxed{4:20\ \text{p.m.}}
\end{array}
$$

Students first convert 15:80 into 16:20. (Change 80 minutes into 1 hour and 20 minutes. Add that amount to 15 hours.) Next, students convert 16:20 into 4:20 P.M. (Subtract 12 from 16. Add the letters P.M.)

COINS AND MONEY AMOUNTS

Starting in Lesson 73, students work problems that refer both to the number of coins and to the amount for a number of particular coins or groups of different coins. The first problems involve multiplication or division. They ask about the number of coins or the amount.

Students start with the basic equation: number × value = amount. After they have put in the two numbers they know, they either multiply or divide to find the missing value.

Here's part of the work from Lesson 73:

d. Problem A: How many nickels are in $3.45?
- We start with the basic equation.
- (Write on the board:)

× value = amount

- You know the value of each nickel. Everybody, what's that value? (Signal.) *5 cents.*
- The problem gives another value—the total amount.
- (Write to show:)

× value = amount
a. □ × .05 = 3.45

- What operation do you use to find the missing number? (Signal.) *Division.*
- Copy the bottom equation; write the division problem. Raise your hand when you've done that much.
- (Write to show:)

× value = amount
a. □ × .05 = 3.45
.05)‾3.45‾

- Here's what you should have: 3 and 45-hundredths divided by 5-hundredths. You'll work that problem later on your calculator.
f. Problem C: A person has 46 nickels. How much money does the person have?
- Does the problem give the number of nickels? (Signal.) *Yes.*
- You know the value of each nickel.
- Write the basic equation. Below, show the equation with two values. Raise your hand when you've done that much.
  (Observe students and give feedback.)

- (Write on the board:)

× value = amount
c.   46 × .05   =□

- Here's what you should have.
- What operation do you use to find the missing number? (Signal.) *Multiplication.*
- So the problem you'll work is 46 times 5-hundredths.

Teaching note: All problems give only one number. Students generate another number—the value of the coin. They write that value as a decimal number. If they write it incorrectly, they will make serious mistakes. Check to make sure that they write .05 for both problems.

The problem-solving steps should be familiar to the students. If they have trouble figuring out how to solve the problems, first make sure that they started with the equation **number times value equals amount** and wrote the value the problem gives and the amount for the coin. If they did this much correctly, the equation shows whether they multiply or divide to solve the problem.

Students use their calculator to solve these problems. Note that they probably would not be able to solve the problems without using their calculator because the operation isn't taught until Lesson 74.

In Lesson 75, students work on multi-step problems that involve more than one type of coin. Students use a table for working these problems. The table is similar to the other tables they've worked with, in that it's possible to add the amounts in two of the columns. The table is different from other tables, in that each row has a different multiplier.

Here's part of the introduction from Lesson 75:

		#	× value	= amount
a.	quarters	7	▮▮▮▮	▮▮▮▮
	dimes	▮	▮▮▮▮	5.10
	nickels	▮	▮▮▮▮	1.45
	total	▮	✕	▮▮▮▮

c. This table is not complete, but you can figure out the missing numbers by completing each row that has a number. The first thing you do is write the number you multiply by for the different coins.

d. Copy the table with the numbers that are shown. Then fill in the middle column. Show the **decimal number** you multiply by. Raise your hand when you've done that much.

- (Write on the board:)

	#	× value	= amount
a. quarters	7	.25	
dimes		.10	5.10
nickels		.05	1.45
total		⤬	

- Here's what you should have.
e. You can complete each row by multiplying or dividing.
- Your turn: Use your calculator. Complete the top three rows. Then add the first column to get a total and add the third column to get a total. Raise your hand when you're finished.
(Observe students and give feedback.)
- (Write to show:)

	#	× value	= amount
a. quarters	7	.25	1.75
dimes	51	.10	5.10
nickels	29	.05	1.45
total	87	⤬	8.30

- Here's what you should have: 7 quarters, 51 dimes, and 29 nickels. So you have a total of 87 coins. They are worth a total of $8.30. Raise your hand if you got everything right.

cross out the place for the total in the middle column. The cross-out discourages them from trying to add or subtract.)

Remind students of the conversions if they try to take shortcuts. Note that if they show the coins in an order different from that shown on the board, no serious problem results.

Starting in Lesson 78, students make tables from word problems.

Here's a problem from that lesson:

a. Roger has $7.30 in quarters, dime and nickels. He has $2.60 in dimes. He has 19 nickels.

1. How many dimes are there?
2. How much is there in nickels?
3. How much is there in quarters?
4. How many coins are there in all?

To solve the problem, students make the table, fill in the missing values, then answer the questions.

Here's the table with the numbers the problem gives and the values for each coin (which the students generate):

	#	× value	= amount
a. quarters		.25	
dimes		.10	2.60
nickels	19	.05	
total		⤬	7.30

They solve the problem by working any row that has two numbers. When they have all but one number in either the first or the last column, they can find that number by adding or subtracting.

	#	× value	= amount
a. quarters	15	.25	3.75
dimes	26	.10	2.60
nickels	19	.05	.95
total	60	⤬	7.30

If students do well in the exercises that precede Lesson 78, they should not have serious difficulties with these problems.

AVERAGE

Students who went through Level E worked problems that ask about averages. The Bridge did not present work with averages. Level F presents a strategy for working average problems that is different from the strategy presented in Level E. The work begins in Lesson 81, with problems that are represented graphically with bars. The explanation of average refers to the area of the shaded part.

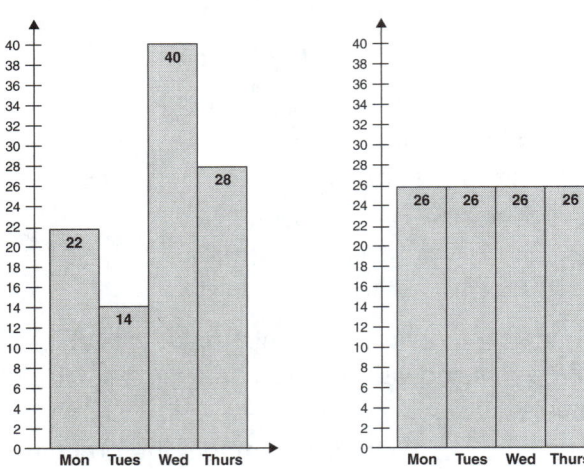

When you find the average, you have the same shaded area. The only difference is that all the bars are the same height. The strategy is to add up the parts (or bars) and divide by the number of parts (or bars).

Here's part of the exercise from Lesson 81:

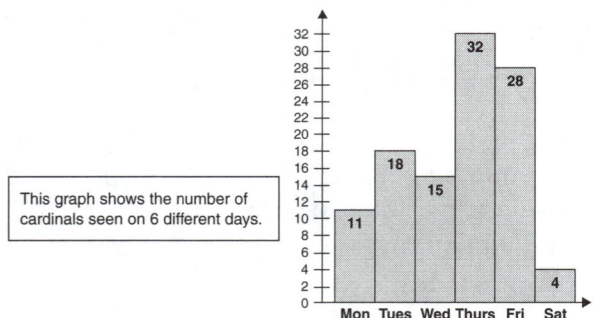

This graph shows the number of cardinals seen on 6 different days.

c. The graph shows the number of cardinals that were observed on 6 days.
• Find the average number of cardinals observed on a day. Add the numbers for the days. Divide by the number of days. Raise your hand when you've answered the question.
(Observe students and give feedback.)

• (Write on the board:)

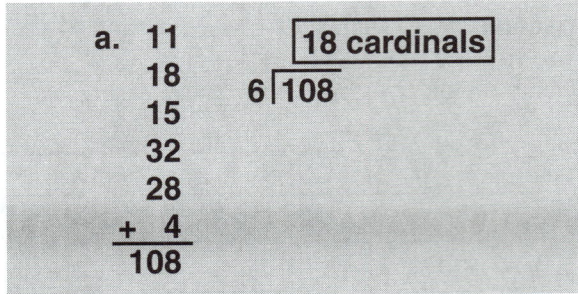

• Here's what you should have. The average is 18 cardinals per day. That means: If you observed the same number of cardinals on 6 days and you saw 108 cardinals, you'd see 18 on each day.

> ***Teaching note:*** If students have trouble, tell them to think of a bar graph. You just find the amount for each bar and add all those amounts. That tells how much you have in all. Then divide by the number of bars.

Later average problems present the information in different ways. Some present it in words. Some present it in tables. Some present it in circle graphs or line graphs.

CIRCLE GRAPHS

In Level F, students learn or review information that permits them to answer a variety of questions shown by circle graphs. By Lesson 73, students know, for example, how to express 1/4 of a circle as a percent (25%) of the circle. They know to convert 1/4 of a circle into degrees. And they know various measurement facts that can be expressed through circle graphs (how a person spends time during a typical day, how much of the income a farmer receives comes from different sources). In Lesson 78 and continuing through the end of the program, students work with a variety of circle-graph problems that present information and ask various types of questions.

Here's the problem from Lesson 78:

> This graph shows the fraction of time a person spent doing different activities during 3 days.

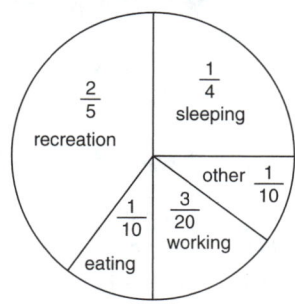

Here is each question and the procedure students use to answer it:

a. How many hours did the person spend sleeping? First convert 3 days into hours:

$$3 \times 24 = 72$$
$$\tfrac{1}{4} \times 72 = \tfrac{72}{4} \quad \boxed{18 \text{ hours}}$$

b. How much more time did the person spend sleeping than eating? First figure out the time spent eating, then subtract:

$$\tfrac{1}{10} \times 72 = \tfrac{72}{10} \quad \boxed{7\tfrac{2}{10} \text{ hours}}$$

$$\begin{array}{r} 18 \\ - 7\tfrac{2}{10} \\ \hline \boxed{10\tfrac{8}{10} \text{ hours}} \end{array}$$

c. What percent of the time was spent for recreation?

$$\tfrac{2}{5}\left(\tfrac{20}{20}\right) = \tfrac{\boxed{40}}{100}$$

The answer is 40 percent.

d. What percent of the time did the person spend working?

$$\tfrac{2}{5}\left(\tfrac{20}{20}\right) = \tfrac{\boxed{40}}{100}$$

The answer is 15 percent.

e. How many more hours did the person spend sleeping than working? First figure out the time spent working, then subtract:

$$\tfrac{3}{20} \times 72 = \tfrac{216}{20} \quad \boxed{10\tfrac{16}{20} \text{ hours}}$$

$$\begin{array}{r} 18 \\ 10\tfrac{16}{20} \\ \hline \boxed{7\tfrac{4}{20} \text{ hours}} \end{array}$$

In later lessons, students work similar problems that present information in a table that accompanies a circle graph:

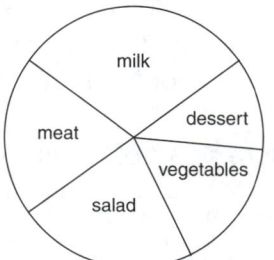

	grams	%
milk	600	30
salad	440	■
meat	■	■
vegetables	360	■
dessert	■	10
total	■	■

To complete the table, students use the ratio strategy of finding a row with two numbers and figuring out the multiplier (1/20 or .05), then applying that multiplier to the other rows. (Completing the table also involves completing the bottom row.) The total circle is 100 percent. With this number in the total row, students can figure out the total weight:

	g	%
milk	600	30
salad	440	22
meat	400	20
vegetables	360	18
dessert	200	10
total	2000	100

Measurement

Level F provides two types of measurement activities. One is measurement that involves related units. Related units are convertible. Inches and feet are related because it's possible to convert inches into feet and vice versa. Level F also has exercises that involve nonconvertible units (such as the number of bottles in a carton or the speed of a vehicle). The basic equation for all the measurement relationships has the larger unit (the whole) on the left and a fraction for the smaller unit (the parts) on the right.

Here's the equation for feet and inches:

$$\boxed{}\ \text{feet} = \frac{\boxed{}\ \text{inches}}{\boxed{}\ \text{inches per foot}}$$

Work on convertible units is introduced in Lesson 7. This work involves the values on the right side of the equation. Given different facts, students write fractions that indicate the basis for converting one unit into the related unit. For instance: **There are 4 seasons in each year.** That statement indicates that 1 season may be exchanged for 1/4 of a year.

In Lesson 7, students first write the denominator for fractions that involve related units.

Here's part of the introduction:

There are 4 seasons in	1 year.
There are 12 months in	1 year.
There are 365 days in	1 year.
There are 3 feet in	1 yard.
There are 36 inches in	1yard.
There are 24 hours in	1 day.
There are 60 minutes in	1 hour.
There are 60 seconds in	1 minute.

a. years and months
b. feet and yards
c. inches and yards
d. hours and minutes

b. For each item, you'll write the denominator of the fraction. Just the denominator.
c. Item A: Years and months.
- One name is the whole and one name is the part. Which name is the part? (Signal.) *Months.*
- Write the denominator of the fraction that shows the number of **months** in **1 year.** You can refer to the table if you need to. Raise your hand when you're finished. √
- (Write on the board:)

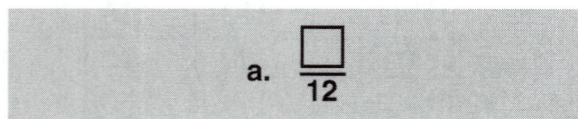

a. $\dfrac{\boxed{}}{12}$

- Here's what you should have. The number is **12.**
d. Item B. Write the denominator of the fraction for **feet** and **yards.** Show how many **feet** are in **each yard.** Raise your hand when you're finished. √
- (Write on the board:)

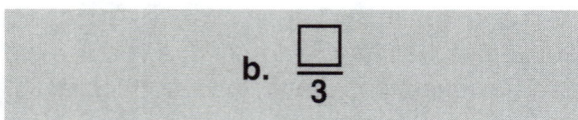

b. $\dfrac{\boxed{}}{3}$

- Here's what you should have. The number is **3.**
e. Your turn: Write denominators for the rest of the items in part 3. Raise your hand when you're finished.
(Observe students and give feedback.)

f. (Write on the board:)

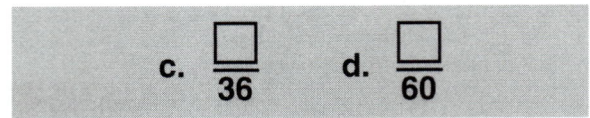

c. $\dfrac{\boxed{}}{36}$ d. $\dfrac{\boxed{}}{60}$

- Here's what you should have for items C and D.
- Item C: Inches and yards. The number of inches in 1 yard is **36.**
- Item D: Hours and minutes. The number of minutes in 1 hour is **60.**

a. | There are 4 **seasons** in each **year.** |

   1) What fraction shows 1 year?
   2) What fraction shows 9 seasons?
   3) What fraction shows 1 season?

b. | There are 12 **months** in a **year.** |

   1) What fraction shows 5 months?
   2) What fraction shows 1 year?
   3) What fraction shows 1 month?

a. | There are 24 **hours** in a **day.** |

   1) What fraction shows 36 hours?
   2) What fraction shows 1 hour?
   3) What fraction shows 1 day?

b. | There are 100 **cents** in each **dollar.** |

   1) What fraction shows 1 dollar?
   2) What fraction shows 1 cent?
   3) What fraction shows 75 cents?

g. Find part 4.
- Each item has a fact about related units. You'll use that fact to make fractions.
h. Item A: There are 4 **seasons** in each **year.**
- The names are **seasons** and **years.** One of the names tells about the whole. The other name tells about the parts.
- Which name tells about the whole? (Signal.) *Years.*
- Which name tells about parts of that whole? (Signal.) *Seasons.*
- The denominator of the fraction shows the number of **parts in 1 whole.** What number is that? (Signal.) *4.*
- Write the fractions for item A. Raise your hand when you're finished.
(Observe students and give feedback.)
- (Write on the board:)

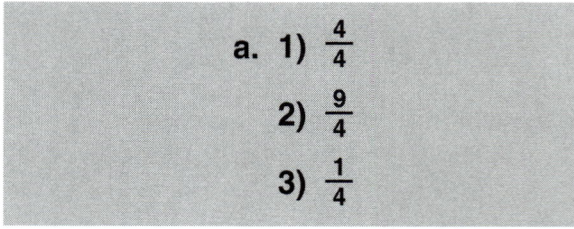

a. 1) $\dfrac{4}{4}$

   2) $\dfrac{9}{4}$

   3) $\dfrac{1}{4}$

- Here's what you should have. The fraction that shows the seasons in 1 year is **4/4.** The fraction that shows 9 seasons is **9/4.** The fraction that shows 1 season is **1/4.**

- i. Item B. The fact is: There are 12 **months** in a **year.**
- Write the fractions for item B. Raise your hand when you're finished.
  (Observe students and give feedback.)
- (Write on the board:)

b. 1) $\frac{5}{12}$

2) $\frac{12}{12}$

3) $\frac{1}{12}$

- Here's what you should have. The fraction that shows 5 months is **5/12.** The fraction that shows 1 year is **12/12.** The fraction that shows 1 month is **1/12.**

Teaching notes: In steps b through f, students write the denominator of the fraction. The denominator is the number of parts in one whole. If students have trouble with any items, repeat them. Students must be firm in the construction of fractions before proceeding. The key is the denominator. It provides the number for converting the smaller unit into the larger unit.

In steps g through i, students make complete fractions that answer different questions. The fractions all have the same denominator because the questions ask about the same relationship. For instance, all questions for item A involve the relationship between seasons and years. Therefore, all of these fractions have a denominator of 4. All questions for B involve the relationship between months and years; therefore, these fractions have a denominator of 12.

To construct the fractions, students first write the appropriate denominator, then write the numerator. If students have trouble, present these tasks:

"What's the fact for these problems?"

"What is the part?"

"Write the denominator that shows the number of parts in a whole. Then write the numerator to show how many parts you have."

Students practice writing fractions through Lesson 9. In Lesson 11, they write the name of the parts shown by different fractions.

Here are some of the items from Lesson 11:

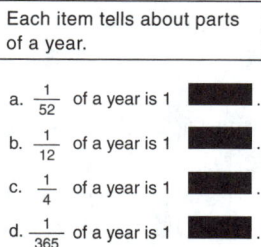

Each item tells about parts of a year.

a. $\frac{1}{52}$ of a year is 1 ▮▮▮.

b. $\frac{1}{12}$ of a year is 1 ▮▮▮.

c. $\frac{1}{4}$ of a year is 1 ▮▮▮.

d. $\frac{1}{365}$ of a year is 1 ▮▮▮.

Students refer to the appropriate fact to determine the name of the part. If students do not know the facts, they may refer to the Table of Weights and Measures at the back of their textbook; however, students should memorize these facts.

These exercises point out that the different fractions simply refer to different divisions of the whole. If the whole is divided into seasons, it is divided into four parts. If it's divided into months, it's divided into 12 parts.

Students work with similar fractions through Lesson 13. Later fractions do not have 1 as the numerator.

Example:

What's 5/7 of a week?

Students write: 5 days.

In Lesson 14, students discriminate between fractions that show related units and those that don't. For example: **5/9 of a week.** No fact involving weeks has nine divisions; therefore, there is no part name for this fraction.

In Lesson 17, students work with mixed numbers. The items present a mixed number with a unit name. Students determine whether the fraction shows related units. They show related units if the denominator of the fraction tells about a familiar part-whole relationship.

Here are some of the items from Lesson 17:

a. $1\frac{3}{5}$ gallons   b. $3\frac{1}{4}$ gallons   c. $9\frac{2}{3}$ gallons

d. $4\frac{3}{8}$ gallons   e. $5\frac{6}{7}$ gallons

Teaching note: If an item shows related units, students rewrite the item with two unit names. The whole number is one unit—the larger unit. The fraction names the number of parts.

For B, students write: 3 gallons and 1 quart. For D, they write: 4 gallons and 3 pints.

In Lesson 19, students go the other way. They construct mixed numbers from statements about related units. For example: **2 gallons and 3 quarts.** The mixed number is 2 and 3/4.

Students determine the whole number by referring to the number of wholes. They construct the fraction by first creating the denominator. The denominator is the number of quarts in each gallon. The numerator is the number of quarts.

In Lesson 22, students write mixed numbers with a unit name. The items are like the earlier ones, but require the unit name. The unit name is the name of the larger unit. This convention may initially be difficult for some students.

Here's the exercise from Lesson 22:

2 years and 7 months is $2\frac{7}{12}$ **years.**

2 years and 44 weeks is $2\frac{44}{52}$ **years.**

3 dollars and 2 quarters is $3\frac{2}{4}$ ▮▮▮▮▮ .

a. You're going to write the mixed number for each description. You're also going to write the unit name. The unit name is always the name of the larger unit in the description.
- You can see 2 years and 7 months. The mixed number is 2 and 7/12. The mixed number tells about **years.** 2 years and 7 months is 2 years and 7/12 of the next year. The whole number is 2. That's 2 **years.** So the unit name for the mixed number is **years.**
- You can see 2 **years** and 44 **weeks.**
- What's the larger unit? (Signal.) *Years.*
- So 2 years and 44 weeks is 2 and 44/52 **years.**
- You can see 3 dollars and 2 quarters.
- Which is the larger unit? (Signal.) *Dollars.*

- So 3 dollars and 2 quarters is 3 and 2/4 what? (Signal.) *Dollars.*
- It's 3 dollars and 2/4 of the next dollar.
- Remember, the name for the mixed number is the name for the larger unit.

a.	4 feet and 11 inches	d.	2 years and 300 days
b.	5 years and 3 months	e.	7 days and 5 hours
c.	8 gallons and 3 quarts	f.	3 weeks and 1 day

b. Find part 2.
c. Item A. You'll write the mixed number and the unit name for 4 feet and 11 inches.
- Which is the larger unit—feet or inches? (Signal.) *Feet.*
- So, what's the unit name for the mixed number? (Signal.) *Feet.*
- Work item A. Raise your hand when you're finished. (Observe students and give feedback.)
- (Write on the board:)

> a. $4\frac{11}{12}$ ft

- Here's the mixed number for 4 feet and 11 inches. It's 4 and 11/12 **feet.**
d. Your turn: Write the mixed number and the unit name for B. Raise your hand when you're finished. (Observe students and give feedback.)
- (Write on the board:)

> b. $5\frac{3}{12}$ yr

- 5 years and 3 months is 5 and 3/12 **years.** Raise your hand if you got it right.
e. Your turn: Work the rest of the items in part 2. Remember the unit names. Raise your hand when you're finished. (Observe students and give feedback.)
f. (Write on the board:)

> c. $8\frac{3}{4}$ gal
>
> d. $2\frac{300}{365}$ yr
>
> e. $7\frac{5}{24}$ days
>
> f. $3\frac{1}{7}$ wk

- Here's what you should have for items C through F.
- Item C: 8 gallons and 3 quarts is 8 and 3/4 gallons.
- Item D: 2 years and 300 days is 2 and 300/365 years.

- Item E: 7 days and 5 hours is 7 and 5/24 days.
- Item F: 3 weeks and 1 day is 3 and 1/7 weeks.

g. Raise your hand if you got everything right.

> **Teaching note:** Make sure that students are very firm on the questions you present in step a. If students know the larger unit names, they know the name for the mixed number.
>
> If students have any problems with this exercise, correct their mistakes; then present the original items orally and require students to say the mixed number. For example: "Listen: 4 feet and 11 inches. Say the mixed number with the unit name."
>
> "Listen: 5 years and 3 months. Say the mixed number with the unit name."

In Lesson 24, students write complete equations with names. On the left is the name for the larger unit of the whole. On the right is the fraction that equals the left value. The key to this fraction is the name for the denominator. It consists of two units. The first is the part. The second is the whole. The numerator of the fraction has the unit that is named first in the denominator.

Here's part of the work from Lesson 24:

a. $2 \rule{1.5cm}{0.25cm} = \dfrac{120 \rule{1.2cm}{0.25cm}}{60 \text{ seconds in each minute}}$

b. $3 \rule{1.5cm}{0.25cm} = \dfrac{72 \text{ hours}}{24 \rule{1.5cm}{0.25cm}}$

c. $5 \rule{1.5cm}{0.25cm} = \dfrac{180 \text{ inches}}{36 \rule{1.5cm}{0.25cm}}$

d. Item A. The unit name is shown for the denominator of the fraction.
- Write the complete equation with numbers and unit names for the numerator and for the whole number. Raise your hand when you're finished.
(Observe students and give feedback.)
- (Write on the board:)

> a. $2 \text{ minutes} = \dfrac{120 \text{ seconds}}{60 \text{ seconds in each minute}}$

- Here's what you should have. The denominator is **seconds in each minute.** So the numerator is **seconds.** The whole number is **minutes.** Raise your hand if you got it right.
e. Item B. The name for the numerator is shown. It's **hours.**

- The denominator does not have a name, but it has a number. From that number, you can figure out what the denominator is. It's hours in each something.
- Write that equation with all the names. Raise your hand when you're finished.
(Observe students and give feedback.)
- (Write on the board:)

> b. $3 \text{ days} = \dfrac{72 \text{ hours}}{24 \text{ hours in each day}}$

- Here's what you should have. The denominator **is hours in each day.** The whole number is **days.**
- The equation is true. If you divided 72 by 24, you'd get 3. So 72 hours divided by 24 hours in each day gives you 3 days. Raise your hand if you got it right.
f. Item C. The name for the numerator is shown.
- Figure out the name for the denominator and write the equation with names. Raise your hand when you're finished.
(Observe students and give feedback.)
- (Write on the board:)

> c. $5 \text{ yards} = \dfrac{180 \text{ inches}}{36 \text{ inches in each yard}}$

- Here's what you should have. The number for the numerator is 36. That's **36 inches in each yard.** The name for the whole number is **yards.**

> **Teaching note:** If students have trouble with the relationship, point out the rules:
> - The denominator names two units.
> - The numerator names the first unit shown in the denominator.
> - The name for the other side of the equation is the name that hasn't been used twice.
>
> For item B: "The name in the numerator is hours. So what's the first unit name in the denominator?" *Hours.*
>
> "The other name is something that is divided into 24 hours. What's that?" *Day.*
>
> "So the denominator name is: hours in each day. Which of those names is not shown twice?" *Day.*
>
> "That's the larger unit. It's the name for the left side of the equation."

In subsequent lessons, students work with similar equations. They also use the equation to answer questions about both of the units (the unit for the part and the unit for the whole).

In Lesson 25, students construct equations to show mixed numbers. Items ask about smaller units.

Example:

How many weeks are in 2 years and 3 weeks?

Students write the equation with numbers:

$$2\frac{3}{52} = \frac{\boxed{107}}{52} \quad \boxed{\textbf{107 weeks}}$$

The answer is 107 weeks.

In Lesson 29, students write complete equations for questions.

Example:

How many yards are in 27 feet?

Students write the equation:

$$\boxed{\textbf{9 yards}} = \frac{\textbf{27 feet}}{\textbf{3 feet per yard}}$$

The answer to the question is 9 yards.

Some questions ask about the smaller unit; some ask about the larger unit. The question above asks about the larger unit. This question asks about the smaller unit: **How many feet are in 72 yards?** *Note:* Students may be able to answer these questions without constructing the equations. However, the exercise calls for the equations. The reason for this is that when students later work with more extensive word problems and with units that are not conventional, they will need to create equations. In other words, don't let students take shortcuts.

In Lesson 31, students work similar problems that do not have numbers involved in related units: **How many months are in 5/4 years?** Students make equivalent fractions with the appropriate denominator. The question asks about months and years; therefore, the equivalent fraction has a denominator of 12. The numerator is 15.

$$\frac{5}{4}\left(\frac{3}{3}\right) = \frac{\boxed{\textbf{15 months}}}{\textbf{12 months per year}}$$

The answer to the question is 15 months.

In Lesson 37, students work similar problems that result in mixed numbers. For example: **How many days are in 79 hours?** Students write the complete equation with names. This exercise

requires them to use everything they have been taught about related units. They show the name on the left as days, the name for the denominator of the fraction as hours per day, and the name for the numerator as hours. They put the number where it goes in the equation: In this case, it's the numerator of the fraction. To find the number of days, students do the division for the fraction: 79/24. The mixed number answer is 3 and 7/24 days.

> *Teaching note:* Students should not have difficulties with these exercises if they have been firmed on the earlier activities. In fact, students should solve these problems very quickly.

In Lesson 39, students work the same type of problems; however, after showing the answer as a mixed number with a unit name, students also show the same answer as two numbers with two unit names. For example, after solving a problem involving inches per yard, students convert the answer, 5 and 31/36 yards, into the description: 5 yards and 31 inches.

As skills with related units are developed, students also work with extensions that involve nonconvertible units that refer to physical things, such as bottles per carton, students per classroom, and dollars per item. These are transition items because they indicate which is the larger unit and which is the smaller. If the item refers to worms in each can, the larger unit is cans, the smaller unit is worms.

Here's part of the exercise from Lesson 37:

Sample item There are 6 bottles per carton.

a. There are 13 dogs in each kennel.
b. The machine makes 25 buttons in each second.
c. There are 23 students in each class.
d. The trolley moves 4 miles per hour.
e. There are 8 slices in each pie.

a. You're going to write equations with names for each sentence.
- The sentence tells the name and **number for the denominator** of your fraction.
b. Look at the sample item: There are 6 bottles per carton.
- What's the name for the denominator? (Signal.) *Bottles per carton.*
- What's the number for the denominator? (Signal.) *6.*

- (Write on the board:)

$$\text{cartons} = \frac{\text{bottles}}{\text{6 bottles per carton}}$$

- Here's the equation with three names and one number. Remember, the name for the larger unit goes on the left.
c. Sentence A: There are 13 dogs in each kennel.
- That's 13 dogs **per** kennel.
- Write the equation with three names and one number. Raise you hand when you're finished. (Observe students and give feedback.)
- (Write on the board:)

$$\text{a.} \quad \text{kennels} = \frac{\text{dogs}}{\text{13 dogs per kennel}}$$

- Here's the equation. Remember, both the numerator and denominator of your fraction have to start with **dogs**.

Teaching note: The construction of the equation is mechanical because the problems give the names for the denominator of the fraction (dogs in each kennel). Although the item implies which is the larger unit, the mechanical steps are important because they are what students do later when the items do not refer to physical things that are nested or physically related.

Remind students, "Write the names for the three parts of the equation. Remember, the name with two units is the denominator or the fraction."

In Lesson 43, students work with units that are not physically related.

Example:

A ball was moving at a rate of 6 feet per second. The ball moved 366 feet. How many seconds did that take?

Students first find the name that refers to two units and write the equation with names and numbers that the problem gives:

$$\boxed{} \text{ seconds} = \frac{\text{366 feet}}{\text{6 feet per second}}$$

Then the students figure out the missing value and answer the question the problem asks:

$$\boxed{\text{61 seconds}} = \frac{\text{366 feet}}{\text{6 feet per second}}$$

In Lesson 46, the most difficult problem type is presented. This type asks about the rate. To work these problems, students first write the equation with the names and numbers that the problem gives.

Example:

It takes a jogger 3 hours to travel 16 miles. How many miles per hour does the jogger travel?

$$3 \text{ hours} = \frac{\text{16 miles}}{\boxed{} \text{ miles per hour}}$$

To find the missing number, students write an equation that starts with the denominator and multiplies by the larger unit:

$$\boxed{} \times 3 = 16$$

Students solve the equation by working a division problem:

$$3\overline{)16} \quad \boxed{5\tfrac{1}{3} \text{ miles per hour}}$$

In Lesson 59, students begin work with related-unit problems that result in answers that are not expressed in the simplest terms. For instance, the answer to the problem may be 4 gallons and 11 quarts. Students convert 11 quarts into 2 and 3/4 gallons and add that value to 4: 6 and 3/4 gallons.

Students work problems that involve addition, subtraction, and multiplication. For some subtraction problems, students must borrow and therefore must convert the value that is given into an improper fraction. For example:

7 weeks and 2 days
− 2 weeks and 5 days

Students convert the larger value into 6 weeks and 9 days, then work the problem.

Note that all these problems parallel the work that students do with time problems that require conversion of answers or conversion of one of the values that are given. (See **Time**.)

For multiplication problems, students multiply by the number of times, then convert the answer, if necessary.

Example:

Each block weighs 4 pounds and 8 ounces. How much do 20 blocks weigh?

The number of times is 20. Students work the problem:

$$\begin{array}{c}
4 \text{ lb} \quad 8 \text{ oz} \\
\times \quad\quad 20 \\
\hline
\end{array}$$

Students multiply each amount by 20 and write the answer below:

$$\begin{array}{c}
4 \text{ lb} \quad 8 \text{ oz} \\
\times \quad\quad 20 \\
\hline
80 \text{ lb} \quad 160 \text{ oz}
\end{array}$$

Then students convert 160 ounces into pounds by dividing by the number of ounces in 1 pound:

$$\begin{array}{c}
4 \text{ lb} \quad 8 \text{ oz} \\
\times \quad\quad 20 \\
\hline
80 \text{ lb} \quad 160 \text{ oz} \\
\boxed{90 \text{ lb}}
\end{array}$$

Students add 10 pounds to 80 pounds. The answer is 90 pounds.

Level F provides students with a model for working various measurement problems that will serve them in dealing with a host of very complicated problems that give students (and adults) great difficulty. These are rate problems, including those that refer to things such as the number of trials per day or the cards in each set. For such related units, there is an equation of the type that students have constructed. The problem may not ask about a simple relationship and may require complicated problem-solving steps, but the first step to solve it is to understand the relationship expressed by the model equation.

Starting with Lesson 86, students work area problems that require conversion of units. For example: **A rectangle is 8 inches wide and 7 feet long.** Students convert 8 inches into a fraction that shows feet: 8/12. Then they multiply: 8/12 times 7 equals 56/12. The area is 4 and 8/12 square feet.

In later lessons, students work mixed-unit problems that involve addition and subtraction.

For example: **Fred has 3 gallons of water. Milton has 22 pints of water. How much more water does Fred have?** Students convert 22 pints into 2 and 6/8 gallons, and then subtract:

$$\begin{array}{c}
3 \\
- 2\frac{6}{8} \\
\hline
\boxed{\frac{2}{8} \text{ gallons}}
\end{array}$$

Here's another example:

The first part of a journey was 12 weeks. The last part of the journey was 33 days. How long was the journey in all? Express the answer in weeks.

Students work the problem:

$$\begin{array}{c}
12 \\
+ 4\frac{5}{7} \\
\hline
\boxed{16\frac{5}{7} \text{ weeks}}
\end{array}$$

Teaching note: These problems may be worked other ways. For example, it is possible to convert the larger unit into the smaller unit. The advantage of working the problems as specified in Level F is that it provides strong reinforcement for the work students have done in expressing smaller units as fractions of a whole.

Geometry

In Level F, students review geometry topics presented in Level E and the Bridge. These include area and perimeter of parallelograms, area and perimeter of triangles, and circumference of circles. The new topics presented in Level F include working with complex shapes (areas that have holes in them, simple polygons that are joined, etc.) and volume of prisms and of three-dimensional figures that come to a point (pyramids, cones). Students also learn facts about angles (the number of degrees in a circle, triangle, etc.).

AREA, PERIMETER, CIRCUMFERENCE, AND DIAMETER

Students review the area and perimeter of rectangles and other parallelograms in Lessons

1 and 2. For area, students use the equation: base × height = area (b × h = A). Note that in Level E students used the equation: A = b × h. If students resist using a new equation, point out: "The equations say the same thing. You're getting good practice by writing it a new way."

Students use initials when they work problems; the first step for a set of problems is to show the equation: b × h = A. Below, they write the equation with the numbers the problem gives. Then they show the answer with a number and a unit name. For perimeter, students are not required to use a "formula." They simply add the length of the sides or add the lengths of two sides and multiply by 2. The answer consists of a number and a unit name.

Here are the problems from Lesson 3:

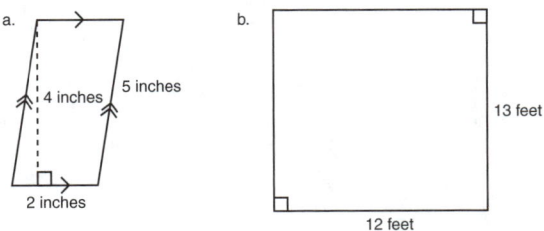

Students figure out both the area and the perimeter of the figures. Here's the work for item A:

$$b \times h = A$$
$$2 \times 4 = A$$
$$\boxed{A = 8 \text{ sq in}}$$

$$\begin{array}{r} 5 \\ 5 \\ 2 \\ +\ 2 \\ \hline \boxed{P = 14 \text{ in}} \end{array}$$

Teaching note: Be strict about the following:

1. Students are to start with the equation for area. If they work more than one problem that involves this equation, don't require them to copy it each time.

2. They show their work or at least show the equation with the numbers involved in their calculations.

3. They show the answer with a number and a unit name. They may abbreviate the name, but the name must be correct. For area, the unit name must be square units. For perimeter, it must be linear (regular) units.

In Lesson 14, students review area of triangles. The equation that they use is:

$$\frac{b \times h}{2} = A$$

Note that this again is the reverse of the equation that students had used in Level E.

The procedures that students follow for working these problems is to start with the equation, rewrite it below with the numbers the problem gives, then write the answer with a number and a unit name. Students should not have any difficulty, except possibly with the notation of height. For triangles that do not have a right angle, students must use the height of the figure, not the length of any side. For this figure:

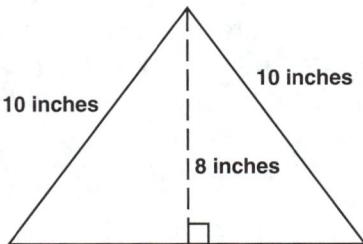

The height is 8 inches, not 10 inches.

In Lesson 24, circumference and diameter of circles is reviewed.

In Lesson 29, area of circles is introduced. For students who have gone through Level E, this work is a review. For students who went through the Bridge, this work may be new. (It was not presented in the Bridge.) Students use the equation: pi × radius × radius = area (π × r × r = A).

Here's part of the exercise from Lesson 29:

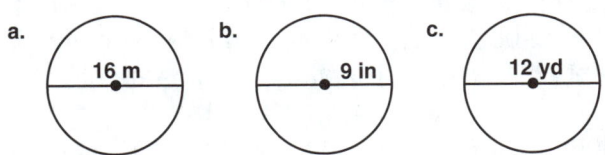

b. For each circle, you'll figure the area.
c. Circle A. The radius is not shown, but the diameter is shown. What's the diameter? (Signal.) *16 meters.*
• So what's the radius? (Signal.) *8 meters.*
• Yes, the radius is 1-half the diameter. The radius times the radius is 8 times 8. What's that? (Signal.) *64.*
• When you multiply 64 by *pi*, you'll have the area of the circle.

- Copy the equation of the area. Put in the number for pi and the number for the radius and figure out the area. The unit name for the answer is square meters. Raise your hand when you're finished. (Observe students and give feedback.)
- (Write on the board.)

a. $\pi \times r \times r = A$
   $3.14 \times 8 \times 8 = A$
   $\boxed{A = 200.96 \text{ sq m}}$

- Here's what you should have. The area is 3 and 14-hundredths times 64. So the area is 200 and 96-hundredths **square meters.**

> **Teaching note:** For each problem that you show on the board, you'll indicate the equation for the area of a circle. Below, you'll show the numbers that the problem gives. Below that problem, you'll show the answer as an equation: A _____sq_____. The answer consists of a number and a unit name.
>
> Part of this work is required by the students; however, students may not show everything that you show. Students may write this as their second step of the problem:
>
> $3.14 \times 64 = A$
>
> or:
>
> $3.14 \times 64 = \boxed{200.96 \text{ sq m}}$
>
> Both variations are acceptable. If the student does not show the complete answer, however, the work is not acceptable.
>
> For subsequent problems, students might not start with the equation for the area of a circle. This variation is acceptable also, as long as the student shows the equation for the first problem in the set.

In Lesson 56, students work problems that refer to a fractional part of an area. For the first problems, the area is given and students compute the area of the part.

Here's a problem from Lesson 56:

a. The area of the square is 160 square centimeters.

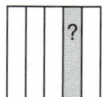

Students work the problems two ways: as a multiplication problem and as a division problem. The multiplication problem is: 1/5 × 160. The answer is 32 square centimeters. The division problem is:

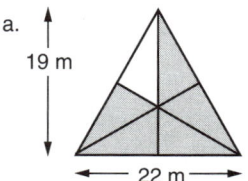

In Lesson 58, students work problems that do not show the area. Students first figure out the area, then find the area of the shaded part.

Here are the problems from Lesson 58:

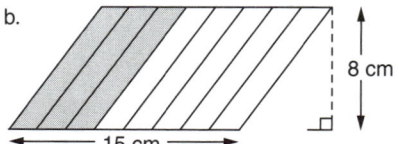

To work problem A, students first find the area of the entire triangle (209 square meters). Then they find the area of the shaded part by working the problem: 5/6 × 209. The answer shown on the calculator has a repeating decimal. Students round the answer to two decimal places: 174.17 square meters.

Complex area is introduced in Lesson 36. The first problem type shows two juxtaposed shapes on the coordinate system.

For example:

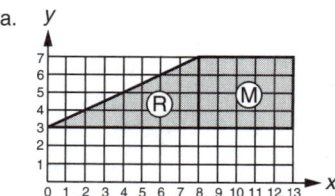

Students first identify the component figures, then find the area of each and add the areas to find the total area.

Here's part of the exercise from Lesson 36:

b. Item A shows a figure that is made up of a rectangle and a triangle. The figures are labeled **R** and **M.**
- **R** is a triangle. Raise your hand when you know the base of the triangle. √
- Everybody, what's the base? (Signal.) *8.*

- Now figure out how high it is. The bottom is at 3. The top is at 7. Raise your hand when you know how high it is. √
- Everybody, how high? (Signal.) 4.
- Figure out the area of the triangle. Show the name **square units** in the answer. Raise your hand when you've done that much.
- (Write on the board:)

$$\boxed{\text{triangle R}}$$

$$\frac{b \times h}{2} = A$$

$$\frac{8 \times 4}{2} = \frac{32}{2}$$

$$\boxed{16 \text{ sq units}}$$

- Here's what you should have. Raise your hand if you got it right.
- Now you have to figure out the base and the height of rectangle **M.** The base starts at 8 on the X axis. Raise your hand when you know the length of the base. √
- Everybody, what's the base? (Signal.) 5.
- The height starts at 3. Everybody, what's the height? (Signal.) 4.
- Figure out the area of rectangle **M.** Then figure out the area of the entire figure. Just add the two areas together. Raise your hand when you're finished. (Observe students and give feedback.)
- (Write on the board:)

$$\boxed{\text{rectangle M}} \qquad \boxed{\text{entire figure}}$$

$$b \times h = A$$
$$5 \times 4 = 20 \qquad \begin{array}{r} 16 \\ + 20 \\ \hline \end{array}$$

$$\boxed{20 \text{ sq units}} \qquad \boxed{A = 36 \text{ sq units}}$$

- Here's what you should have. The total area of the figure is 36 square units.

Teaching note: The way you show the work is the way you'll show it for later multi-step problems. You label each part (the triangle, the rectangle, and the entire figure). Students might not show these labels. Remind them that they can write the names to keep track of the parts of the problem.

These problems do not give a unit name. Students write the answer as either **squares** or **square units.**

The problems are shown on the coordinate system, which means that students can take some shortcuts. Instead of finding the area of R, they can find the area of the rectangle that is described by R (8 times 4), then divide by 2. You might want to point out that when right triangles are on the coordinate system, they show why the equation for the area of a triangle works. The triangle is clearly 1/2 of the rectangle that contains the triangle.

Later students work with shapes that are composed of three or more figures. Often, it's possible to decompose these figures more than one way; however, you will tend to show the most efficient way.

In Lesson 51, students work problems involving figures that have holes. The strategy is to find the area of the entire figure, find the area of the hole, then subtract the hole from the figure.

Here's part of the work from Lesson 51:

c. Figure A is a rectangle with a small parallelogram in the middle.
- Find the area of the entire rectangle as if it didn't have that hole in it. Raise your hand when you have done that much. √
- (Write on the board:)

a. $\boxed{\text{rectangle}}$ $7 \times 12 = 84$ sq units

- Here's the area of the rectangle.
- Now figure out the area of the hole and subtract that area from the area of the rectangle. Raise your hand when you're finished. (Observe students and give feedback.)
- (Write to show:)

a. $\boxed{\text{rectangle}}$ $7 \times 12 = 84$ sq units

$$\boxed{\text{hole}} \quad 4 \times 3 = 12 \text{ sq units}$$

$$\boxed{\text{figure}} \quad \begin{array}{r} 84 \\ - 12 \\ \hline \end{array}$$

$$\boxed{A = 72 \text{ sq units}}$$

- The hole is 12 square units. When you subtract 12 from 84 you get 72 square units. That's the area of the figure with the hole in it.

In Lesson 53, students work problems that have more than one hole. To work these problems, students find the area of the largest shape, find the area of each hole, add the area of the holes and subtract that total from the area of the largest shape.

Here's a problem from Lesson 53:

A builder wants to figure out the cost of siding for this wall. The wall will have a hole for the door and a hole for the window. The rest of the wall will be covered with siding.

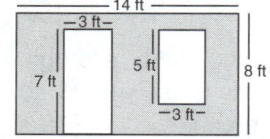

b. Find the area of the wall that needs siding.

Here's how you show the work for this problem:

entire wall b × h = A
14 × 8 = A
A = 112 sq ft

door 3 × 7 = 21 sq ft

window 3 × 5 = 15 sq ft

both holes 21 + 15 = 36 sq ft

siding 112 − 36 = 76 sq ft

These problems reinforce the work that students are doing in other tracks and problem types. For signed-number operations, they combine more than one negative value. They do a parallel operation in working problems that have figures with more than one hole. Students combine the area of the holes, then treat the total as a negative value that is combined with a positive value (the area of the largest figure).

The final application of area problems with holes is introduced in Lesson 55. Here's the problem from that lesson:

This diagram shows a wall with holes for two windows and a door. Siding costs $2.80 per square foot. Figure out the cost of siding for the part of the wall that does not have holes.

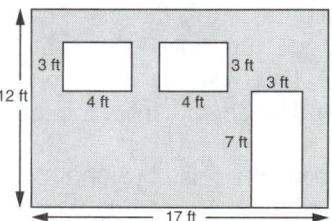

Students first find the area of the shaded part, then compute the cost of siding, which costs $2.80 per square foot.

This problem should not be difficult if students are firm on the preceding work. It is a simple extension of what they have done in finding the area of figures that have holes and working multi-step problems that involve multiplication.

Students continue to work problems similar to those above through Lesson 85. Some of the applications involve a circle as the largest figure or as a hole.

VOLUME

The work on volume begins in Lesson 71 and continues through Lesson 87. Students work with rectangular and triangular prisms, cylinders, and figures that come to a point (cones and pyramids).

Prisms and Cylinders

In Lesson 71, students work on the volume of a prism. For students who have gone through the Bridge, this work may be new. Students use the equation: Area of base × height = Volume.

Here's a problem that students solve in Lesson 71:

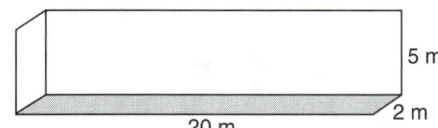

Here's the work for the problem:

$$\text{Area of } b \times h = V$$
$$40 \times 5 = V$$

$$\boxed{V = 200 \text{ cu m}}$$

> **Teaching note:** Expect students to have the following difficulties:
> 1. They may use improper unit names in the answer. The units are cubic units.
> 2. Students may become confused about the base of the figure and the base of the rectangle that forms the base.
>
> The items that students work initially have the base in red. After they become practiced at working these problems, the figures are shown without red bases. The simplest way to avoid confusion over the base is to remind students: "First find the area of the red part. That's the base. Do the calculations for that part. After you find that area, multiply by the height of the box."

In Lesson 74, the first triangular prisms are presented. Students use the same equation that applies to rectangular prisms or boxes. Students may have more difficulties with the base. Again, remind them, "Just find the area of the red part. Do what it takes. Then multiply by the height of the box."

Cylinders are introduced in Lesson 83. The procedures are the same as they are for the other figures. Students are reminded, "The only difference between figuring out the volume of cylinders and boxes is how you find the area of the base. After you figure out the base, you multiply by the height of the figure. That gives you the volume."

Pyramids and Cones

In Lesson 85, students are presented with a procedure for finding the volume of figures that come to a point. That procedure is: First find the area of the base; then multiply by the height; then divide by 3. In other words, the volume of these figures is 1/3 the volume of prisms with the same base and height. Here are the problems from Lesson 85:

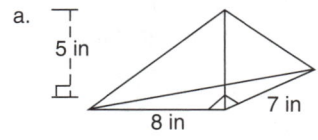
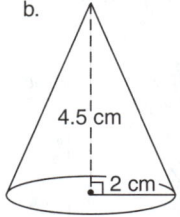
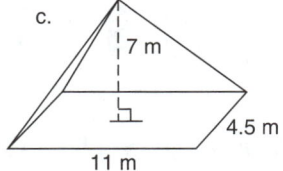
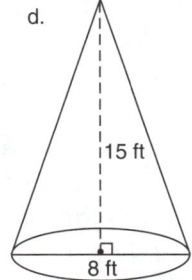

> **Teaching note:** If students follow the procedure of first figuring out the base and then working the rest of the problem, they will not become confused. If they don't follow this procedure, they may have difficulties with a triangular base.
> Make sure that students write the equation for the volume $\left(\frac{\text{Area of } b \times h}{3} = v\right)$ and show the number for each part (the base, the height).

GEOMETRY FACTS

In Level F, students are taught facts about circles and polygons. In Lesson 44 students learn the following facts about polygons:

Triangles have three sides.
Quadrilaterals have four sides.
Pentagons have five sides.
Hexagons have six sides.
Octagons have eight sides.

In Lesson 47, students learn facts about angles:

A circle has 360 degrees.
Half a circle has 180 degrees.
The corner of a page has 90 degrees.
A triangle has 180 degrees.

Starting in Lesson 73, students work problems that require application of what they have learned about angles. Problems are of the form: **An angle is 40% of a circle. How many degrees are in the angle?** Students figure out 40% of a circle by working the problem: 40/100 360. The answer is 144 degrees.

In Lesson 76, students apply what they've learned to work problems involving circle graphs:

Copy and complete the table.

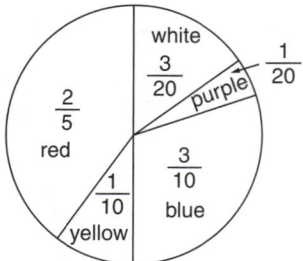

	fraction	degrees
red	■	■
blue	■	■
white	■	■
yellow	■	■
purple	■	■

There are several ways to work the problem. One is to find a common denominator, then enter the numerators in the first column of a ratio table. Another is to use the fractions that are shown in the first column and find the degrees by working a separate problem for each row.

Here's the table that shows the fractions:

	fraction	degrees
red	$\frac{2}{5}$	
blue	$\frac{3}{10}$	
white	$\frac{3}{20}$	
yellow	$\frac{1}{10}$	
purple	$\frac{1}{20}$	

In Lesson 76, students complete the table by working a separate multiplication problem for each row. The problem for the blue part is 3/10 × 360. The answer is 108.

In Lessons 81 and 82, students work similar problems with fractions that already have a common denominator. They enter the numerators only in the first column of the ratio table. Then they multiply to find the degrees.

Signed Numbers

Level F introduces signed numbers. The first work that students do involves combining terms that are added and those that are subtracted. These exercises begin in Lesson 59 and show

students that more than one minus value may be combined.

Here's part of the exercise from Lesson 59:

a. $88 - 15 - 13 - 19 =$ ■

b.
$$\begin{array}{r} 62 \\ -\ 48 \\ -\ 14 \\ \hline \blacksquare \end{array}$$

b. You're going to work each problem by first figuring out the total you subtract, then subtracting that total.

c. Problem A. You're subtracting 15 and 13 and 19. Figure out that total and write it. Just add 15, 13, and 19. Raise your hand when you know that total. √
- Everybody, what's the total you'll subtract? (Signal.) 47.
- Write the problem you'll work. √
- (Write on the board:)

$$\begin{array}{r} \text{a.} \quad 88 \\ -\ 47 \\ \hline \end{array}$$

- You'll work 88 minus 47. Do it and write the answer. Raise your hand when you're finished. √
- (Write to show:)

$$\begin{array}{r} \text{a.} \quad 88 \\ -\ 47 \\ \hline \boxed{41} \end{array}$$

- Here's what you should have.

d. Problem B. Figure out the total you're subtracting and write the new problem and the answer. Raise your hand when you're finished. (Observe students and give feedback.)
- (Write on the board:)

$$\begin{array}{r} \text{b.} \quad 62 \\ -\ 62 \\ \hline \boxed{0} \end{array}$$

- Here's what you should have. You subtracted 62. The answer is zero.

Teaching note: In step c, students write the total for the numbers that are subtracted. Do not require them to write the answer as a signed number. The answer is 47. When they write 47 in the problem 88 minus 47, they are to show the minus sign.

Students should have no trouble with these problems. The work they do avoids references to signs and rules for combining.

In Lesson 61, students work similar problems that require combining both positive and negative values.

Here's the problem set from Lesson 61:

a. $0 + 26 - 15 + 104 - 2 - 8 = \blacksquare$

b. $0 - 13 + 28 + 120 + 89 - 99 - 43 = \blacksquare$

c. $0 + 51 - 141 - 68 + 312 = \blacksquare$

> **Teaching note:** This work reinforces the idea that the order of the values is not important and that they can be "regrouped" and then combined. Although the regrouping is not overtly required, students are actually working this problem when they work A:
>
> $$(+ 26 + 104) + (- 15 - 2 - 8).$$

In Lesson 63, students learn the rule that numbers without signs are positive numbers. The problems shown start with a positive value so they do not have a sign: **10 − 2 − 3.** They are given a new order for these problems, e.g., 2 3 10. Students write the problem in this order. The order requires a sign for each value: $- 2 - 3 + 10$. Then students work the problem on their calculator—entering both the sign and the number for each value.

Here's part of the exercise from Lesson 63:

b. $\boxed{18 - 12 - 4 = \blacksquare}$

  new order: 4   12   18

c. $\boxed{4 - 2 + 5 = \blacksquare}$

  new order: 5   4   2

e. Problem B. The original problem is shown in the box. You'll work the values in the order shown below.
• Write the problem you'll work. Show signs for all the numbers. Raise your hand when you've written the problem. √
• (Write on the board:)

> b. $- 4 - 12 + 18 =$

• Here's the problem you'll work: Minus 4 minus 12 plus 18.
• Do it and write the answer your calculator shows. √
• Everybody, what's the answer to problem B? (Signal.) *2.*
f. Problem C: 4 minus 2 plus 5.
• Work that problem in your head. √
• Everybody, what's the answer? (Signal.) *7.*

• Show the problem rewritten with signs for every value. Raise your hand when you've done that much.
  (Observe students and give feedback.)
• (Write on the board:)

> c. $+ 5 + 4 - 2 =$

• Here's what you should have: Plus 5 plus 4 minus 2.
• When you work that problem on your calculator, you should end up with 7. When you enter plus 5, your calculator will show 5, because plus 5 equals 5. Raise your hand when you've worked the problem on your calculator. √
• Everybody, what did you end up with? (Signal.) *7.*

> **Teaching notes:** For item B, the calculator will probably not display the first value as −4 until students press the minus for −12. However, as long as the keys are pressed in this order: $- 4 - 12 + 18 =$, the answer will be correct.
>
> For the problem, $+ 5 + 4 - 2 =$, the calculator will not show 5 with a sign. In step f, you point out that the calculator does this because + 5 is just 5, which is what the calculator displays.

In Lesson 64, students are introduced to a number line that has both positive and negative values. The exercise points out that the operation of adding or subtracting on such a number line is the same as on a number line that has no negative values. To add, you go to the right. That's the direction for larger numbers. To subtract, you go to the left. That's the direction for smaller numbers.

One exercise that students do on Lesson 64 is to show addition and subtraction from different points on the number line.

Here's part of the exercise:

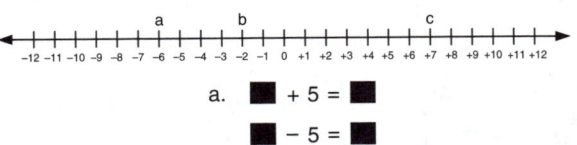

a. $\blacksquare + 5 = \blacksquare$

    $\blacksquare - 5 = \blacksquare$

f. There's a number line with three letters on it: A, B, and C. Below is an incomplete problem that adds 5 and an incomplete problem that subtracts 5. You'll write the two problems for each letter.
g. Touch A on the number line. √
• What's the number at A? (Signal.) *Minus 6.*
• So the first problem you'll work is minus 6 plus 5.

- Write that problem. Draw an arrow below the plus 5 to show the direction you'll move on the number line when you add 5. Raise your hand when you've written the problem and the arrow. √
- (Write on the board:)

> **a.** $-6+5=$
> →

- Here's what you should have. The problem is minus 6 plus 5. The arrow goes in the plus direction. You'll go 5 places in that direction.
- Touch minus 6 on the number line and go 5 places. Write the number you end up at. Remember the sign. Raise your hand when you're finished. (Observe students and give feedback.)
- (Write to show:)

> **a.** $-6+5=\boxed{-1}$
> →

- Here's what you should have. You ended up at minus 1.
- Now work the other problem for A. Show the starting number and minus 5. Then write the arrow below the minus 5 to show the direction you'll go on the number line. Raise your hand when you've written the problem and the arrow. √
- (Write on the board:)

> **a.** $-6-5=$
> ←

- Here's what you should have: Minus 6 minus 5.
- Touch A on the number line and go 5 places in the minus direction. Write the number you end up at. Remember the sign. Raise your hand when you're finished. (Observe students and give feedback.)
- (Write to show:)

> **a.** $-6-5=\boxed{-11}$
> ←

- Here's what you should have. You ended up at minus 11.

Teaching note: At this point in the program, students do not write a larger operational sign between signed values (e.g., $-6++5$). The reason is that the plus operational sign has no effect on the sign of the number that follows it. The problem is validly rewritten as $-6+5$. Later, students will be introduced to the conventional notation; however, at this point in the program, it is not necessary either for their understanding or for mathematical integrity.

In Lesson 65, students are introduced to signed number lines that are oriented vertically. Students are prompted to think of these as being like a thermometer (with the negative numbers below zero and positive numbers above zero) or like a water level (with the negative numbers below the water and the positive numbers above). The vertical number line is useful in thinking about the coordinate system. Positive values are above zero and to the right of zero.

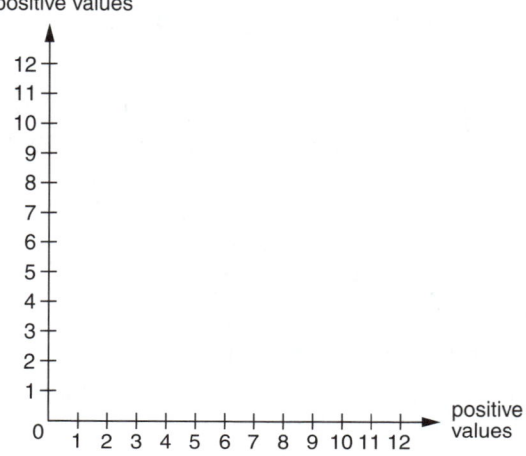

In Lesson 65, students write complete equations from displays on number lines. For example:

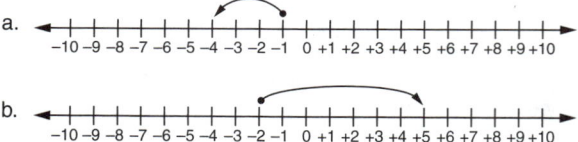

For A, students write: $-1-3=-4$. For B, students write: $-2+7=+5$.

Lesson 66 introduces the notion of **absolute value** (distance from zero). Students are shown number pairs. Students identify which of the numbers is farther from zero. The test is to count. The number that you say later when you count is the number that is farther from zero and has the larger absolute value.

In Lesson 67, students apply part of the "rule" for working problems with signed values. If the signs of the numbers shown are the same, you add. If the signs are different, you subtract.

Here's part of the work from Lesson 67:

a. + 2   b. − 3   c. − 8
    − 9   − 4   + 3
  ──────   ──────   ──────
   − ■   − ■   − ■

i. You're going to copy these problems and work them. The correct sign is already shown for the answer. You'll copy that sign. But don't worry about it. You'll learn about it later. Your job is to figure out the number.

j. Problem A: Plus 2 minus 9.
• Are the signs the same or different? (Signal.) *Different.*
• So do you add or subtract? (Signal.) *Subtract.*
• Start with the number that is farther from zero and say the ordinary subtraction problem. (Signal.) *9 minus 2.*
  (Repeat step j until firm.)

k. Copy the problem and write the answer. Don't use your calculator. Raise your hand when you're finished.
  (Observe students and give feedback.)
• (Write on the board:)

  a. + 2
      − 9
    ──────
     − 7

• Here's what you should have: Plus 2 minus 9 equals minus 7.

l. Problem B. Minus 3 minus 4.
• Are the signs the same or different? (Signal.) *Same.*
• So do you add or subtract? (Signal.) *Add.*
• Copy the problem and write the answer. Raise your hand when you're finished.
  (Observe students and give feedback.)
• (Write on the board:)

  b. − 3
      − 4
    ──────
     − 7

• Here's what you should have. You added: Minus 3 and minus 4 equals minus 7. Raise your hand if you got it right.

Teaching note: The sign is shown for the answer so that students are able to concentrate on the operation, not on the signs. They simply determine whether the signs of the values shown are the same or different and add or subtract. If the signs are different, students may have difficulty in working the problem. They are to start with the number that is farther from zero and subtract the other number. If students have trouble, do the following:

1. Tell them to circle the number that is farther from zero. They are to circle just the number, not the sign.

2. Tell them to say the ordinary subtraction problem that starts with the value they circled.

3. Remind them not to attend to any of the signs shown in the problem when saying the subtraction problem. "After you figure out that you're subtracting, say a regular subtraction problem that starts with _____. Say that problem." If they continue to have trouble, require them to write the problem that starts with the circled number.

In Lesson 71, students learn the rule for the sign in the answer: "You copy the sign of the number that is farther from zero." If students have trouble, direct them to write the problem and circle the number that is farther from zero. For problems that require subtraction, that is the number you start with when you say the subtraction problem. It also has the sign for the answer:

In Lesson 78, students work multiplication problems of the form:

  7 − 2 − 3
      × 5
  ──────────

This is a familiar problem type (see **Distributive Property**.) Students work the problem by copying the sign shown for each value that has a sign. In Lesson 78, students rewrite the problem so that all the values have signs. They apply the rule that if a value does not have a sign, it is a plus value.

Here's the work for the problem above:

$$7 - 2 - 3$$
$$\times\ 5$$
$$+\ 35 - 10 - 15 = \boxed{+10}$$

In Lesson 83, students learn the rule that if they multiply by a minus value, they do not copy the signs for the top values. They write the opposite of each sign. Students work pairs of problems. One member of the pair multiplies by a plus value, the other by a minus value.

Here's a pair of problems from Lesson 84:

$$\begin{array}{r} \text{a.} \quad -6-5+2 \\ \times \quad +3 \\ \hline = \blacksquare \end{array} \qquad \begin{array}{r} \text{a.} \quad -6-5+2 \\ \times \quad -3 \\ \hline = \blacksquare \end{array}$$

> **Teaching note:** The rule is simple. You look at the value you multiply by. That tells whether you'll copy the signs of the other values in the problem or write the opposite of each sign. The rule works for all combinations and requires far less learning than the traditional rules:
> plus $\times$ plus = plus;
> minus $\times$ plus = minus;
> minus $\times$ minus = plus;
> plus $\times$ minus = minus.

Students apply these rules to different types of problems through Lesson 88.
Examples:

$$\begin{array}{r} -3 \\ \times -5 \\ \hline \end{array} \qquad \begin{array}{r} -1+12+2-10 \\ \times +2 \\ \hline \end{array} \qquad \begin{array}{r} +6-10 \\ \times -2 \\ \hline \end{array}$$

$$-6\,(+2) = \qquad +8\,(+9) = \qquad \begin{array}{r} +4 \\ \times -6 \\ \hline \end{array}$$

Lesson 88 introduces the conventional notation for signed numbers that are combined through addition and subtraction. Students learn to interpret the large plus and large minus signs. The plus indicates that you combine the value before the sign with the value after the sign. The minus indicates that you combine the value before the sign with the **opposite** of the value after the sign.

The tasks in Lesson 88 and Lesson 89 require students to rewrite the problem without the large plus or minus. If the sign is plus, students simply copy the sign of the following value. For example: $-4+-5$ becomes $-4-5$.

If the sign is a minus, students write the opposite of the following sign: $-4--5$ becomes $-4+5$.

Note that these are variations of the multiplication rules (which results from the fact that the $+/-$ sign rules can be explained in terms of multiplying by 1, either positive or negative).

Here's part of the exercise from Lesson 88:

a. $^-3 + {}^+2 =$ b. $^+5 - {}^+8 =$ c. $^+10 - {}^-5 =$
d. $^+9 + {}^-7 =$ $^-3 - {}^+9 =$

b. You're going to rewrite these problems so they don't have the large operational sign.
c. Problem A has a large plus sign. So are you going to copy the following sign or write the opposite of that sign? (Signal.) *Copy it.*
- Write the problem without the large plus sign and write the answer. Raise your hand when you're finished.
(Observe students and give feedback.)
- (Write on the board:)

> a. $-3 + 2 = \boxed{-1}$

- Here's what you should have. The large plus sign tells you to copy the sign for plus 2. The answer is minus 1. Raise your hand if you got it right.
d. Problem B. Is the large operational sign a plus or a minus? (Signal.) *Minus.*
- So do you copy the sign of 8 or write the opposite? (Signal.) *Write the opposite.*
- Write the simple problem and the answer. Raise your hand when you're finished.
(Observe students and give feedback.)
- (Write on the board:)

> b. $+5 - 8 = \boxed{-3}$

- Here's what you should have.
e. Your turn: Rewrite the rest of the items in part 9. Raise your hand when you're finished.
(Observe students and give feedback.)
f. (Write on the board:)

> c. $+10 + 5 = \boxed{+15}$
>
> d. $+9 - 7 = \boxed{+2}$
>
> e. $-3 - 9 = \boxed{-12}$

- Here's what you should have for each problem. Raise your hand if you got everything right.

In Lesson 90, students write the elaborated notation from written directions, such as "Combine plus 7 with the opposite of plus 3." Students write the elaborated notation, then write the simplified problem and the answer:

$$^+7 - {}^+3 =$$
$$+7 - 3 = +4$$

In Lesson 89 students extend the procedures used for multiplying signed values to division problems. If the sign after the division is a plus, the sign in the answer is the sign of the first value. If the sign after the division sign is a minus, the sign in the answer is the opposite sign. The procedure is also applied to fractions.

Here are the problems presented in Lesson 90:

a. $+9\overline{\smash{)}{-72}}$ b. $-4\overline{\smash{)}{-36}}$ c. $+40 \div -10$

d. $\dfrac{-15}{-15}$ e. $+28 \div +14$

Exponents

Level F introduces exponents to show repeated multiplication of the same value. The value that is multiplied is the base. The exponent indicates the number of times the value is used as a factor.

The work with exponents begins in Lesson 74.

Here's part of the introduction. This work follows an explanation of what the base number is and how to figure out the exponent.

a. $4 \times 4 \times 4 = $ ■   d. $9 \times 9 \times 9 = $ ■

b. $34 \times 34 = $ ■   e. $2 \times 2 \times 2 \times 2 \times 2 = $ ■

c. $M \times M \times M \times M = $ ■   f. $B \times B \times B = $ ■

c. Problem A is 4 times 4 times 4. What's the base in that problem? (Signal.) *4.*
- What's the exponent? (Signal.) *3.*
- Problem B: 34 times 34. What's the base? (Signal.) *34.*
- What's the exponent? (Signal.) *2.*
- Problem C: M times M times M times M. What's the base? (Signal.) *M.*
- What's the exponent? (Signal.) *4.*
(Repeat step c until firm.)

d. Your turn: For each problem in part 2, show the base and the exponent. Don't copy the problem. (Observe students and give feedback.)
- (Write on the board:)

a.	4^3
b.	34^2
c.	M^4
d.	9^3
e.	2^5
f.	B^3

- Check your work. Here's what you should have for each problem.
- Raise your hand if you got everything right.

Lesson 75 presents problems that go both ways. Here's the set of problems from Lesson 75:

a. ▬▬▬▬ = 6^3 d. $5 \times 5 =$ ▬

b. ▬▬▬▬ = 1^4 e. ▬▬▬▬ = M^5

c. $f \times f \times f \times f =$ ▬   f. $9 \times 9 \times 9 =$ ▬

For some of the problems, students write the multiplication. For others, they write the exponential notation.

In Lesson 78, students learn to read exponential notation. They read 5^3 as 5 to the third power. They read N^4 as N to the fourth power.

In Lesson 83, students learn that a group of multiplied values can be divided into smaller groups, each with a base and an exponent. For example, students rewrite $4 \times 4 \times 4 \times 4 \times 4$ or $(4 \times 4)(4 \times 4 \times 4)$ as $4^5 = 4^2 \times 4^3$.

Here's the set of problems from Lesson 83:

Copy and complete each boxed equation.

a. $8 \times 8 \times 8 \times 8 \times 8 \times 8$
   $8^6 =$ ▨ × ▨

b. $7 \times 7 \times 7 \times 7 \times 7$
   $7^5 =$ ▨ × ▨

d. $9 \times 9 \times 9 \times 9 \times 9 \times 9 \times 9$
   $9^7 =$ ▨ × ▨

d. $5 \times 5 \times 5 \times 5$
   $5^4 =$ ▨ × ▨

e. $10 \times 10 \times 10 \times 10 \times 10 \times 10 \times 10 \times 10$
   $10^8 =$ ▨ × ▨

Teaching note: The rules for combining the parts is implied. If the base is the same, the exponents for the parts are added. This rule is not explicit in the program; however, it is something that students should be able to state with a little prompting. (They have the understanding they need to figure out the rule.)

Also implied by the program is the rule for dividing by values that have the same base. Starting with Lesson 86, students rewrite fractions that show the same base for the multiplied values in the numerator and denominator.

The rule that students follow to simplify fractions is to determine whether the base number is shown more times in the numerator or in the denominator. The answer to the question tells where to write the

base for the exponential notation. If the base appears more times in the numerator than in the denominator, the base for the exponential notation is written in the numerator.

$$\frac{3 \times 3 \times 3 \times 3 \times 3 \times 3}{3 \times 3} = 3^4$$

$$\frac{7 \times 7 \times 7 \times 7}{7 \times 7 \times 7 \times 7 \times 7 \times 7 \times 7 \times 7} = \frac{1}{7^4}$$

Here's part of the exercise from Lesson 86:

a. $\dfrac{5}{5 \times 5 \times 5 \times 5}$ b. $\dfrac{6 \times 6 \times 6}{6 \times 6 \times 6 \times 6 \times 6}$ c. $\dfrac{3 \times 3 \times 3 \times 3 \times 3 \times 3}{3 \times 3}$

f. Problem B. Is the base shown more times in the numerator or in the denominator? (Signal.) *Denominator.*
• How many more times? (Signal.) *2.*
• So what's the exponent? (Signal.) *2.*
• Write what the fraction equals. Raise your hand when you're finished.
  (Observe students and give feedback.)
• (Write on the board:)

b. $\dfrac{1}{6^2}$

• Here's what you should have. The fraction equals 1 over 6 to the second.
g. Problem C. What's the base? (Signal.) *3.*
• Is the base shown more times in the numerator or in the denominator? (Signal.) *Numerator.*
• Write it where it goes. Then figure out how many more times it appears in the numerator and write the exponent. Raise your hand when you're finished.
  (Observe students and give feedback.)
• (Write on the board:)

c. 3^4

• Here's what you should have. The base appears 4 more times in the numerator. So the fraction equals 3 to the fourth. That should be on top.

Teaching note: The questions provide the basis for an understanding of how the notation system works and how division of values with the same base works. Although the rules are not stated in the program, this work implies the subtraction rules for division: To divide exponential values with the same base, subtract the exponents.

For example:

$$\frac{6 \times 6 \times 6 \times 6}{6} = 6^3$$

The fraction is written as a division problem: 6 to the fourth power divided by 6. The answer is 6 to the third power $(4 - 1 = 3)$.

In Lesson 87, students are introduced to a base raised to the power zero. Students answer the question: How many more times is the base shown in the numerator than in the denominator? For an item such as,

$$\frac{7^4}{7^4}$$

the answer is "zero times."

That answer indicates the exponential notation: 7^0. Any non-zero base with an exponent of zero equals 1.

Simple Machines

In Level F, students solve problems that involve the work performed by simple machines—levers, wheels, inclined planes, and pulleys. For all of these applications, students use the equation for the forces and distances involved in the problem: **force × distance (in) = force × distance (out).** Students also use the equation for work: **force × distance = work.**

The basic notion of the machine is one of balance. The product for "in" balances the product for "out." This notion does not actually occur in real life because of friction, but discounting friction, the equation is accurate (and it is generally used to provide the mathematical answer to the problem).

Lesson 88 introduces levers. The problems show diagrams that give three of the four values. Students figure out the missing value.

Here are problems from Lesson 88:

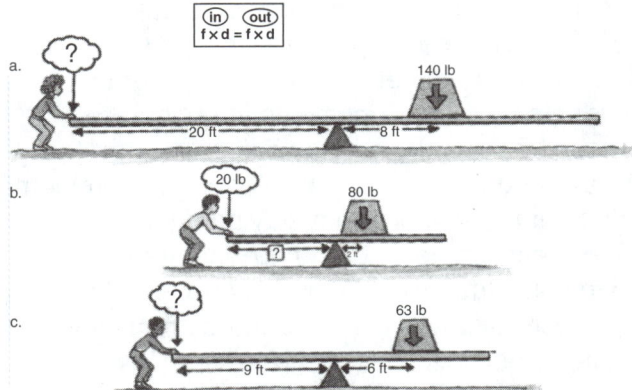

Teaching note: To work each problem, students start with the equation for forces and distances. Below, they rewrite the equation with the three numbers the problem gives.

Here's part of what students would write for problem A:

$$f \times d = f \times d$$
$$f \times 20 = 140 \times 8$$

Students compute the value on the right side of the equation (1120) and then work the problem: $f \times 20 = 1120$. Students work the division problem: $20\overline{)1120}$ to figure out the answer, which is 56 pounds. Note that the answer has a number and a unit name.

For all these problems, the "in" side of the equation refers to the effort a person puts into the machine. The "out" side of the equation is the result. All problems are shown so that the effort in is shown on the left. The reason for this convention is simply that it is easier for students to apply the equation for forces and distances if the input is on the left. Some students would otherwise write the reverse equation:

$$\overset{\text{out}}{f} \times d = \overset{\text{in}}{f} \times d$$

Although this equation is correct and will work, it may create some confusion that is avoided by the conventions used in the program.

In the following lessons, students work a variety of lever problems. In Lesson 89, they are introduced to the term **fulcrum.** Problems that students work cover the same range as those in Lesson 88.

In Lesson 91, students are introduced to a problem type that results in this type of calculation:

$$f \times d = f \times d$$
$$16 \times 20 = 64 \times d$$

To find the distance, students rewrite the equation with the unknown on the left: $64 \times d = 320$. Then they work the division problem: $320 \div 64$.

In Lesson 92, students are introduced to the wheel and axle. For these problems, diagrams show the distances and the forces. For example:

a. Somebody is trying to turn a wheel. The person is exerting a force of 40 pounds, 3 feet from the center of the wheel. You're holding the wheel steady by exerting a force. Your force is 16 pounds. How far from the center of the circle is your force?

b. The diagram shows that a force near the center of the wheel moves 6 inches with a force of 80 pounds. The outside of the wheel moves 21 inches. What is the force on the outside of the wheel?

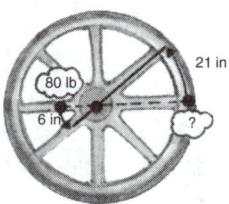

Students use the same equation they use for levers: force × distance = force × distance.

> **Teaching note:** The distances may be distances from the center of the circle, as in problem A, or they may be "circular distances" as in problem B. As long as the corresponding distances are used on both sides of the equation, the equation will work.

In Lesson 94, Level F introduces the notion of work. The product on either side of the equation is the work: force × distance = work.

Students solve some problems by finding either the force or the distance. They solve other problems by specifying the amount of work that is done. The initial problems presented are work problems. The units that they use for work are products: feet × pounds = foot-pounds.

Example:

A girl moves a lever 3 feet with a force of 39 pounds. How much work does she do?

Students work the problem:

$$f \times d = w$$
$$39 \times 3 = 117$$
$$\boxed{w = 117 \text{ ft-lb}}$$

In the remaining lessons, students work projects that extend what they have learned about simple machines. In Lesson 95, students apply the equation for forces and distances to an inclined plane. The force along the incline times the distance along the incline equals the weight times the distance straight up to the top of the incline.

Here are two problems from Lesson 95:

a. What's the force required to raise the weight 8 feet, using the inclined plane?

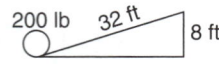

b. If 25 pounds of force is used to move the weight to the end of the inclined plane, how far does the weight move?

For problem A, students write the problem as:
$$f \times d = f \times d$$
$$f \times 32 = 200 \times 8$$
For problem B, students write:
$$f \times d = f \times d$$
$$25 \times d = 125 \times 5$$

Note that students may write the second problem without first writing the equation for the forces and distances. This omission is acceptable if they show the equation for the first problem.

In Lesson 96, students work problems that ask about work accomplished by moving an object up an inclined plane. Students also work on projects involving simple machines.

In Lesson 97, students figure out how a screw works like an inclined plane. In Lessons 98 and 99, students work with a simple pulley system to determine the distances and the forces.

Projects

Starting in Lesson 91, students work on projects. For most of the work, students are in teams. Assign permanent teams of four students each.

All of the projects extend the skills the have been taught in Level F. Each project is specified for a lesson period; however, some of the projects may require more than a period. All students are expected to contribute to the completion of the project.

The work on projects is somewhat different from the more structured activities that students have done because not all the steps are specified. Also, not all the problems are solvable using the patterns or problem-solving steps that have been presented earlier in the program. Students may have questions about how to present their work and may feel uneasy or unsure about how to show the work. If a problem does not follow a problem-solving pattern they have practiced, tell them to do what they have to do to solve the problem, but try to use the rules and information they have learned about solving similar problems.

If students have trouble figuring out how to solve or approach a problem, give them hints or suggestions, but try not to specify the problem-solving steps. "Remember, this problem works something like a ratio-table problem, but you may need more than one ratio table. Let's see which team can come up with a way to solve this problem." Call on and praise teams that consider different possibilities and "map out" or try to plan steps in solving the problem. If a team produces a clever solution, let that team know that their work is exceptional. Give the team a special opportunity to present their work to another classroom or to their classmates.

Show the teams that you have high expectations of them. Make sure that you provide times for each team to report on their work.

During teamwork, members of the team are to discuss strategies, assign component tasks to team members, and complete the project by producing one copy of the team's work. To keep the projects running smoothly, reinforce teams that are performing. If a team gets stuck on what to do, members are to raise their hands. Respond by pointing students in possible directions, not by giving them the solution. If members of a team disagree about how to solve the problem or how to present the work, tell the members that they should try all the alternatives and see which one seems most appropriate.

A final feature of the work on projects is that teams may need copies of diagrams, coordinate systems, or circles. The material to be copied appears at the back of this *Teacher's Guide.* Reproduce the material before the lesson. A good plan is to provide each team with two or three copies of the material. Tell teams, "Use one of the copies for your initial work. Use the other copy for your finished work."

For Lesson 91, you will reproduce Graph A:

Graph A

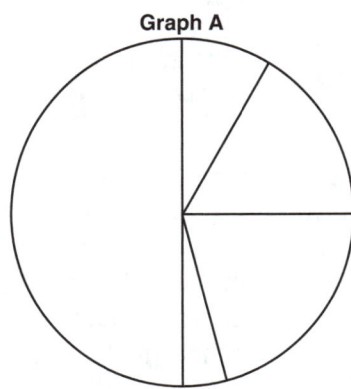

In Lesson 91, students study symmetry and then construct a symmetrical (mirror image) circle graph from half of the graph.

Graph A

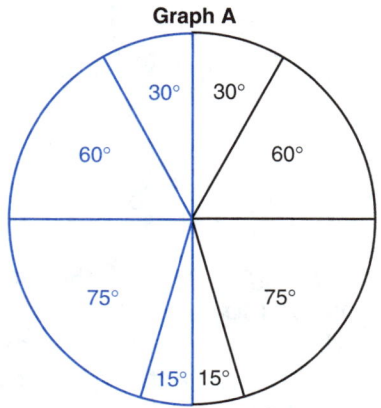

Teaching note: To solve the problem, students apply what they know about circles, degrees, and the protractor. Students first measure the various angles (using a protractor). Next, they construct the mirror image of the half-completed graph. For each slice, they construct a slice with the same number of degrees.

For Lesson 92, you will reproduce a pie graph that shows 10-degree divisions on half of the graph.

Graph B

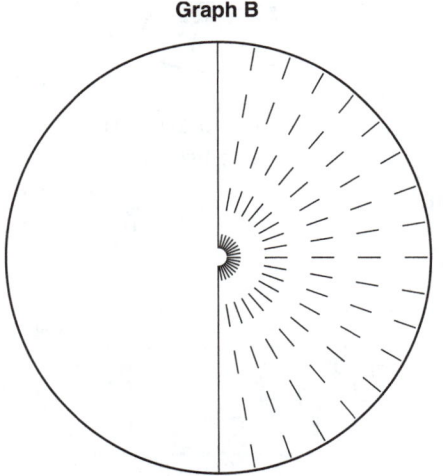

Below is a graph that appears in the textbook for Lesson 92.

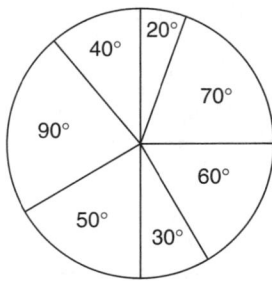

Students copy this graph onto Graph B. They do not use a protractor to create the slices for this graph. Instead, they use what they know about opposite angles. To create the 40-degree segment, students count off a segment that is 40 degrees from vertical on the bottom right side of the figure and draw a straight line to create the opposite angle on the top left of the figure. The completed graph is shown below.

Graph B

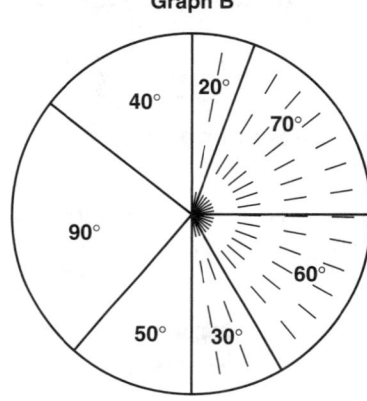

In Lesson 92, students also use the properties of symmetrical figures to find their area.

For example:

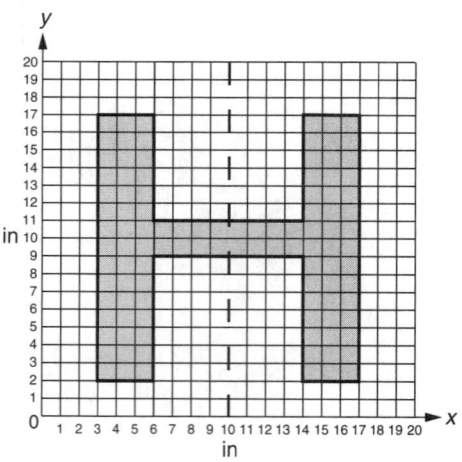

Teams first figure out the area of half the figure, then multiply by 2 to find the area of the entire figure.

---

large rectangle	$3 \times 15 = 45$ sq in
small rectangle	$4 \times 2 = 8$ sq in
half figure	$45 + 8 = 53$ sq in
entire figure	$53 \times 2 = \boxed{106 \text{ sq in}}$

Teams then confirm their calculations by figuring out the area of a rectangle, the perimeter of which touches the four outside corners of the H, and then subtracting the combined area of the "holes."

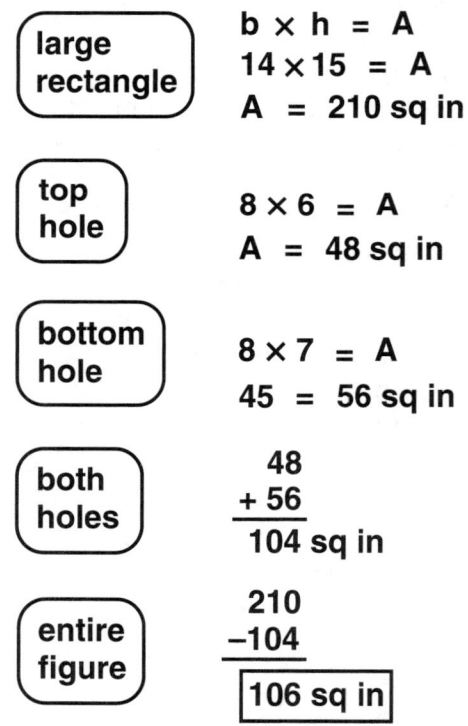

large rectangle	$b \times h = A$ $14 \times 15 = A$ $A = 210$ sq in
top hole	$8 \times 6 = A$ $A = 48$ sq in
bottom hole	$8 \times 7 = A$ $45 = 56$ sq in
both holes	$\begin{array}{r} 48 \\ + 56 \\ \hline 104 \text{ sq in} \end{array}$
entire figure	$\begin{array}{r} 210 \\ -104 \\ \hline \boxed{106 \text{ sq in}} \end{array}$

In Lesson 93, students work on an elaborate project that involves probability. Here are the main steps involved in the project: Teams first determine the probability for the possible outcomes for a pair of dice (with the outcomes being the numbers 2 through 12). Students do this by labeling one of the dice "left" and one "right" and showing the various possibilities, which are:

# of dots	combinations = left + right	possibilities	degrees
2	1 | 1	1	
3	1 | 2 2 | 1	2	
4	1 | 3 2 | 2 3 | 1	3	
5	1 | 4 2 | 3 3 | 2 4 | 1	4	
6	1 | 5 2 | 4 3 | 3 4 | 2 5 | 1	5	
7	1 | 6 2 | 5 3 | 4 4 | 3 5 | 2 6 | 1	6	
8	2 | 6 3 | 5 4 | 4 5 | 3 6 | 2	5	
9	3 | 6 4 | 5 5 | 4 6 | 3	4	
10	4 | 6 5 | 5 6 | 4	3	
11	5 | 6 6 | 5	2	
12	6 | 6	1	
total		36	360

Next, teams make a circle graph that shows the number of degrees for each probability.

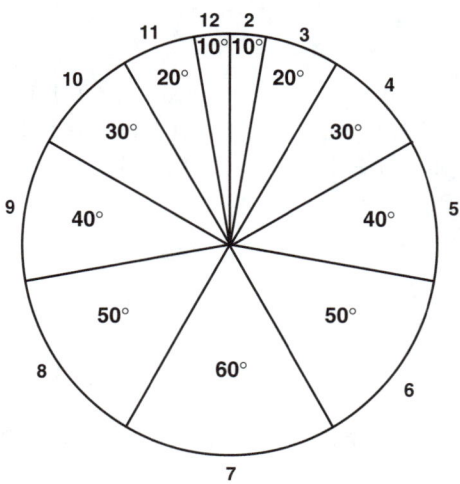

Next, students compute the expected outcomes for rolling the dice 72 times.

# of dots	combinations = left + right	possibilities	degrees	excepted #	tally	actual #
2	1 | 1	1	10°	2		
3	1 | 2 2 | 1	2	20°	4		
4	1 | 3 2 | 2 3 | 1	3	30°	6		
5	1 | 4 2 | 3 3 | 2 4 | 1	4	40°	8		
6	1 | 5 2 | 4 3 | 3 4 | 2 5 | 1	5	50°	10		
7	1 | 6 2 | 5 3 | 4 4 | 3 5 | 2 6 | 1	6	60°	12		
8	2 | 6 3 | 5 4 | 4 5 | 3 6 | 2	5	50°	10		
9	3 | 6 4 | 5 5 | 4 6 | 3	4	40°	8		
10	4 | 6 5 | 5 6 | 4	3	30°	6		
11	5 | 6 6 | 5	2	20°	4		
12	6 | 6	1	10°	2		
total		36	360°	72		

Students then conduct an experiment and complete columns to show the actual numbers for each outcome. Students use these numbers to figure out averages and create bar graphs.

> **Teaching note:** Students should be able to do the various component tasks; however, the work may require several lesson periods.

In Lesson 94, students use descriptions of points on a coordinate system to construct figures. The figures prove to be letters, and when all the letters are constructed, they spell a word:

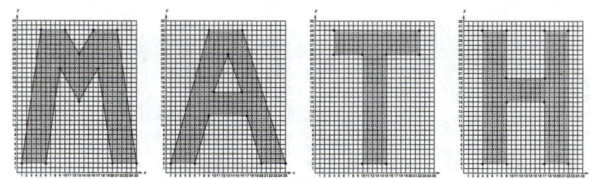

For this project, each team will need possibly eight copies of the coordinate grid.

Lesson 95 extends the notion of symmetry to a series of numbers.

Here are the problems in Lesson 95:

a. Find the sum of the numbers from 1 through 22.
b. Find the sum of the numbers from 1 through 40.
c. Find the sum of the **odd** numbers from 1 through 23.

To solve these problems, students "fold the series in half." For example, for problem A, students create 11 pairs of values, each of which has a sum of 23. To find the total, students multiply 23 by 11.

> ***Teaching note:*** If students have trouble with a problem, tell them to show the pairs of numbers that are implied, for example, in problem C:
>
> | 1 | 23 |
> |---|----|
> | 3 | 21 |
> | 5 | 19 |
> | 7 | 17 |
> | 9 | 15 |
> | 11 | 13 |

In Lesson 96, students work problems that involve inclined planes. They use the same equation they used for other simple machines: force × distance (in) = force × distance (out).

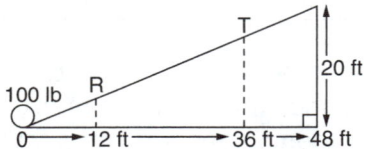

a. What is the vertical distance from the floor to point R?

b. What is the vertical distance from the floor to point T?

c. How much work is required to move the weight to point R?

d. How much work is required to move the weight to point T?

The "out" side of the equation is the side that shows the weight moving vertically. The side with the weight moving up the incline is the "in" side of the equation. Students may show the equation with the "out" side on the left. Have them label the sides.

In Lesson 96, students also relate the distances shown for an inclined plane to what they have learned about triangles. The distances in the figure below show a series of nested triangles.

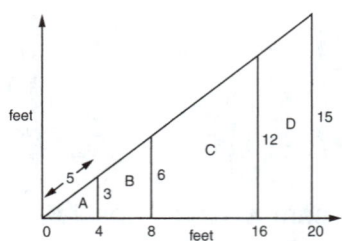

a. How does the force change as the distance increases?

b. What is the fraction you multiply by for any inclined distance to get the corresponding vertical distance?

c. How could you make a table to show the distance?

In Lesson 97, students figure out the relationship between an inclined plane and a screw. Students cut out a triangle and convert it into a screw. (They do this by creating a spiral.)

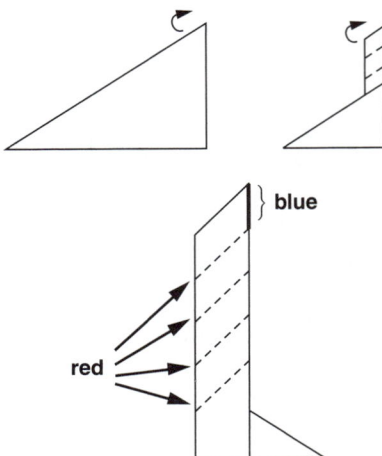

After relating a screw to an inclined plane, students show the distances for a screw by using the corresponding distances of the inclined plane. The distance straight up is the "out" distance for the force. The distance along the edge of the spiral is the distance for the "in" force. (Students color the edge for the "out" force blue and the edge for the incline red.)

In Lesson 98, students apply a folding strategy to solve geometry problems that involve repeated patterns.

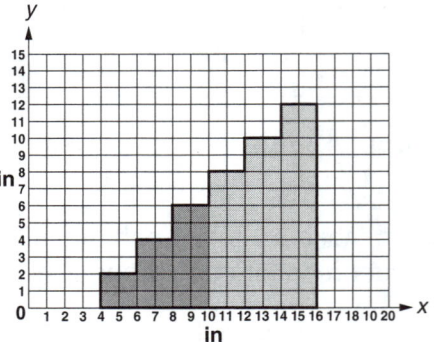

Students first figure out the midline in the problem. They then figure out a strategy for rearranging the parts so that each column is the same height.

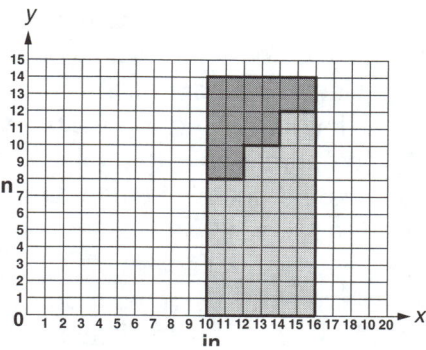

For the example above, students fold parts in much the same way they fold a number line to create pairs that have the same value. Remind students that these problems work the same way as the earlier problems involving number series. The only difference is that the problem is now solved as an area problem, and the pairs form a rectangle.

Also in Lesson 98, students work a simple pulley problem. They use a paper clip that can slide freely on a string as the weight. One end of the string is fixed, and the other moves up. Students determine that as the string moves up 1 unit, the weight moves 1/2 a unit. Also the weight moves if a force equal to 1/2 the weight is exerted on the end of the string. The equation is the same as that used for the other simple machines: $f \times d = f \times d$.

In Lesson 99, students work another type of problem that has a recurring pattern. This type **describes** the movement (instead of presenting it through a diagram).

Here are the problems from Lesson 99:

a. An ant wants a supply of 100 seeds. The ant collects seeds and eats some of them. After the ant collects 8 seeds, the ant eats 3 seeds. How many seeds will the ant collect in all before the ant has a supply of 100 seeds?

b. It takes Mr. Wilson 10 minutes to complete each frame. He works for 50 minutes and then has a 10-minute break. He starts work at 7 a.m. If he makes 30 frames, at what time does he finish? If he worked without taking any breaks, when would he finish?

c. A tank has a leak. The water leaks from the tank at the rate of 2 gallons per minute. The tank holds 200 gallons. The tank starts out empty and is filled at the rate of 7 gallons per minute. How much time is required to fill the tank? How many gallons go into the tank before it is filled?

Also in Lesson 99, students figure out how they could arrange strings for a pulley system that would require a force that is only 1/4 the weight being raised. (With the single-pulley system, the force was 1/2 the weight.)

> **Teaching note:** Students may have a lot of trouble with this project unless you prompt them.
>
> Here are some good prompts:
> 1. When you worked with the string last time, there was one loop, and the weight was attached to just one loop. Put two paper clips on your string and see if you can make the string so it has two loops with the paper clips at the bottom of those loops. Make sure both paper clips can slide freely. Make sure that one end of your string is fastened and cannot move.
> 2. Attach something that will serve as your weight to the two paper clips. Make sure that the weight is attached to both paper clips.
>
>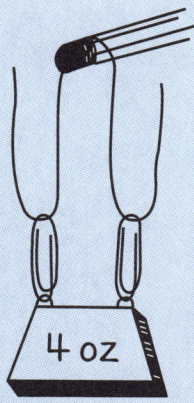
>
> 3. Check your distances to make sure that as the weight moves up 1 unit, the free end of the string moves up 4 units.

In Lesson 100, students work a three-dimensional problem that has a "hole." For example, a large box has a smaller cube-shaped box inside. Students are to find the net volume (the volume of the larger box minus the volume of the cube).

SUMMARY

Students who complete the projects presented in Level F will have learned new tool skills and then applied them to complex projects. The projects give you and the students an idea of the mathematical power the students have developed. As you do the projects, you and the students may identify other possible projects. If time permits, do them. The purpose of teaching core skills and operations is to apply them to real-life settings. Students who complete Level F have a repertoire of skills and the experiences required to meet the challenges presented as they move to higher levels of math and to tackle even more difficult real-life applications. Both you and your students will be impressed with their performance.

Appendix A

Connecting Math Concepts

Level F Cumulative Test 1
(Lessons 1–30)

Materials Note: Students will need lined paper and a calculator.

Note: Students are not to use calculators for any part of the test except Part 13.

Direct students who are new to *Connecting Math Concepts,* Level F to skip Part 8.

a. This is a test. You should only have your test and a sharpened pencil on your desk.
b. Work Parts 1 through 12.
• Raise your hand when you've finished Part 12.
• (Observe students but do not give feedback.)
c. (After students have completed Part 12, permit them to use a calculator to complete Part 13. Observe.)

CUMULATIVE TEST 1 SCORING CHART			
PART	**SCORE**	**POSSIBLE SCORE**	**PASSING SCORE**
1	2 for each item	6	Parts 1, 2 combined 8
2	2 for each item	4	
3	EACH ITEM	6	6
	Answer 2 / Name 1 / Total 3		
4	2 for each item	4	Parts 4, 5, 6 combined 13
5	3 for each item	6	
6	3 for each item	6	
7	1 for each item	4	4
8	3 for each item	6	Parts 8, 9, 10 combined 12
9	3 for each item	3	
10	3 for each item	6	
11	2 for each item	8	6
12	3 for each item	6	Parts 12, 13 combined 9
13	2 for each item	6	
	TOTAL	71	

Note: Bracketed exercises teach preskills for boldface remedies. For students who fail a part of the test but have mastered the preskills, present only the boldface remedies for that part.

CUMULATIVE TEST 1 PERCENT SUMMARY					
SCORE	**%**	**SCORE**	**%**	**SCORE**	**%**
71	100	63	89	56	78
70	99	62	87	55	77
69	97	61	86	54	76
68	96	60	85	53	75
67	94	59	83	52	73
66	93	58	82	51	71
65	92	57	80	50	70
64	90				

CUMULATIVE TEST 1 REMEDIES	
PART	**LESSON and (EXERCISE)**
1	**1 (5), 2 (5), 3 (5), 5 (1), 6 (1)**
2	[9 (3), 10 (3), 13 (3)] **14 (2), 15 (3), 16 (3), 17 (5), 18 (7, part 9)**
3	**1 (7), 2 (7), 3 (7), 14 (7), 15 (6)**
4	[6 (2), 7 (4)] **27 (6), 28 (5), 29 (5)**
5	[11 (4)] **12 (4), 13 (4), 14 (6), 15 (2), 18 (6)**
6	[7 (2), 8 (1), 9 (1)] **25 (5), 26 (4), 27 (5)**
7	**24 (3), 25(2)**
8	[1 (4), 2 (2)] **3 (4), 4 (4), 18 (2), 19 (2)**
9	[5 (3), 6 (4, 5)] **7 (5), 8 (3), 9 (4, steps a–c)**
10	[6 (3)] **13 (1), 14 (4)**
11 a, d	**2 (6), 3 (2), 4 (2), 5 (4)**
11 b, c	**8 (2), 10 (2), 11 (5), 18 (5)**
12	[16 (2), 17 (3)] **18 (4)**
13	**24 (5), 25 (3), 26 (2), 27 (3), 28 (4)**

Connecting Math Concepts

Level F Cumulative Test 2
(Lessons 1–60)

Materials Note: Students will need lined paper and a calculator.

Note: Students are not to use calculators for any part of the test except Parts 10 and 11.

a. This is a test. You should only have your test and a sharpened pencil on your desk.
b. Work Parts 1 through 9.
• Raise your hand when you've finished Part 9.
• (Observe students but do not give feedback.)
c. (After students have completed Part 9, permit them to use a calculator to complete Parts 10 and 11. Observe.)

CUMULATIVE TEST 2 PERCENT SUMMARY

SCORE	%	SCORE	%	SCORE	%
59	100	53	90	47	80
58	98	52	88	46	78
57	97	51	86	45	76
56	95	50	85	44	75
55	93	49	83	43	73
54	92	48	82	42	71

CUMULATIVE TEST 2 SCORING CHART

PART	SCORE	POSSIBLE SCORE	PASSING SCORE
1	2 for each item	4	Parts 1, 2, 3
2	2 for each item	4	combined
3	2 for each question	4	10
4	2 for each item	6	Parts 4, 5
5	3 for each item	6	combined 9
6	2 for each cell	4	4
7	2 for each question	6	Parts 7, 8
8	3 for each item 9	9	combined 12
9	2 for each item	4	4
10	EACH ITEM	6	5
	Digits for answer 2 / Decimal point for placement 1 / Total 3		
11	3 for each item	6	6
	TOTAL	59	

Note: Bracketed exercises teach preskills for boldface remedies. For students who fail a part of the test but have mastered the preskills, present only the boldface remedies for that part.

CUMULATIVE TEST 2 REMEDIES

PART	LESSON and (EXERCISE)
1	[24 (4), 25 (1), 26 (1), 27 (1), 28 (3)] **29 (3), 31 (5), 32 (1), 33 (1), 34 (1), 35 (1), 36 (5)**
2	[46 (2), 47 (2)] **47 (5), 48 (3), 49 (5)**
3	**35 (2), 43 (1)**
4	**47 (3)** [47 (7)] **48 (5)**
5	**56 (3), 57 (1)**
6	[7 (2), 8 (1), 9 (1)] [11 (3), 12 (1), 13 (2), 14 (1, 5), 15 (1, 5), 16 (4), 17 (4), 18 (3), 19 (1)] **34 (5), 35 (5), 38 (6, part 8)**
7	[7 (3), 8 (4), 9 (2), 10 (1), 11 (1, 4)] **12 (4), 13 (4), 18 (6)**
8	[49 (3), 51 (4)] [52 (3), 53 (4), 54 (1, 4), 55 (2), 56 (2), 57 (3), 58 (4)] **59 (1), 60 (1)**
9	[1 (7), 2 (7), 14 (7), 15 (6)] [51 (2), 52 (4)] **53 (5), 54 (5), 55 (5)**
10	[53 (2), 54 (6)] **55 (6), 56 (1)**
11	**36 (1), 37 (3), 38 (1)**

Connecting Math Concepts

Level F Final Cumulative Test
(Lessons 1–100)

> **Materials Note:** Each student will need a copy of the Final Test (pages 109–122), lined paper, and a calculator.

SECTION 1

> **Note:** Pass out copies of Section 1 (pages 109–111).

a. The Final Test is a very long test that shows just how much you have learned in Level F.
b. This test has three sections. You'll work the first eight parts today. That's Section 1. During the next two lessons, you'll complete the test.
c. Start by filling out the information at the top of the first page.
• Then work very carefully and show just how smart you are. You must show your work for each part. If you need to use lined paper, show the part number you're working.
• Raise your hand when you've completed Part 8. (Observe students but do not give feedback.)

SECTION 2

> **Note:** Pass out copies of Section 2 (pages 112–115).

a. You're going to work Section 2 of the Final Test today. During the next lesson you'll complete the test.
b. You'll work Parts 9 through 18 today. Show your work for each part. Raise your hand when you've completed Part 18.
(Observe students but do not give feedback.)

SECTION 3

> **Note:** Pass out copies of Section 3 (pages 116–122). Students are not to use a calculator for any part of the test except Part 27.

a. You're going to finish the Final Test today.
b. You'll work Parts 19 through 27.
• You'll need a calculator for Part 27. So when you've completed Part 26, raise your hand to let me know you're ready to use your calculator.
(Observe students but do not give feedback.)

MARKING THE TEST

• (Collect the students' papers. Use the answer key (pages 123–127) to score the tests and award points. A good score is 90% or above.)

FINAL CUMULATIVE TEST PERCENT SUMMARY					
SCORE	%	SCORE	%	SCORE	%
329	100	293–296	89	260–263	79
326–328	99	290–292	88	257–259	78
323–325	98	287–289	87	254–256	77
320–322	97	283–286	86	251–253	76
316–319	96	280–282	85	247–250	75
313–315	95	277–279	84	244–246	74
310–312	94	274–276	83	241–243	73
306–309	93	270–273	82	237–240	72
303–305	92	267–269	81	234–236	71
300–302	91	264–266	80	231–233	70
297–299	90				

	FINAL CUMULATIVE TEST SCORING CHART			
PART	**SCORE**		**POSSIBLE SCORE**	**PASSING SCORE**
1	1 for each missing cell		12	10
2	2 for each item		10	8
3	1 for each item		4	4
4	2 for each item		26	22
5	2 for each item		10	8
6	3 for each item		12	9
7	2 for each item		32	26
8	3 for each item		9	6
9	EACH ITEM		6	Parts 9, 10 combined
	Multiplication 1 · Answer 2 · Total 3			10
10	EACH ITEM		6	
	Exponents 2 · Answer 1 · Total 3			
11	1 for each item		3	3
12	3 for each item		9	3
13	EACH ITEM		18	15
	Sign 1 · Number 2 · Total 3			
14	1 for each item		4	3
15	EACH ITEM		12	10
	Sign 1 · Number 2 · Total 3			
16	2 for each item		10	8
17	3 for each item		6	6
18	2 for each item		12	10
19	2 for each item		20	16
20	1 for each missing cell		15	13
21	2 for each item		24	20
22	EACH ITEM		10	8
	Number 1 · Unit name 1 · Total 2			
23	EACH ITEM		8	6
	Decimal 2 · Mixed number 2 · Total 4			
24	2 for each item		22	18
25	EACH ITEM		9	6
	Number 2 · Unit name 1 · Total 3			
26	2 for each item		8	6
27	2 for each item		12	10
	TOTAL		**329**	

Note: Bracketed exercises teach preskills for boldface remedies. For students who fail a part of the test but have mastered the preskills, present only the boldface remedies for that part.

	FINAL CUMULATIVE TEST REMEDIES
PART	**LESSON and (EXERCISE)**
1	[1 (2, 3), 2 (1, 3)] [3 (1, 6)] **3 (3), 4 (3, 5), 5 (5)**
2 a, d	**46 (2), 47 (2)**
2 b, c, e	**21 (1), 22 (5), 23 (5)**
3	[44 (3), 45 (3), 46 (3)] **47 (7)**
4 a, c, d, f, m	[29 (3), 31 (5), 32 (1)] **33 (1), 34 (1), 35 (1), 36 (5), 37 (2), 38 (5), 39 (1)**
4 b	**25 (5), 26 (4), 27 (5)**
4 e	[16 (4)] **31 (3), 32 (3), 33 (6)**
4 g, h	**17 (4), 18 (3), 19 (1), 34 (5), 35 (5)**
4 i, j	[11 (3), 12 (1), 13 (2), 14 (1), 15 (1)] **8 (1), 9 (1)**
4 k, l	**19 (4), 21 (2), 22 (1), 23 (2)**
5	**41 (1), 42 (1, 4), 43 (3), 44 (1)**
6	[9 (3), 10 (3)] **16 (3), 17 (5)** [61 (1), 62 (1), 64 (4)] **67 (5), 68 (5), 69 (1), 80 (1), 81 (6), 83 (2)**
7 a, j, m	[1 (4), 2 (2)] **5 (2), 6 (3)**
7 b, d, g, o	**48 (2), 49 (1)**
7 f, p	**2 (6), 3 (2), 4 (2)**
7 c, h, k, l	**8 (2), 10 (2), 11 (5), 18 (5), 61 (4)**
7 e, i, n	**45 (5), 47 (5), 48 (3), 49 (5)**
8	[49 (3), 51 (4)] [52 (3), 53 (4), 54 (1, 4), 55 (2), 56 (2), 57 (3), 58 (4)] **59 (1), 60 (1), 62 (6), 63 (3), 67 (2), 77 (4), 78 (2), 79 (3)**
9	[(74 (1)] **75 (4), 76 (4), 77 (2), 78 (4)**
10 a	[74 (1)] **86 (5), 87 (4)**
10 b	[74 (1)] **83 (1), 84 (2), 85 (2)**
11	**24 (3), 25 (2)**
12 a, b	[(1 (7), 2 (7)] **86 (1), 87 (6), 88 (6)**
12 c	**46 (4), 47 (4)**
13 a, b, f	**[78 (5), 79 (1), 81 (4), 82 (1), 83 (4), 84 (5), 85 (3), 86 (4), 87 (2), 88 (2)]**
13 c, d, e	[61 (3), 62 (3)] [63 (1), 64 (1), 65 (1)] [64 (5), 65 (4), 66 (1, 3), 67 (1)] [67 (3), 68 (1), 69 (5)] **[71 (4), 72 (3), 73 (3)]**
14	**47 (3), 48 (5, steps a–c)**
15	**88 (5), 89 (2, 7), 90 (3)**
16	[51 (2), 52 (4)] **53 (5), 54 (5), 55 (5), 56 (4), 57 (6), 59 (2)**
17	**36 (1), 37 (3), 38 (1), 43 (1), 44 (6), 45 (6), 46 (6), 47 (1)**
18 a, b	**44 (4), 45 (1)**
18 c	**86 (3), 87 (1)**
18 d, e, f	**46 (4), 47 (4)**
18 g, h	[1 (4), 2 (2)] [3 (4), 4 (4)] [5 (3), 6 (4, 5), 7 (5), 8 (3), 9 (4)] **12 (2), 13 (5), 14 (3), 15 (4), 16 (1), 17 (1)**
18 i, j	[6 (3)] [11 (2), 12 (3)] **13 (1) 14 (4)**
19 a–e	**26 (5), 27 (4)** [28 (1), 29 (4), 30 (1)] [31 (1), 32 (5)] **33 (1), 34 (4), 35 (3), 36 (3), 37 (6), 38 (4), 39 (6)**
19 f	**86 (3), 87 (1)**

PART	LESSON and (EXERCISE)
FINAL CUMULATIVE TEST	
REMEDIES	
20	[81 (3), 82 (5)] **83 (3), 84 (6), 85 (5)**
21 a, b	**61 (5), 62 (2), 63 (5)** [61 (2), 62 (5), 63 (2)] **64 (2), 65 (2), 66 (2)**
21 c, f	((same as Part 8))
21 d, e, j, k	[81 (1), 82 (3), 83 (6), 84 (1)] **85 (4), 86 (2)**
21 g, h	[75 (1), 76 (3)] **77 (3), 78 (1), 79 (2)**
21 i	**81 (5), 82 (4), 84 (7)**
21 l	[7 (1, 3), 8 (4, 5), 9 (2, 5), 10 (1)] **11 (1)**
22 a, b, c, d	**1 (7), 2 (7, 8), 3 (7), 14 (7), 15 (6)**
22 e	[36 (4), 37 (4), 38 (3), 39 (3), 48 (4), 49 (4)] [51 (2), 52 (4)] **53 (5), 54 (5), 56 (4), 57 (6)**
23	[35 (4), 36 (2)] **37 (1), 39 (2), 41 (2)**
24 a, c	**53 (2), 54 (6), 55 (6), 56 (1)**
24 b	**42 (6), 43 (5)**
24 d	**21 (3), 22 (4), 23 (1), 24 (2), 25 (6)**
24 e, j, k	[71 (1), 72 (4), 73 (1)] **74 (6), 75 (6), 77 (6)**
24 f, h	**23 (4), 24 (6), 26 (6), 27 (2), 28 (6)**
24 g, i	[66 (5)] **81 (1), 82 (3), 83 (6), 84 (1, 4)**
25 a	**85 (1), 86 (6), 87 (5)**
25 b, c	**71 (2), 72 (5), 74 (5), 75 (2), 76 (2)**
26	[1 (4), 2 (2), 6 (3), 9 (4, step a)] **68 (7, Part 12)**
27 a, c, d	**24 (5), 25 (3), 26 (2), 27 (3), 28 (4)**
27 b	**29 (1), 31 (4), 32 (2), 33 (3), 35 (6, Part 8)**
27 e, f	**57 (1), 58 (5), 59 (5), 68 (4), 69 (6)**

Part 1 Show the proper mixed number for each item.

a. $6\frac{14}{5}$ = ☐   b. $3\frac{8}{4}$ = ☐   c. $9\frac{19}{10}$ = ☐

Part 2 Work each problem. For each item show the answer as a proper mixed number.

a. $\begin{array}{r} 39 \\ -\ 7\frac{3}{8} \\ \hline \end{array}$ ☐

b. $\begin{array}{r} 4 \\ 16\frac{2}{10} \\ +\ 6\frac{12}{10} \\ \hline \end{array}$ ☐

Part 3 Find the area of each figure.

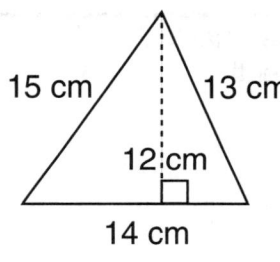

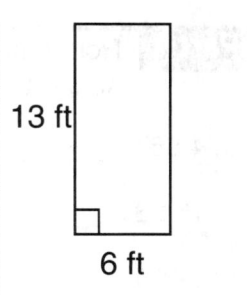

Area = _____   Area = _____

Part 4 Rewrite each decimal value as a fraction. Then work each problem.

a. $.09 \times 4 =$ ☐

b. $2.07 \times 10 =$ ☐

Part 5 — Work each problem and answer the questions.

a. 32% of the class were girls. The class had 25 students.
How many boys were there in the class?

_____

b. .8 of the questions were true/false. There were 50 questions
on the test. How many questions were not true/false?

_____

Part 6 — For each item, show the mixed number and the fraction it equals. Answer the questions.

a. How many feet are in $12\frac{1}{3}$ yards? _____

b. How many inches are in $5\frac{4}{12}$ feet? _____

Part 7 — Round each decimal to the nearest hundredth.

a. 4.567 _____

b. 16.331 _____

c. 3.029 _____

d. 7.205 _____

Part 8 — Complete each item.

a. $36 - 12 = \boxed{}$?

$\boxed{} + \boxed{} = \boxed{}$

$\boxed{} \times 2 = 60$

b. $11 \times 7 = \boxed{}$?

$\boxed{} - \boxed{} = \boxed{}$

$\boxed{} \div 4 = 15$

Part 9 Answer the question.

A girl started out with some seeds. Then the number she had trippled. Then she gave her brother 9 seeds. Now she has 24 seeds left. How man seeds did she start out with?

_____

Part 10 Work each item.

a. 5 identical bags of flour weigh 22 pounds. How much do 8 bags of flour weigh?

_____

b. It takes 15 minutes to walk 9 equal blocks. How long does it take to walk 6 blocks?

_____

Part 11 Write each problem as a column problem and work it.

a. $32.5 + 16.22 + .07 =$ _____

b. $196.4 \times 14 =$ _____

c. $.08 \times 3.61 =$ _____

d. $39 - 22.14 =$ _____

Part 12 Work each item. Use shortcuts if you can.

a. $3 \times \dfrac{490}{20} =$ _____

b. $1000 \times \dfrac{60}{200} =$ _____

Part 13 Use your calculator to work each item.

 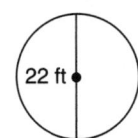 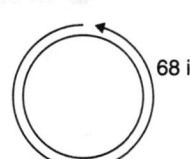 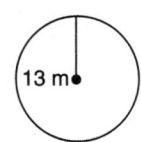

a. Figure out the radius.

_____

b. Figure out. the diameter.

_____

c. Figure out the circumference.

_____

NAME _____

DATE _____

Part 1 Answer each question.

a. How many hours are in 2 days? _____

b. How many years are in 60 months? _____

Part 2 Complete each equation.

a. $\dfrac{8}{3}$ $\left(\right) = \boxed{} = 1$

b. $\dfrac{48}{10}$ $\left(\right) = \boxed{} = 1$

Part 3 Answer each question.

The bride buys 4 times as many tulips as roses. She buys 32 roses.
Each rose costs $1.70. Each tulip costs $.65.

How many tulips did she buy? _____

How much did the bride spend on her flowers? _____

Part 4 Answer each question.

a. How many degrees are in a triangle? _____

b. How many degrees are in the corner of a rectangle? _____

c. How many degrees are in a half circle? _____

Part 5 Find the area of the shaded part.

a. 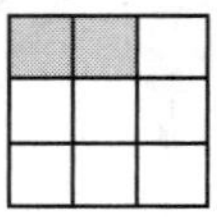 The area of the entire rectangle is 72 square feet.

What is the area of the shaded part? _____

b. 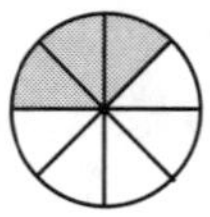 The area of the entire circle is 60 square feet.

What is the area of the shaded part? _____

Part 6 Write the answer to each item.

a. $9\dfrac{27}{365}$ years is $\boxed{}$ years and $\boxed{}$ days.

b. 8 pounds and 11 ounces is $\boxed{}$ pounds.

Part 7   Answer each question.

a. 65% of the students walk to school. There are 420 students.

How many students walk to school? _____

How many students don't walk to school? _____

b. 40% of the kids went horseback riding. The rest went swimming.

There were 85 kids. How many went swimming? _____

Part 8   Answer each question.

a. A girl is 7 years and 8 months old. Her brother was born
   when she was 5 years 14 months old. How old is her brother? _____

b. On Monday George worked 8 hours and 45 minutes.
   On Tuesday, he worked 6 hours and 50 minutes.

   How long did George work in all? _____

c. A gas tank can hold 11 gallons and 2 quarts. The tank needs 4 gallons

   and 5 quarts to be full. How much fuel is in the tank? _____

Part 9   Write each item as a division problem and work it.

a. $\dfrac{5.4}{4}$ b. $\dfrac{.392}{8}$

Part 10 Work the item.

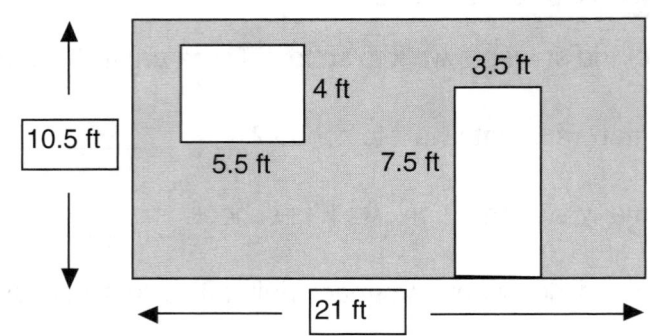

This diagram shows a wall with holes for a door and a window. Figure out the area of the wall that will be painted. _____

Part 11 Work each problem. Show the cost of the items. Show the tax. Show the total.

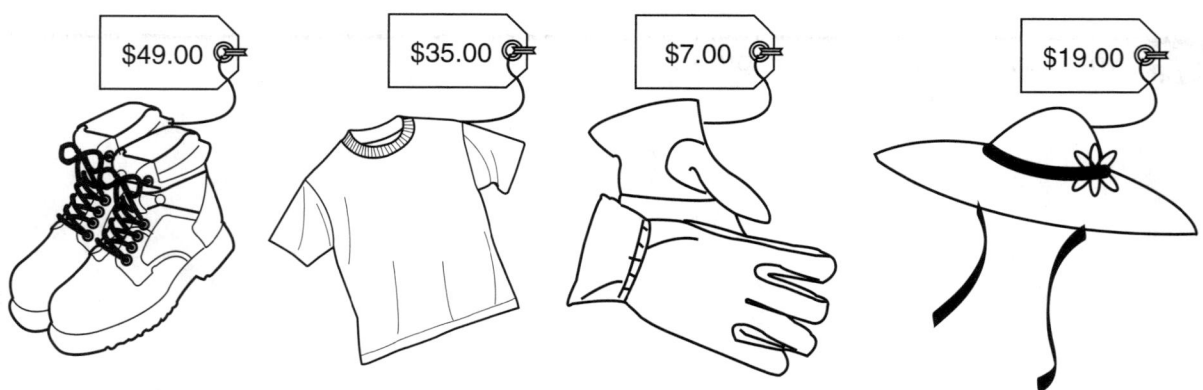

a. Scott purchases the boots and the hat.
   The tax is 7%. How much does Scott pay?

b. Toni purchases the gloves and the hat.
   The tax is 5%. How much does Toni pay?

SECTION 1

Part 1 Complete each table.

a.

fraction	decimal	percent
$\frac{2}{100}$		
	58.64	
		268%
		4%

b.

fraction	mixed number
$\frac{26}{7}$	
	$3\frac{1}{8}$
	$20\frac{1}{2}$
$\frac{5}{3}$	

Part 2 Work each item.

a. What's the reciprocal of 7? _____

b. What's $\frac{2}{3}$ of 51? _____

c. What's 20% of 15? _____

d. What's the reciprocal of $\frac{13}{8}$? _____

e. What's $\frac{2}{5}$ of 2.05? _____

Part 3 Write the name of each figure.

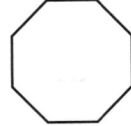      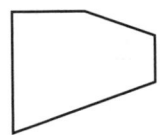   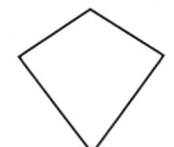

a. _____   b. _____   c. _____   d. _____

Part 4   Work each item.

a. How many years are in 50 months? _____

b. How many seasons are in 3 years and 1 season? _____

c. How many days are in 12 weeks? _____

d. How many hours are in $1\frac{7}{24}$ days? _____

e. How many hours are in $\frac{3}{4}$ of a day? _____

f. How many yards are in 16 feet? _____

g. Write $7\frac{3}{4}$ gallons with two unit names. _____

h. Write 27 pints with two unit names. _____

i. What fraction of a pound is 15 ounces? _____

j. What fraction shows the number of pounds in 1 ounce? _____

k. Write 3 pounds and 7 ounces as a mixed number with one unit name. _____

l. Write 2 minutes and 14 seconds as a mixed number with one unit name. _____

m. How many minutes is 98 seconds? _____

Part 5   Write the reduced fraction for each percent.

a. 25% = ☐   b. 20% = ☐   c. 75% = ☐   d. 60% = ☐   e. 50% = ☐

Part 6   Work each item. Box the answer.

a.
$$3\frac{1}{5}$$
$$-\ \frac{3}{8}$$

b.
$$2\frac{4}{5}$$
$$+1\frac{1}{5}$$

c.
$$10\frac{3}{5}$$
$$-6\frac{10}{12}$$

d.
$$2\frac{2}{3}$$
$$+\ \frac{5}{8}$$

Part 7 — Work each item.

a. $3 \times \boxed{} = 7$

g. $\frac{1}{8} \times 5\frac{1}{3} = \boxed{}$

l. $\begin{array}{r} 1.6 \\ \times\, 5.4 \\ \hline \end{array}$

b. $\frac{13}{5} \times \frac{1}{2} = \boxed{}$

h. $5.3 \times 100 = \boxed{}$

m. $\boxed{} \times 4 = 200$

c. $\begin{array}{r} 2.05 \\ \times\, 7 \\ \hline \end{array}$

i. $35 \left(\boxed{}\right) = \boxed{} = 1$

h. $\frac{10}{15} \left(\boxed{}\right) = \boxed{} = 1$

d. $\frac{12}{8} \times \frac{5}{8} = \boxed{}$

j. $\boxed{} \times 5 = 3$

o. $\begin{array}{r} 7\frac{4}{5} \\ \times\, 1\frac{1}{9} \\ \hline \end{array}$

e. $\frac{1}{9} \left(\boxed{}\right) = \boxed{} = 1$

k. $\begin{array}{r} 3.75 \\ \times\, .02 \\ \hline \end{array}$

p. $\begin{array}{r} .3 \\ 2.08 \\ +\, 26. \\ \hline \end{array}$

f. $4.36 - .294 = $ _____

Part 8 — Work each item.

a. Three identical containers hold 3 gallons and 5 pints each. How much do all of the containers together hold?

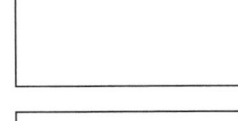

b. A salesman took 2 trips in a week. The first trip took 2 days and 17 hours. The second trip took 1 day and 18 hours. How long did the salesman's trips take in all?

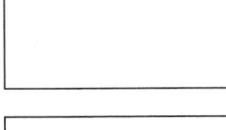

c. A carpenter cut 8 boards. Each board was 4 feet 9 inches long. What was the total length of the boards?

END of SECTION 1

SECTION 2

Part 9 Write the multiplication problem for each exponent. Then write the number it equals.

a. $5^3 =$ [   ] = [   ]

b. $2^5 =$ [   ] = [   ]

Part 10 Write a complete equation for each item. Show the base number and exponent.

a. $\dfrac{2 \times 2 \times 2}{2 \times 2 \times 2 \times 2 \times 2} =$

b. $(3 \times 3)(3 \times 3 \times 3 \times 3) = 3$ 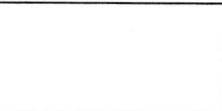 $=$ [   ] $\times$ [   ]

Part 11 Round each value to hundredths.

a. 2.3666 _____

b. 13.9804 _____

c. .0182 _____

Part 12 Work each item.

a. A man bought 7 gallons of water. He also bought 18 quarts of water. How much water did he have in all?

b. A field is 56 feet wide and 12 yards long. What's the area of the field in **square yards?**

c. If there are 56 coins in 8 containers, how many coins are there in each container?

NAME ____________________

DATE ____________________

Part 13 Work each item.

a. $\begin{array}{r} ^{-}4 \\ \times\ ^{-}6 \\ \hline \end{array}$

b. $+\ 24(^{-}2) =$ ________

c. $\begin{array}{r} ^{-}3.4 \\ -\ 5 \\ \hline \end{array}$

d. $\begin{array}{r} ^{-}1\ 5 \\ -\ 2\ 5 \\ \hline \end{array}$

b. $+\ 29 - 12 =$ ________

f. $\begin{array}{r} ^{-}3 + 2 + 5 \\ \times \quad\quad ^{-}4 \\ \hline \end{array}$

Part 14 Answer each question.

a. How many degrees are in a corner of a page? ________

b. How many degrees are in a circle? ________

c. How many degrees are in a triangle? ________

d. How many degrees are in a half circle? ________

Part 15 Rewrite each item without the large sign and work it.

a. $^{-}6 + ^{-}2 =$ ☐

b. $+16 - ^{-}10 =$ ☐

c. $^{-}48 \div ^{+}3 =$ ☐

d. $^{-}2 \div ^{-}98 =$ ☐

Part 16 Work each item. Box the answer to each question.

Figure Q

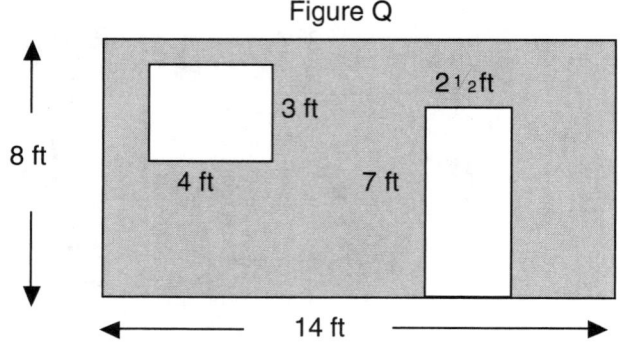

Figure Q shows a wall that is to be papered. The wallpaper costs 75¢ per square foot.

a. How many square feet of wallpaper are needed?

b. What is the cost of the wallpaper for this wall?

Figure R

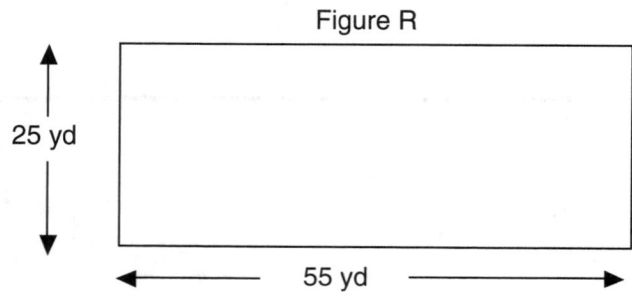

Figure R shows a field. The farmer who owns the field will plant it with oats and fence it.

c. Oats cost $.05 per square yard. What is the cost of planting oats?

d. Fencing the field costs $11 per yard. What is the cost of fencing the field?

e. What the total cost of planting and fencing the field?

Part 17 Work each item. Box the answer to each question.

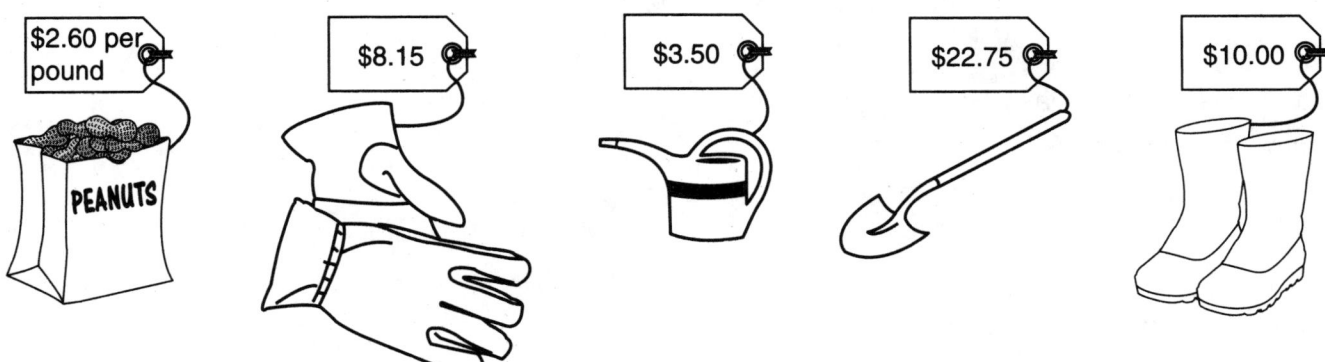

$2.60 per pound   PEANUTS

$8.15

$3.50

$22.75

$10.00

a. Hilda buys 3 pairs of gloves and 1 shovel. The tax is 8 percent. How much does Hilda pay for her purchases?

b. Tim purchases 4 pairs of boots and $\frac{1}{2}$ pound of nuts. Including 8 percent tax, how much is his total purchase?

Part 18 Work each item. Box each answer.

a. Mike is $\frac{8}{3}$ the age of Amy. Mike is 48 years old. How many years older than Amy is he?

b. What is Amy's age?

c. Bruno is $\frac{3}{5}$ as old as his father. His father is 60 years old. How old is Bruno?

d. The sale price of the coat is 45% of the regular price. By purchasing the coat on sale, the person would save $66. What's the regular price of the coat?

e. What's the sale price?

f. A circle is divided into 7 equal parts. One snowflake falls on the circle. What's the probability of the snowflake falling on any one of those parts?

END of SECTION 2

SECTION 3

Part 19 Work each item. Box the answer to each question.

a. A student is $\frac{1}{28}$ of his class. How many students are in his class?

b. If there are 72 members in the club, what's the fraction for each member?

c. 78 people work in the Holt Building. 50 of them are women. What's the probability that the first person you see in the Holt building is not a woman?

d. There are 34 shoes per carton. How many shoes are in 5 cartons?

e. If there are 80 glasses in 4 boxes, how many glasses are there per box?

f. If a car goes 320 miles on 8 gallons of gas, how many miles per gallon does the car get?

Part 19   (continued)

g. Start with a number and divide it by 6. Then add 6. Then multiply by 6. You end up with 66. What's the number you started with?

h. Molly had $125. She spent $50. Then she bought something for $12. Then she received her paycheck. She ended up with $75. How much was her paycheck?

i. 4 identical pens weigh 3 ounces. What's the weight of 7 pens?

j. There are 5 moths for every 2 butterflies. If there are 400 butterflies, how many moths are there?

Part 20   Somebody takes 70 trials at spinning the spinner. Complete the table that shows the percents, the expected numbers, and the actual numbers for each color. Here are the actual numbers the person had for three colors: 5, 30, 17.

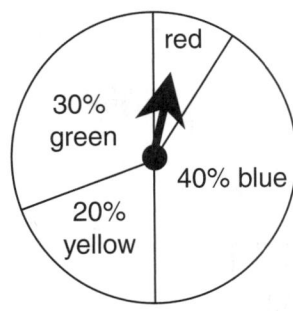

	Percent	Expected Number	Actual Number
red			
yellow			
green			
blue			
Total			

Part 21 Work each item. Box each answer.

a. A person started work at 7:24 A.M. The person finished at 1:15 P.M. How long did the person work?

b. Mary left on a bike ride at 10:45 AM. She rode for 2 hours and 20 minutes. At what time did she stop?

c. Each shelf is 2 feet 7 inches long. How many feet of shelf material are needed for 3 shelves?

d. $\frac{1}{4}$ of the sand weighed 15 tons. What did all of the sand weigh?

e. The gravel is divided into 8 equal piles. The total weight of the gravel is 4,600 pounds. How much does each pile weigh?

f. A tank had 4 gallons and 1 quart in it. 2 gallons and 3 quarts were removed. How much was left in the tank?

g. Ginger has 60 coins in all. She has $2 in nickels. She has 6 quarters. The rest of her money is in dimes. How much money does she have in all?

i. How many dimes does Ginger have?

h. Use the chart to find the average amount of money each person had.

Jan	$3.20
Fran	$2.30
Ann	$0
Dan	$5
Van	$10.50

Part 21 (continued)

j. Ann has $\frac{5}{3}$ pies. She divides the pies so that each person

receives $\frac{1}{9}$ pie. How many people can she serve?

k. A load of gravel weighs 14 tons. It is divided into

piles that weigh $\frac{2}{5}$ of a ton each. How many piles

are there?

l. $\frac{3}{5}$ of the children are boys. There are 50 children.

How many are girls?

Part 22 Work each item.

$4\frac{3}{5}$ ft

12 ft

a. Find the perimeter. _____

b. Find the area. _____

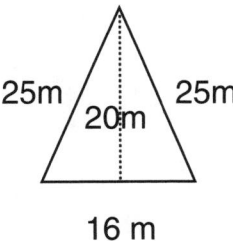

25m   25m
  20m
  16 m

c. Find the perimeter. _____

d. Find the area. _____

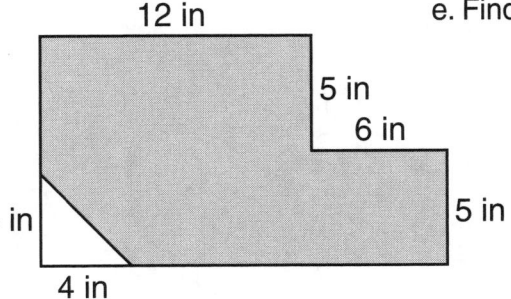

12 in

5 in

6 in

4 in

4 in

5 in

e. Find the area of the shaded part. _____

Part 23 Work each problem two times. Show each
answer as a decimal and as a mixed number.

a. $35\overline{)126.}$ decimal   _____

b. $16\overline{)24.}$ decimal   _____

mixed number _____

mixed number _____

Part 24 Do the division for each item. Show each
answer as a decimal number or a whole number.
Box your answers.

a. $\dfrac{7}{5} =$

d. $12\overline{)324}$

g. $\dfrac{4}{7} \div \dfrac{4}{7} =$

j. $.9\overline{).657}$

b. $\dfrac{4}{5} =$

e. $.03\overline{)72}$

h. $100\overline{)376}$

k. $.02\overline{)7.80}$

c. $\dfrac{9.8}{4} =$

f. $40\overline{)8080}$

i. $\dfrac{\frac{3}{1}}{6}$

Part 25 Find the volume of each figure.

a.

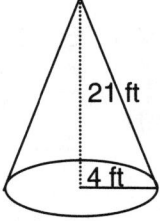

21 ft

4 ft

b.

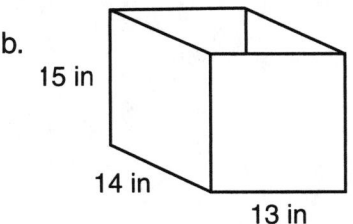

15 in

14 in

13 in

c.

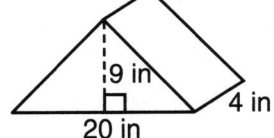

9 in

4 in

20 in

Part 26 Work each item.

a. 1107 − R = 92

R = ☐

b. 143 + 68 = D

D = ☐

c. 7 × B = 51

B = ☐

d. M + 95 = 201

M = ☐

Part 27 Work each item.

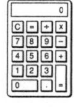

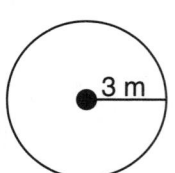
3 m

a. What's the diameter? _____

b. What's the area? _____

c. What's the circumference? _____

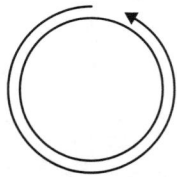
25 in

d. What's the radius? _____

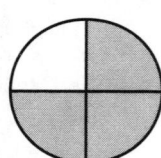

e. The area of the circle is 52 square inches.
What's the area of the shaded part? _____

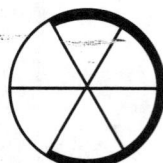

f. The circumference is 20 centimeters.
What's the length of the black part? _____

Top-left page (103)

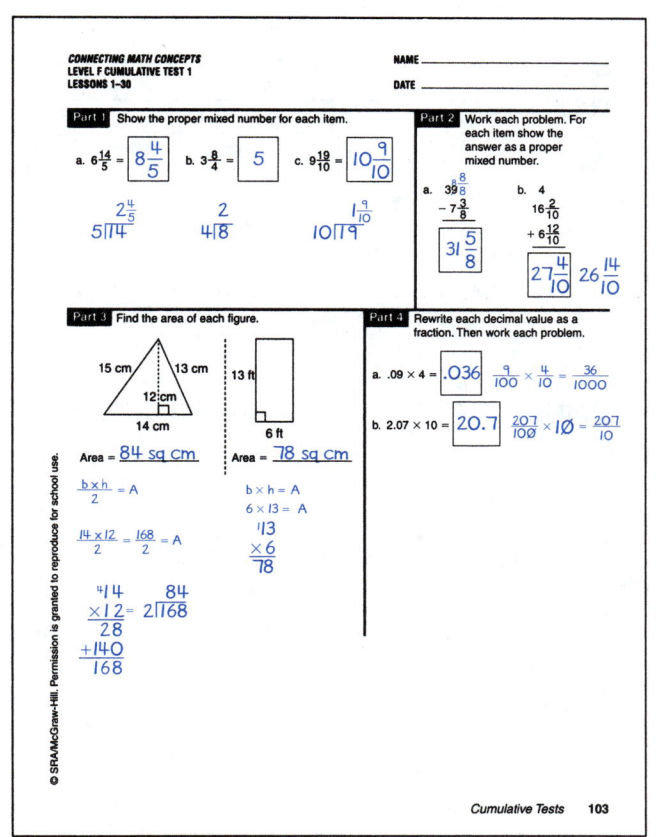

Part 1 Show the proper mixed number for each item.

a. $6\frac{14}{5} = 8\frac{4}{5}$ b. $3\frac{8}{4} = 5$ c. $9\frac{19}{10} = 10\frac{9}{10}$

$$5\overline{)14} \quad 2\frac{4}{5} \qquad 4\overline{)8} \quad 2 \qquad 10\overline{)19} \quad 1\frac{9}{10}$$

Part 2 Work each problem. For each item show the answer as a proper mixed number.

a. $39\frac{8}{8}$
$- 7\frac{3}{8}$
$\boxed{31\frac{5}{8}}$

b. 4
$16\frac{2}{10}$
$+ 6\frac{12}{10}$
$\boxed{27\frac{4}{10}} \ 26\frac{14}{10}$

Part 3 Find the area of each figure.

15 cm 13 cm
12 cm
14 cm

13 ft
6 ft

Area = $\underline{84}$ sq cm

Area = $\underline{78}$ sq cm

$\frac{b \times h}{2} = A$

$\frac{14 \times 12}{2} = \frac{168}{2} = A$

$\begin{array}{r} ^4 14 \\ \times 12 \\ \hline 28 \\ + 140 \\ \hline 168 \end{array} \quad \begin{array}{r} 84 \\ 2\overline{)168} \end{array}$

$b \times h = A$
$6 \times 13 = A$

$\begin{array}{r} ^1 13 \\ \times 6 \\ \hline 78 \end{array}$

Part 4 Rewrite each decimal value as a fraction. Then work each problem.

a. $.09 \times 4 = \boxed{.036} \quad \frac{9}{100} \times \frac{4}{10} = \frac{36}{1000}$

b. $2.07 \times 10 = \boxed{20.7} \quad \frac{207}{100} \times 10 = \frac{207}{10}$

Top-right page (104)

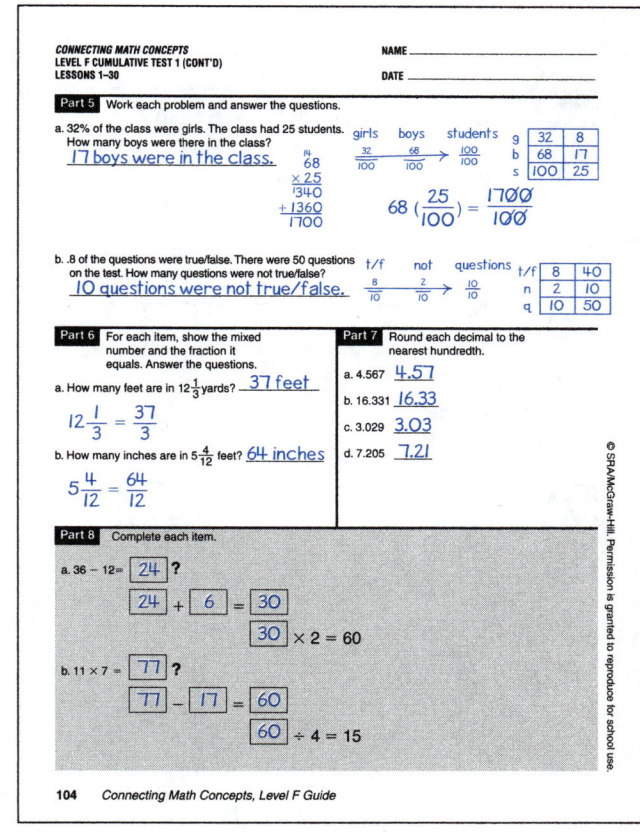

Part 5 Work each problem and answer the questions.

a. 32% of the class were girls. The class had 25 students. How many boys were there in the class?

$\underline{17 \text{ boys were in the class.}}$

girls boys students
$\frac{32}{100} \quad \frac{68}{100} \quad \frac{100}{100}$

	g	32	8
	b	68	17
	s	100	25

$\begin{array}{r} ^{14}68 \\ \times 25 \\ \hline 340 \\ +1360 \\ \hline 1700 \end{array}$

$68\left(\frac{25}{100}\right) = \frac{1700}{100}$

b. .8 of the questions were true/false. There were 50 questions on the test. How many questions were not true/false?

$\underline{10 \text{ questions were not true/false.}}$

t/f not questions
$\frac{8}{10} \quad \frac{2}{10} \rightarrow \frac{10}{10}$

	t/f	8	40
	n	2	10
	q	10	50

Part 6 For each item, show the mixed number and the fraction it equals. Answer the questions.

a. How many feet are in $12\frac{1}{3}$ yards? $\underline{37 \text{ feet}}$

$12\frac{1}{3} = \frac{37}{3}$

b. How many inches are in $5\frac{4}{12}$ feet? $\underline{64 \text{ inches}}$

$5\frac{4}{12} = \frac{64}{12}$

Part 7 Round each decimal to the nearest hundredth.

a. 4.567 $\underline{4.57}$

b. 16.331 $\underline{16.33}$

c. 3.029 $\underline{3.03}$

d. 7.205 $\underline{7.21}$

Part 8 Complete each item.

a. $36 - 12 = \boxed{24}$?

$\boxed{24} + \boxed{6} = \boxed{30}$

$\boxed{30} \times 2 = 60$

b. $11 \times 7 = \boxed{77}$?

$\boxed{77} - \boxed{17} = \boxed{60}$

$\boxed{60} \div 4 = 15$

Bottom-left page (105)

Part 9 Answer the question.

A girl started out with some seeds. Then the number she had tripled. Then she gave her brother 9 seeds. Now she has 24 seeds left. How man seeds did she start out with?

$\underline{11 \text{ seeds}}$

$\boxed{11} \times 3 = \boxed{33}$

$\boxed{33} - 9 = 24$

Part 10 Work each item.

a. 5 identical bags of flour weigh 22 pounds. How much do 8 bags of flour weigh?

$35\frac{1}{5}$ pounds

$\begin{array}{r} ^1 22 \\ \times 8 \\ \hline 176 \end{array} \quad \begin{array}{r} 35^1 \\ 5\overline{)176} \end{array}$

$\frac{5}{22}\left(\frac{\frac{8}{5}}{\frac{8}{5}}\right) = \frac{8}{\frac{176}{5}}$

b. It takes 15 minutes to walk 9 equal blocks. How long does it take to walk 6 blocks?

$\underline{10 \text{ minutes}}$

$\frac{15}{9}\left(\frac{\frac{6}{9}}{\frac{6}{9}}\right) = \frac{90}{\frac{90}{6}} \quad \begin{array}{r} ^3 15 \\ \times 6 \\ \hline 90 \end{array}$

Part 11 Write each problem as a column problem and work it.

a. $32.5 + 16.22 + .07 = \underline{48.79}$

$\begin{array}{r} 32.50 \\ 16.22 \\ + .07 \\ \hline \boxed{48.79} \end{array}$

b. $196.4 \times 14 = \underline{2749.6}$

$\begin{array}{r} ^{3}^{2}196.4 \\ \times \quad 14 \\ \hline 7856 \\ 19640 \\ \hline \boxed{2749.6} \end{array}$

c. $.08 \times 3.61 = \underline{.2888}$

$\begin{array}{r} ^4 3.61 \\ \times .08 \\ \hline .2888 \end{array}$

d. $39 - 22.14 = \underline{16.86}$

$\begin{array}{r} ^3 39.00 \\ - 22.14 \\ \hline \boxed{16.86} \end{array}$

Part 12 Work each item. Use shortcuts if you can.

a. $3 \times \frac{490}{29} = \frac{147}{2}, 73\frac{1}{2} \quad \begin{array}{r} 49 \\ \times 3 \\ \hline 147 \end{array}$

b. $1000 \times \frac{60}{200} = \frac{600}{2}, 300$

Part 13 Use your calculator to work each item.

a. Figure out the radius.   22 ft
$\underline{11 \text{ ft}}$

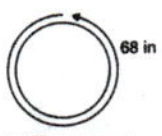

b. Figure out the diameter.   68 in
$\underline{21.66 \text{ in}}$
$\pi \times D = C$
$3.14 \times D = 68$
$D = \frac{68}{3.14}$

c. Figure out the circumference.   13 m
$\underline{81.64 \text{ m}}$
$\pi \times D = C$
$3.14 \times 26 = C$
$81.64 = C$

Bottom-right page (106)

Part 1 Answer each question.

a. How many hours are in 2 days? $\underline{48 \text{ hours}}$
$2 \text{ days} \times 24 \text{ hours} = \boxed{48}$

b. How many years are in 60 months? $\underline{5 \text{ years}}$
$\frac{60}{12} = \boxed{5}$

Part 2 Complete each equation.

a. $\frac{8}{3}\left(\frac{3}{8}\right) = \frac{\boxed{24}}{\boxed{24}} = 1$

b. $\frac{48}{10}\left(\frac{10}{48}\right) = \frac{\boxed{480}}{\boxed{480}} = 1$

Part 3 Answer each question.

The bride buys 4 times as many tulips as roses. She buys 32 roses. Each rose costs $1.70. Each tulip costs $.65.

How many tulips did she buy? $\underline{128 \text{ tulips}}$

How much did the bride spend on her flowers? $\underline{\$137.60}$

$4 \times 32 = t$
$t = \boxed{128}$

R
$\begin{array}{r} \$1.70 \\ \times 32 \\ \hline 340 \\ + 5100 \\ \hline \$54.40 \end{array}$

T
$\begin{array}{r} 128 \\ \times .65 \\ \hline 640 \\ + 7680 \\ \hline \$83.20 \end{array}$

$\begin{array}{r} \$54.40 \\ + 83.20 \\ \hline \$137.60 \end{array}$

Part 4 Answer each question.

a. How many degrees are in a triangle? $\underline{180°}$

b. How many degrees are in the corner of a rectangle? $\underline{90°}$

c. How many degrees are in a half circle? $\underline{180°}$

Part 5 Find the area of the shaded part.

a. The area of the entire rectangle is 72 square feet. What is the area of the shaded part? $\underline{16 \text{ square feet}}$

$\frac{2}{9} \times 72 = \frac{144}{9} = \boxed{16 \text{ sq ft}}$

b. The area of the entire circle is 60 square feet. What is the area of the shaded part? $\underline{22.5 \text{ square feet}}$

$\frac{3}{8} \times 60 = \frac{180}{8} = \boxed{22\frac{1}{2} \text{ sq ft}}$

Part 6 Write the answer to each item.

a. $9\frac{27}{365}$ years is $\boxed{9}$ years and $\boxed{27}$ days.

b. 8 pounds and 11 ounces is $8\frac{11}{16}$ pounds.

Top Left (Page 107)

Part 7 Answer each question.

a. 65% of the students walk to school. There are 420 students.

How many students walk to school? __273 students__

How many students don't walk to school? __147 students__

	walk	not	students
	65/100	35/100	100/100

w	65	273
nw	35	147
s	100	420

$420 \times .65$
2100
25200
273.00

$420 - 273 = 147$

85
.60
51.00

b. 40% of the kids went horseback riding. The rest went swimming.

There were 85 kids. How many went swimming? __51 kids__

	h back	swim	kids
	40/100	60/100	100/100

hback	40	34
swim	60	51
kids	100	85

Part 8 Answer each question.

a. A girl is 7 years and 8 months old. Her brother was born when she was 5 years 14 months old. How old is her brother? __1 year 6 months__

$$\begin{array}{r} {}^6 7y\ {}^{20}8m \\ -\ 5y\ 14m \\ \hline 1y\ \ 6m \end{array}$$

b. On Monday George worked 8 hours and 45 minutes. On Tuesday, he worked 6 hours and 50 minutes. How long did George work in all? __15 hours and 35 minutes__

$$\begin{array}{r} 8h\ 45m \\ +\ 6h\ 50m \\ \hline 14h\ 95m \end{array}$$
or
14h 95m
15h 35m

c. A gas tank can hold 11 gallons and 2 quarts. The tank needs 4 gallons and 5 quarts to be full. How much fuel is in the tank? __6 gallons and 1 quart__

$$\begin{array}{r} {}^{10}11g\ {}^6 2qt \\ -\ 4g\ 5qt \\ \hline 6g\ 1qt \end{array}$$

Part 9 Write each item as a division problem and work it.

a. $\dfrac{5.4}{4}$
$$\begin{array}{r} 1.35 \\ 4\overline{)5.40} \\ 12 \end{array}$$

b. $\dfrac{.392}{8}$
$$\begin{array}{r} .049 \\ 8\overline{).392} \\ 7 \end{array}$$

Top Right (Page 108)

Part 10 Work the item.

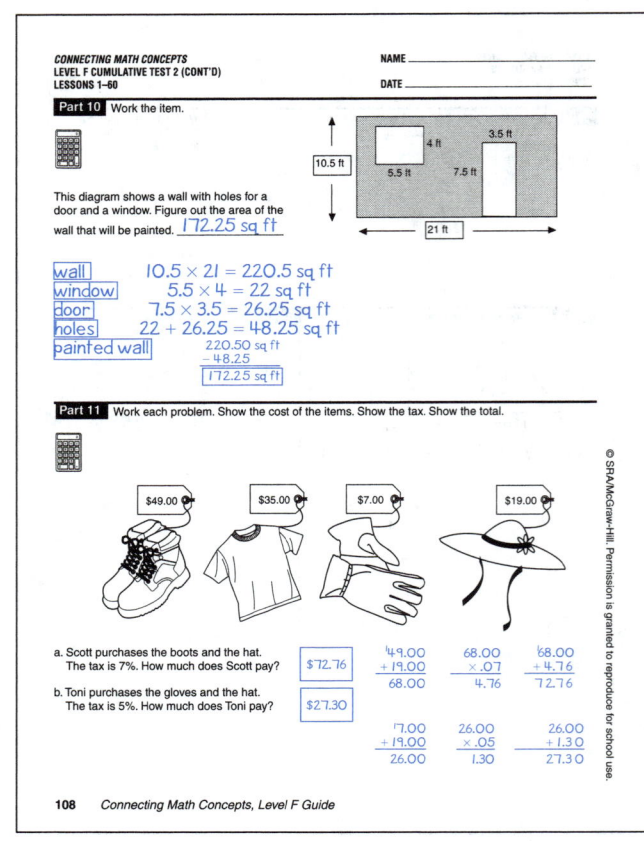

This diagram shows a wall with holes for a door and a window. Figure out the area of the wall that will be painted. __172.25 sq ft__

10.5 ft, 4 ft, 3.5 ft, 5.5 ft, 7.5 ft, 21 ft

wall	$10.5 \times 21 = 220.5$ sq ft
window	$5.5 \times 4 = 22$ sq ft
door	$7.5 \times 3.5 = 26.25$ sq ft
holes	$22 + 26.25 = 48.25$ sq ft
painted wall	220.50 sq ft

$$\begin{array}{r} 220.50 \\ -\ 48.25 \\ \hline 172.25\ \text{sq ft} \end{array}$$

Part 11 Work each problem. Show the cost of the items. Show the tax. Show the total.

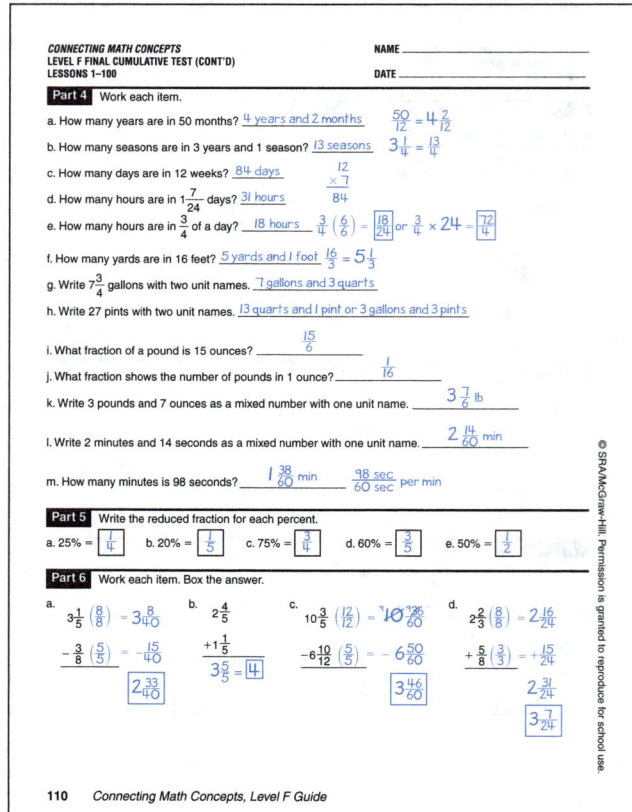

$49.00 $35.00 $7.00 $19.00

a. Scott purchases the boots and the hat. The tax is 7%. How much does Scott pay? __$72.76__

$$\begin{array}{r} 49.00 \\ +\ 19.00 \\ \hline 68.00 \end{array} \quad \begin{array}{r} 68.00 \\ \times\ .07 \\ \hline 4.76 \end{array} \quad \begin{array}{r} 68.00 \\ +\ 4.76 \\ \hline 72.76 \end{array}$$

b. Toni purchases the gloves and the hat. The tax is 5%. How much does Toni pay? __$27.30__

$$\begin{array}{r} 7.00 \\ +\ 19.00 \\ \hline 26.00 \end{array} \quad \begin{array}{r} 26.00 \\ \times\ .05 \\ \hline 1.30 \end{array} \quad \begin{array}{r} 26.00 \\ +\ 1.30 \\ \hline 27.30 \end{array}$$

Bottom Left (Page 109)

CONNECTING MATH CONCEPTS
LEVEL F FINAL CUMULATIVE TEST
LESSONS 1–100
SECTION 1

NAME _____
DATE _____

Part 1 Complete each table.

a.

fraction	decimal	percent
-2/100	.02	2%
58 64/100	58.64	58 64%
268/100	2.68	268%
4/100	.04	4%

b.

fraction	mixed number
26/7	3 5/7
25/8	3 1/8
41/2	20 1/2
5/3	1 2/3

Part 2 Work each item.

a. What's the reciprocal of 7? __1/7__

b. What's $\frac{2}{3}$ of 51? __102/3 or 34__ $\frac{2}{3} \times 51 = \frac{102}{3}$

c. What's 20% of 15? __3__ $\frac{20}{100} \times 15 = \frac{30}{10} = 3$

d. What's the reciprocal of $\frac{13}{8}$? __8/13__

e. What's $\frac{2}{5}$ of 2.05? __.82 or 4.10/5__ $\frac{2}{5} \times 2.05 = \frac{4.10}{5}$ $5\overline{)4.10}$

Part 3 Write the name of each figure.

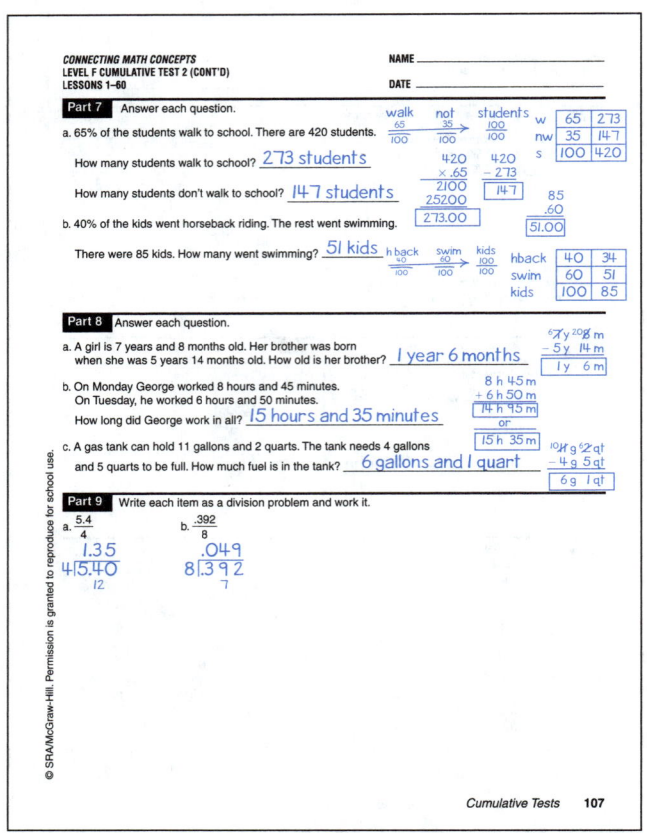

a. __octagon__ b. __triangle__ c. __pentagon__ d. __quadrilateral__

Bottom Right (Page 110)

Part 4 Work each item.

a. How many years are in 50 months? __4 years and 2 months__ $\frac{50}{12} = 4\frac{2}{12}$

b. How many seasons are in 3 years and 1 season? __13 seasons__ $3\frac{1}{4} = \frac{13}{4}$

c. How many days are in 12 weeks? __84 days__ $\begin{array}{r} 12 \\ \times 7 \\ \hline 84 \end{array}$

d. How many hours are in $1\frac{7}{24}$ days? __31 hours__

e. How many hours are in $\frac{3}{4}$ of a day? __18 hours__ $\frac{3}{4}\left(\frac{6}{6}\right) = \frac{18}{24}$ or $\frac{3}{4} \times 24 = \frac{72}{4}$

f. How many yards are in 16 feet? __5 yards and 1 foot__ $\frac{16}{3} = 5\frac{1}{3}$

g. Write $7\frac{3}{4}$ gallons with two unit names. __7 gallons and 3 quarts__

h. Write 27 pints with two unit names. __13 quarts and 1 pint or 3 gallons and 3 pints__

i. What fraction of a pound is 15 ounces? __15/16__

j. What fraction shows the number of pounds in 1 ounce? __1/16__

k. Write 3 pounds and 7 ounces as a mixed number with one unit name. __$3\frac{7}{16}$ lb__

l. Write 2 minutes and 14 seconds as a mixed number with one unit name. __$2\frac{14}{60}$ min__

m. How many minutes is 98 seconds? __$1\frac{38}{60}$ min__ $\frac{98 \text{ sec}}{60 \text{ sec}}$ per min

Part 5 Write the reduced fraction for each percent.

a. 25% = 1/4   b. 20% = 1/5   c. 75% = 3/4   d. 60% = 3/5   e. 50% = 1/2

Part 6 Work each item. Box the answer.

a. $$\begin{array}{r} 3\frac{1}{5}\left(\frac{8}{8}\right) = 3\frac{8}{40} \\ -\ \frac{3}{8}\left(\frac{5}{5}\right) = -\ \frac{15}{40} \\ \hline \boxed{2\frac{33}{40}} \end{array}$$

b. $$\begin{array}{r} 2\frac{4}{5} \\ +1\frac{1}{5} \\ \hline 3\frac{5}{5} = \boxed{4} \end{array}$$

c. $$\begin{array}{r} 10\frac{3}{5}\left(\frac{12}{12}\right) = {}^9 10\frac{\cancel{36}}{60} \\ -6\frac{10}{12}\left(\frac{5}{5}\right) = -\ 6\frac{50}{60} \\ \hline \boxed{3\frac{46}{60}} \end{array}$$

d. $$\begin{array}{r} 2\frac{2}{3}\left(\frac{8}{8}\right) = 2\frac{16}{24} \\ +\ \frac{5}{8}\left(\frac{3}{3}\right) = +\frac{15}{24} \\ \hline 2\frac{31}{24} \\ \boxed{3\frac{7}{24}} \end{array}$$

Panel 1 (page 111)

Part 7 Work each item.

a. $3 \times \boxed{\frac{7}{3}} = 7$

g. $\frac{1}{8} \times 5\frac{1}{3} = \boxed{\frac{16}{24}}$

l.
$$\begin{array}{r} 1.6 \\ \times\ 5.4 \\ \hline 64 \\ 800 \\ \hline 8.64 \end{array}$$

b. $\frac{13}{5} \times \frac{1}{2} = \boxed{\frac{13}{10}}$ (or $1\frac{3}{10}$)

h. $5.3 \times 100 = \boxed{530}$

m. $\boxed{50} \times 4 = 200$

c.
$$\begin{array}{r} 2.05 \\ \times\ 7 \\ \hline 14.35 \end{array}$$

i. $35 \left(\boxed{\frac{1}{35}}\right) = \boxed{\frac{35}{35}} = 1$

h. $\frac{10}{15} \left(\boxed{\frac{15}{10}}\right) = \boxed{\frac{150}{150}} = 1$

d. $\frac{12}{8} \times \frac{5}{8} = \boxed{\frac{60}{64}}$

j. $\boxed{\frac{3}{5}} \times 5 = 3$

o. $7\frac{4}{5}$
$\frac{39}{5} \times \frac{10}{9} = \frac{390}{45}$
$\times 1\frac{1}{9}$
$$\begin{array}{r} 8 \\ 45\overline{)390} \\ \underline{-360} \\ 30 \end{array}$$
$\frac{390}{45}$ or $8\frac{30}{45}$

e. $\frac{1}{9} \left(\boxed{9}\right) = \boxed{\frac{9}{9}} = 1$

k.
$$\begin{array}{r} 1 1 \\ 3.75 \\ \times\ .02 \\ \hline .0750 \end{array}$$

p.
$$\begin{array}{r} .30 \\ 2.08 \\ +26.00 \\ \hline 28.38 \end{array}$$

f. $4.36 - .294 = \underline{4.066}$
$$\begin{array}{r} 4.360 \\ -\ .294 \\ \hline \boxed{4.066} \end{array}$$

Part 8 Work each item.

a. Three identical containers hold 3 gallons and 5 pints each. How much do all of the containers together hold?
$\boxed{10\ gal\ 7\ pt}$

$$\begin{array}{r} 3\ gal\ 5\ pt \\ \times\quad 3 \\ \hline 9\ gal\ 15\ pt \end{array}$$

b. A salesman took 2 trips in a week. The first trip took 2 days and 17 hours. The second trip took 1 day and 18 hours. How long did the salesman's trips take in all?
$\boxed{4\ day\ 11\ hr}$

$$\begin{array}{r} 2\ day\ 17\ hr \\ +1\ day\ 18\ hr \\ \hline 3\ day\ 35\ hr \end{array}$$

c. A carpenter cut 8 boards. Each board was 4 feet 9 inches long. What was the total length of the boards?
$\boxed{38\ ft}$

$$\begin{array}{r} 4\ ft\ 9\ in \\ \times\quad 8 \\ \hline 32\ ft\ 72\ in \end{array}$$

END of SECTION 1

Panel 2 (page 112)

CONNECTING MATH CONCEPTS
LEVEL F FINAL CUMULATIVE TEST (CONT'D)
LESSONS 1–100
SECTION 2

NAME
DATE

Part 9 Write the multiplication problem for each exponent. Then write the number it equals.

a. $5^3 = \boxed{5 \times 5 \times 5} = \boxed{125}$

b. $2^5 = \boxed{2 \times 2 \times 2 \times 2 \times 2} = \boxed{32}$

Part 10 Write a complete equation for each item. Show the base number and exponent.

a. $\dfrac{2 \times 2 \times 2}{2 \times 2 \times 2 \times 2 \times 2} = \boxed{\frac{1}{4}}$

b. $(3 \times 3)(3 \times 3 \times 3) = 3^{\boxed{6}} = \boxed{3^2} \times \boxed{3^4}$

Part 11 Round each value to hundredths.

a. 2.3666 ___2.37___

b. 13.9804 ___13.98___

c. .0182 ___.02___

Part 12 Work each item.

a. A man bought 7 gallons of water. He also bought 18 quarts of water. How much water did he have in all?
$\boxed{11\ gal\ 2\ qt}$ or $\boxed{11\frac{1}{2}\ gallons}$

$$\begin{array}{r} 7\ gal \\ +4\frac{2}{4}\ gal \\ \hline 11\frac{2}{4}\ gal \end{array}$$ or $\left(\frac{18}{4} = 4\frac{2}{4}\right)$

b. A field is 56 feet wide and 12 yards long. What's the area of the field in **square yards**?
$\boxed{224\ sq\ yd}$

$b \times h = A$
$\frac{56}{3} \times 12 = \frac{672}{3}$

c. If there are 56 coins in 8 containers, how many coins are there in each container?
$\boxed{7\ coins\ per\ container}$

$8 = \dfrac{56\ coins}{7\ coins\ per\ container}$

Panel 3 (page 113)

Part 13 Work each item.

a.
$$\begin{array}{r} ^-4 \\ \times\ ^-6 \\ \hline +24 \end{array}$$

b. $+ 24(^-2) = \underline{-48}$

c.
$$\begin{array}{r} ^-3.4 \\ -\ 5 \\ \hline -8.4 \end{array} \left(\begin{array}{r} +4 \\ \times\ ^-4 \\ \hline ^-16 \end{array}\right)$$

d.
$$\begin{array}{r} ^-1\ 5 \\ -\ 2\ 5 \\ \hline -40 \end{array}$$

b. $+ 29 - 12 = \underline{+17}$

f. $^-3 + 2 + 5$
$\times\ ^-4$
$^-12 - 8 - 20 = ^-16$ or

Part 14 Answer each question.

a. How many degrees are in a corner of a page? ___90°___

b. How many degrees are in a circle? ___360°___

c. How many degrees are in a triangle? ___180°___

d. How many degrees are in a half circle? ___180°___

Part 15 Rewrite each item without the large sign and work it.

a. $^-6 \div ^-2 = \boxed{^-6 - 2 = ^-8}$

c. $^-48 \div ^+3 = \boxed{\frac{^-48}{3} = ^-16}$

b. $+16 - ^-10 = \boxed{+16 + 10 = 26}$

d. $^-2 \div ^-98 = \boxed{\frac{^-2}{^-98} = \frac{2}{98}}$

Panel 4 (page 114)

Part 16 Work each item. Box the answer to each question.

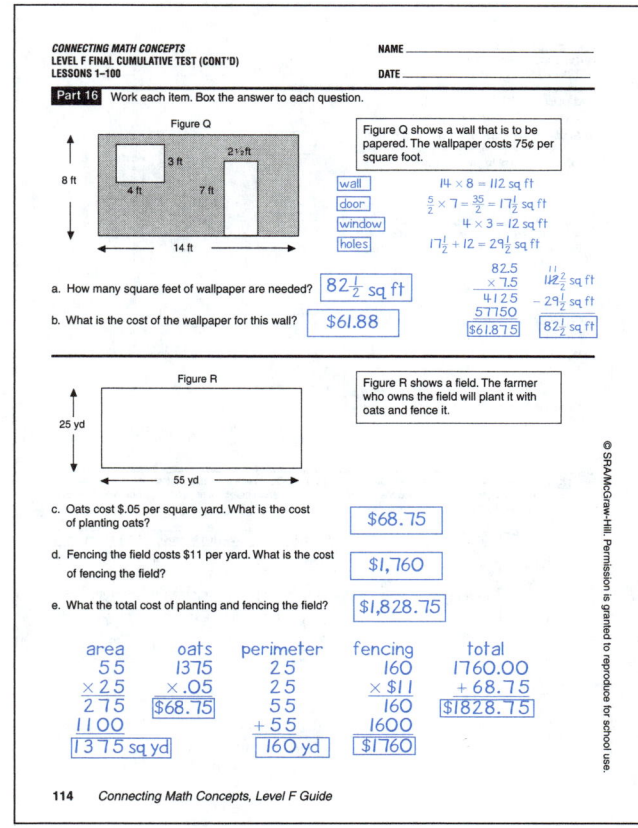

Figure Q

Figure Q shows a wall that is to be papered. The wallpaper costs 75¢ per square foot.

wall	$14 \times 8 = 112$ sq ft
door	$\frac{5}{2} \times 7 = \frac{35}{2} = 17\frac{1}{2}$ sq ft
window	$4 \times 3 = 12$ sq ft
holes	$17\frac{1}{2} + 12 = 29\frac{1}{2}$ sq ft

a. How many square feet of wallpaper are needed? $\boxed{82\frac{1}{2}\ sq\ ft}$

b. What is the cost of the wallpaper for this wall? $\boxed{\$61.88}$

$$\begin{array}{r} 82.5 \\ \times\ 7.5 \\ \hline 4125 \\ 57750 \\ \hline \boxed{\$61.875} \end{array}$$

$$\begin{array}{r} 112\frac{2}{2}\ sq\ ft \\ -29\frac{1}{2}\ sq\ ft \\ \hline \boxed{82\frac{1}{2}}\ sq\ ft \end{array}$$

Figure R

Figure R shows a field. The farmer who owns the field will plant it with oats and fence it.

25 yd
55 yd

c. Oats cost $.05 per square yard. What is the cost of planting oats? $\boxed{\$68.75}$

d. Fencing the field costs $11 per yard. What is the cost of fencing the field? $\boxed{\$1,760}$

e. What the total cost of planting and fencing the field? $\boxed{\$1,828.75}$

area	oats	perimeter	fencing	total
55	1375	2.5	160	1760.00
$\times 2.5$	$\times .05$	2.5	$\times \$11$	$+ 68.75$
275	$\boxed{\$68.75}$	55	160	$\boxed{\$1828.75}$
1100		$+55$	1600	
$\boxed{1375\ sq\ yd}$		$\boxed{160\ yd}$	$\boxed{\$1760}$	

Part 17 Work each item. Box the answer to each question.

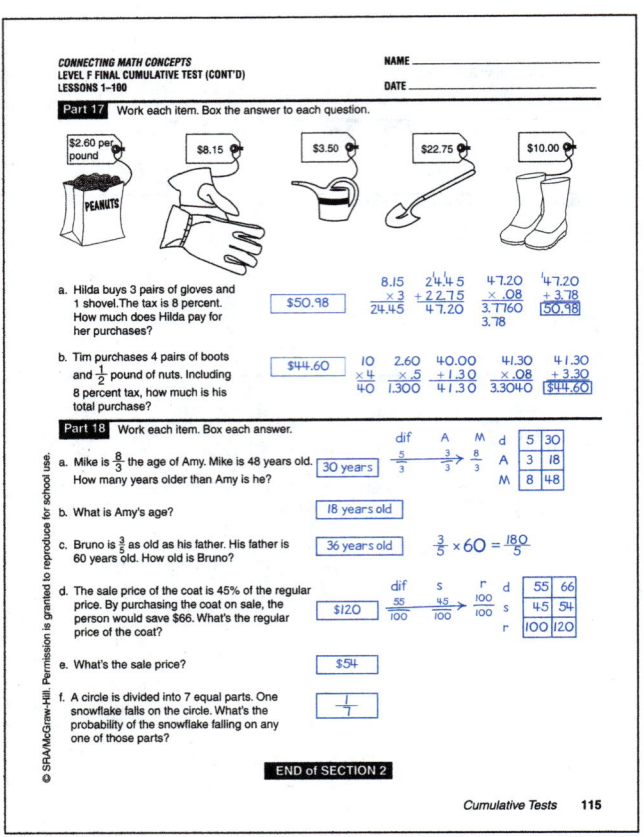

$2.60 per pound | $8.15 | $3.50 | $22.75 | $10.00

a. Hilda buys 3 pairs of gloves and 1 shovel. The tax is 8 percent. How much does Hilda pay for her purchases?

$50.98

$$\begin{array}{r}8.15\\ \times 3\\ \hline 24.45\end{array} \qquad \begin{array}{r}24.45\\ +22.75\\ \hline 47.20\end{array} \qquad \begin{array}{r}47.20\\ \times .08\\ \hline 3.7760\end{array} \qquad \begin{array}{r}47.20\\ +3.78\\ \hline 50.98\end{array}$$

b. Tim purchases 4 pairs of boots and $\frac{1}{2}$ pound of nuts. Including 8 percent tax, how much is his total purchase?

$44.60

$$\begin{array}{r}10\\ \times 4\\ \hline 40\end{array} \qquad \begin{array}{r}2.60\\ \times .5\\ \hline 1.300\end{array} \qquad \begin{array}{r}40.00\\ +1.30\\ \hline 41.30\end{array} \qquad \begin{array}{r}41.30\\ \times .08\\ \hline 3.3040\end{array} \qquad \begin{array}{r}41.30\\ +3.30\\ \hline 44.60\end{array}$$

Part 18 Work each item. Box each answer.

a. Mike is $\frac{8}{3}$ the age of Amy. Mike is 48 years old. How many years older than Amy is he?

30 years

$$\begin{array}{c}\text{dif} \quad A \quad M\\ \frac{3}{3} \quad \frac{3}{3} \quad \frac{8}{3}\end{array}$$

d	5	30
A	3	18
M	8	48

b. What is Amy's age?

18 years old

c. Bruno is $\frac{3}{5}$ as old as his father. His father is 60 years old. How old is Bruno?

36 years old

$$\frac{3}{5} \times 60 = \frac{180}{5}$$

d. The sale price of the coat is 45% of the regular price. By purchasing the coat on sale, the person would save $66. What's the regular price of the coat?

$120

$$\begin{array}{c}\text{dif} \quad s \quad r\\ \frac{55}{100} \quad \frac{45}{100} \quad \frac{100}{100}\end{array}$$

d	55	66
s	45	54
r	100	120

e. What's the sale price?

$54

f. A circle is divided into 7 equal parts. One snowflake falls on the circle. What's the probability of the snowflake falling on any one of those parts?

$\frac{1}{7}$

END of SECTION 2

CONNECTING MATH CONCEPTS
LEVEL F FINAL CUMULATIVE TEST (CONT'D)
LESSONS 1–100

NAME _____

DATE _____

SECTION 3

Part 19 Work each item. Box the answer to each question.

a. A student is $\frac{1}{28}$ of his class. How many students are in his class?

28 students

b. If there are 72 members in the club, what's the fraction for each member?

$\frac{1}{72}$

c. 78 people work in the Holt Building. 50 of them are women. What's the probability that the first person you see in the Holt building is not a woman?

$\frac{28}{78}$

$$\begin{array}{ccc}W & N & P\\ \frac{50}{78} & \frac{28}{78} & \rightarrow \frac{78}{78}\end{array}$$

d. There are 34 shoes per carton. How many shoes are in 5 cartons?

170 shoes

$$\begin{array}{r}\overset{2}{34}\\ \times 5\\ \hline 170\end{array}$$

e. If there are 80 glasses in 4 boxes, how many glasses are there per box?

20 glasses

$$4\overline{)80}\ \ 20$$

f. If a car goes 320 miles on 8 gallons of gas, how many miles per gallon does the car get?

40 mpg

$$8\overline{)320}\ \ 40$$

Part 19 (continued)

g. Start with a number and divide it by 6. Then add 6. Then multiply by 6. You end up with 66. What's the number you started with?

30

$$\boxed{30} \div 6 = \boxed{5}$$
$$\boxed{5} + 6 = \boxed{11}$$
$$\boxed{11} \times 6 = 66$$

h. Molly had $125. She spent $50. Then she bought something for $12. Then she received her paycheck. She ended up with $75. How much was her paycheck?

$12

$$125 - 50 = \boxed{75}$$
$$\boxed{75} - 12 = \boxed{63}$$
$$\boxed{63} + \boxed{12} = 75$$

i. 4 identical pens weigh 3 ounces. What's the weight of 7 pens?

$5\frac{1}{4}$ oz, $\frac{21}{4}$ oz

$$\frac{4}{3}\left(\frac{\frac{7}{4}}{\frac{4}{4}}\right) = \frac{7}{21}\ 4$$

j. There are 5 moths for every 2 butterflies. If there are 400 butterflies, how many moths are there?

1,000 moths

$$\frac{\text{moths}}{\text{butterflies}} \quad \frac{5}{2}\left(\frac{200}{200}\right) = \frac{1000}{400}$$

Part 20 Somebody takes 70 trials at spinning the spinner. Complete the table that shows the percents, the expected numbers, and the actual numbers for each color. Here are the actual numbers the person had for three colors: 5, 30, 17.

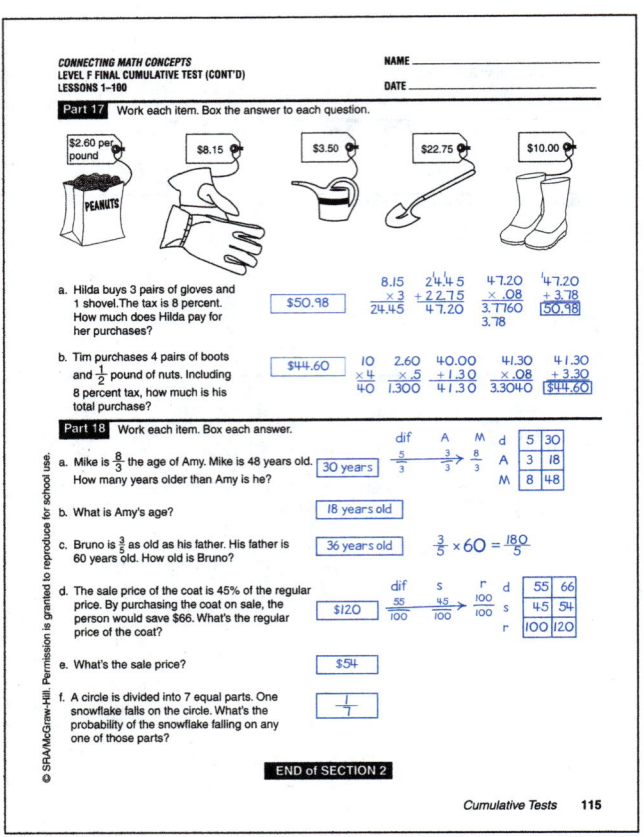

30% green, 40% blue, 20% yellow, red

	Percent	Expected Number	Actual Number
red	10	7	5
yellow	20	14	17
green	30	21	18
blue	40	28	30
Total	100	70	70

Part 21 Work each item. Box each answer.

a. A person started work at 7:24 A.M. The person finished at 1:15 P.M. How long did the person work?

5 hr 51 min

$$\begin{array}{r}2\ 75\\ \cancel{1}3\cancel{1}5\\ -7:24\\ \hline 5:51\end{array}$$

b. Mary left on a bike ride at 10:45 A.M. She rode for 2 hours and 20 minutes. At what time did she stop?

1:05 P.M.

$$\begin{array}{r}10:45\\ +2:20\\ \hline 12:65\end{array}$$

c. Each shelf is 2 feet 7 inches long. How many feet of shelf material are needed for 3 shelves?

7 ft 9 in

$$\begin{array}{r}2\ \text{ft}\ 7\ \text{in}\\ \times 3\\ \hline 6\ \text{ft}\ 21\ \text{in}\end{array}$$

d. $\frac{1}{4}$ of the sand weighed 15 tons. What did all of the sand weigh?

60 tons

$$15 \div \frac{1}{4} = 15 \times 4 = 60$$

e. The gravel is divided into 8 equal piles. The total weight of the gravel is 4,600 pounds. How much does each pile weigh?

575 lbs

$$8\overline{)4600}\ \ 575$$

f. A tank had 4 gallons and 1 quart in it. 2 gallons and 3 quarts were removed. How much was left in the tank?

1 gal 2 qt

$$\begin{array}{r}3\ \text{gal}\ 5\ \text{qt}\\ \cancel{4}\ \text{gal}\ \cancel{1}\ \text{qt}\\ -2\ \text{gal}\ 3\ \text{qt}\\ \hline 1\ \text{gal}\ 2\ \text{qt}\end{array}$$

g. Ginger has 60 coins in all. She has $2 in nickels. She has 6 quarters. The rest of her money is in dimes. How much money does she have in all?

$4.90

q	6	.25	1.50
d	14	.10	1.40
n	40	.05	2.00
t	60	×	4.90

i. How many dimes does Ginger have?

14 dimes

h. Use the chart to find the average amount of money each person had.

Jan	$3.20
Fran	$2.30
Ann	$0
Dan	$5
Van	$10.50

$4.20

$$\begin{array}{r}4.20\\ 5\overline{)21.00}\end{array}$$

Page 119 (top-left)

Part 21 (continued)

j. Ann has $\frac{5}{3}$ pies. She divides the pies so that each person
receives $\frac{1}{9}$ pie. How many people can she serve? [15 people] $\frac{5}{3} \div \frac{1}{9} = \frac{5}{3} \times 9 = \frac{45}{3}$

k. A load of gravel weighs 14 tons. It is divided into
piles that weigh $\frac{2}{5}$ of a ton each. How many piles
are there? [35 piles] $14 \div \frac{2}{5} = 14 \times \frac{5}{2} = \frac{70}{2}$

l. $\frac{3}{5}$ of the children are boys. There are 50 children.
How many are girls? [20 girls] $\frac{3}{5} \times 50 = \frac{150}{5}$

b	3	30
g	2	20
c	5	50

Part 22 Work each item.

$4\frac{3}{5} + 4\frac{3}{5} + 12 + 12 = 32\frac{6}{5}$

$b \times h = A$
$12 \times \frac{23}{5} = \frac{276}{5}$

a. Find the perimeter. $33\frac{1}{5}$ ft

12 ft

b. Find the area. $55\frac{1}{5}$ sq ft

c. Find the perimeter. 66 m

25m 20m 25m

16 m

d. Find the area. 160 sq m

$\frac{b \times h}{2} = A \quad \frac{16 \times 20}{2} = \frac{320}{2} = $ [160 sq m]

$\begin{array}{r} 25 \\ 25 \\ +16 \\ \hline 66m \end{array}$

e. Find the area of the shaded part. 142 sq in

12 in
5 in
6 in
4 in 5 in
4 in

left rectangle $12 \times 10 = 120$ sq in
or   right rectangle $6 \times 5 = 30$ sq in
missing triangle $\frac{4 \times 4}{2} = 8$ sq in
$150 - 8 = 142$ sq in

Page 120 (top-right)

Part 23 Work each problem two times. Show each
answer as a decimal and as a mixed number.

a. $35\overline{)126.0}$ decimal ___3.6___
$\begin{array}{r} 3.6 \\ \hline 105 \\ 210 \\ 210 \end{array}$

mixed number $3\frac{21}{35}$ or $3\frac{3}{5}$

b. $16\overline{)24.0}$ decimal ___1.5___
$\begin{array}{r} 1.5 \\ \hline 16 \\ 80 \\ 80 \end{array}$

mixed number $1\frac{8}{16}$ or $1\frac{1}{2}$

Part 24 Do the division for each item. Show each
answer as a decimal number or a whole number.
Box your answers.

a. $\frac{7}{5} = 5\overline{)7.0}$ [1.4]
$\begin{array}{r} 5 \\ 20 \end{array}$

d. $12\overline{)324}$ [27]
$\begin{array}{r} 24 \\ 84 \\ 84 \end{array}$

g. $\frac{4}{7} \div \frac{4}{7} = \square$ $\frac{4}{7} \times \frac{7}{4} = 1$

j. $9\overline{)657}$ [.73]
$\begin{array}{r} 63 \\ 27 \end{array}$

b. $\frac{4}{5} = 5\overline{)4.0}$ [.8]
$\begin{array}{r} 40 \end{array}$

e. $.03\overline{)72}$ [2400] $.03\overline{)72.00}$
$\begin{array}{r} 40 \end{array}$

h. $100\overline{)376}$ [3.76]

k. $.02\overline{)7.80}$ [390]

c. $\frac{9.8}{4} = 4\overline{)9.80}$ [2.45]
$\begin{array}{r} 8 \\ 18 \\ 16 \\ 20 \end{array}$

f. $40\overline{)8080}$ [202]

i. $\frac{3}{1} \frac{3 \div \frac{1}{6}}{\frac{1}{6}} \quad 3 \times 6 = $ [18]

Page 121 (bottom-left)

Part 25 Find the volume of each figure.

$\frac{\text{Area of } b \times h}{3} = v$

$\pi \times r \times r = A$
$3.14 \times 4 \times 4 = 50.24$ sq ft

a. [351.68 cu ft]
21 ft
4 ft

$\frac{50.24 \times 21}{3} = v$

$\frac{1055.04}{3} = v$

$v = 351.68$ cu ft

$\begin{array}{r} 3.14 \\ \times 16 \\ \hline 1884 \\ 3140 \\ 50.24 \end{array}$

$\begin{array}{r} 351.68 \\ 3\overline{)1055.04} \end{array}$

b. [2,730 cu in]
15 in
14 in 13 in

$\text{Area of } b \times h = v$
$182 \times 15 = v$
$v = 2730$ cu in

$b \times h = A$
$13 \times 14 = 182$ sq in

$\begin{array}{r} 182 \\ \times 15 \\ \hline 910 \\ 1820 \\ 2730 \end{array}$

c. [360 cu in]
9 in
20 in 4 in

$\frac{\text{Area of } b \times h}{2} = v$

$\frac{90 \times 4}{2} = v$

$v = 360$ cu in
or
$\frac{4 \times 20 \times 9}{2} = \frac{720}{2} = v$

$v = 360$ cu in

$\frac{b \times h}{2} = A$

$\frac{20 \times 9}{2} = \frac{180}{2} = 90$

Page 122 (bottom-right)

Part 26 Work each item.

a. $1107 - R = 92$ b. $143 + 68 = D$ c. $7 \times B = 51$ d. $M + 95 = 201$

R = [1015]   D = [211]   B = $\frac{51}{7}$ M = [106]
or
$7\frac{2}{7}$

$\begin{array}{r} 1107 \\ -92 \\ \hline 1015 \end{array}$
$\begin{array}{r} 143 \\ +68 \\ \hline 211 \end{array}$
$\begin{array}{r} 201 \\ -95 \\ \hline 106 \end{array}$

Part 27 Work each item.

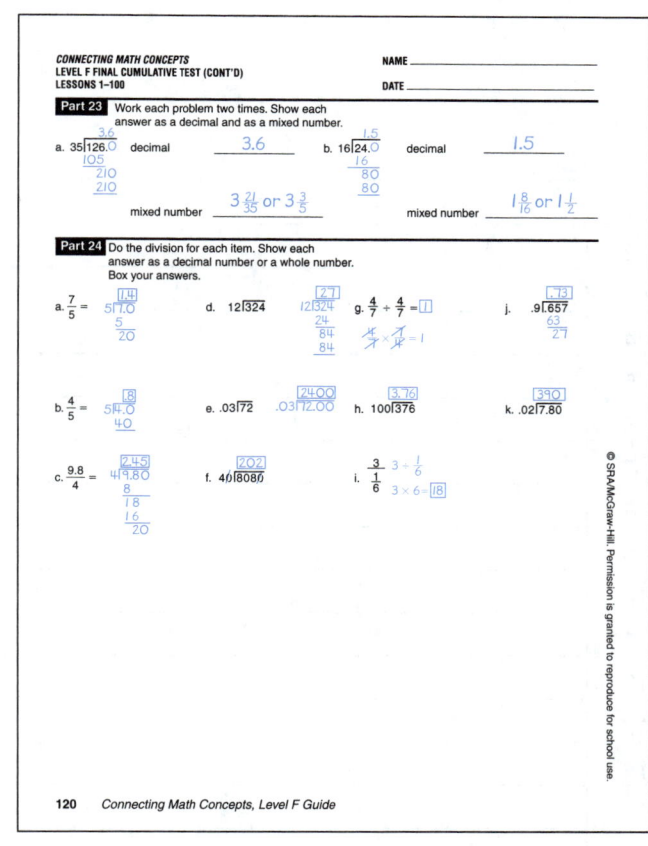

a. What's the diameter? ___6 m___
b. What's the area? ___28.26 sq m___
c. What's the circumference? ___18.84 m___

3 m

$\pi \times r \times r = A$
$3.14 \times 3 \times 3 = A$
[A = 28.26 sq m]

$\pi \times d = c$
$3.14 \times 6 = c$
[c = 18.84 m]

25 in

d. What's the radius? ___3.98 in___

$\pi \times d = c$
$3.14 \left(\frac{25}{3.14} \right) = 25$
$d = 7.96$
[r = 3.98]

e. The area of the circle is 52 square inches.
What's the area of the shaded part? ___39 sq in___

$52 \times \frac{3}{4} = \frac{156}{4} = $ [39 sq in]

f. The circumference is 20 centimeters.
What's the length of the black part? ___13.33 cm or $13\frac{2}{6}$ cm___

$20 \times \frac{4}{6} = $ [13.33 cm]

Remedy Summary CMC F

Name	Cumulative Test 1 Check parts not passed												
	1	2	3	4	5	6	7	8	9	10	11	12	13
1.													
2.													
3.													
4.													
5.													
6.													
7.													
8.													
9.													
10.													
11.													
12.													
13.													
14.													
15.													
16.													
17.													
18.													
19.													
20.													
21.													
22.													
23.													
24.													
25.													
26.													
27.													
28.													
29.													
30.													

Remedy Summary CMC F

Name	Cumulative Test 2 Check parts not passed										
	1	2	3	4	5	6	7	8	9	10	11
1.											
2.											
3.											
4.											
5.											
6.											
7.											
8.											
9.											
10.											
11.											
12.											
13.											
14.											
15.											
16.											
17.											
18.											
19.											
20.											
21.											
22.											
23.											
24.											
25.											
26.											
27.											
28.											
29.											
30.											

Remedy Summary CMC F

Name	Final Cumulative Test Check parts not passed																										
	1	2	3	4	5	6	7	8	9	10	11	12	13	14	15	16	17	18	19	20	21	22	23	24	25	26	27
1.																											
2.																											
3.																											
4.																											
5.																											
6.																											
7.																											
8.																											
9.																											
10.																											
11.																											
12.																											
13.																											
14.																											
15.																											
16.																											
17.																											
18.																											
19.																											
20.																											
21.																											
22.																											
23.																											
24.																											
25.																											
26.																											
27.																											
28.																											
29.																											
30.																											

Appendix B

Objectives

	Objectives	Lessons
Division	Work a long division problem that has a two-digit divisor and a two-digit quotient.	21-25
	Work a division problem in which both the dividend and divisor end in one or more zeros.	23, 24
	Use "shortcuts" to work a mixed set of division problems.	28
	Write mixed-number answers to problems that divide by 10, 100 or 1,000.	29
	Use a calculator to work a division problem that does not have a whole-number answer.	44-46
Combining Terms and Distributive Property	Work a problem that requires distribution.	58-60
	Work a problem that subtracts more than one value.	59
	Combine the values in a problem that adds and subtracts more than one value.	61, 62

NUMBER RELATIONSHIPS

Objectives	Lessons
Write an equation to show a mixed number and the improper fraction it equals.	1-3
Write an equation to show an improper mixed number and the proper mixed number it equals.	1-3, 5, 6
Write an equation to show a fraction and the decimal value it equals.	1-3
Complete a table that shows mixed numbers and corresponding decimal values.	3
Complete a table that shows mixed numbers and corresponding fractions.	4
Complete a table to show fractions with denominators of 10, 100, 1,000; the corresponding decimal values; and corresponding mixed numbers.	4, 5
Write an equation to show the decimal value and the equivalent fraction.	6
Complete a set of equations to show fractions and the equivalent mixed numbers.	6, 7
Write percents for a set of simple fractions.	41, 44
Derive a fraction from a percent that is related to a familiar percent.	42, 43
Write fractions for a set of common percents.	42
Convert a fraction that does not have a denominator of 100 into a percent value.	71, 72

OPERATIONAL RELATIONSHIPS

	Objectives	Lessons
Inverse Operations	Use inverse operations to solve a set of problems that have the first number missing.	1, 2
	Work a two-equation problem that requires inverse operations.	3
	Work a three-equation problem that requires inverse operations.	4
	Show a missing factor as a fraction.	5
	Work a set of multiplication problems in which one of the factors is missing.	6
	Use inverse operations to solve a problem in which the middle equation has three boxes.	18, 19
	Figure out the missing denominator in an equation that shows a whole number and the equivalent fraction.	45
	Complete a ratio table with more than three rows.	74, 75
	Work inverse-operation problems to find missing values in a ratio table.	76-78, 80
	Solve an equation that has a single term on the left and the unknown on the right.	89
	Rewrite and solve four-value equations that have the unknown on the right.	89, 90
Place Value	Write an equation to show a decimal value that ends in one or more zeros and the simplified decimal value.	1, 2
	Round a decimal value to the nearest hundredth.	24, 25

FRACTION OPERATIONS

	Objectives	Lessons
	Construct a complex fraction that equals 1 to solve an equivalent-fraction problem.	11, 12
	Use a calculator to work a problem that multiplies a fraction times a whole number.	51
	Use a calculator to work a problem that multiplies a fraction times a whole number or decimal.	52
	Add or subtract fractions with unlike denominators.	61, 62, 64
	Work a mixed set of fraction problems with unlike denominators that require multiplication, addition or subtraction.	65
Fraction Simplification	Simplify a fraction in which both the numerator and denominator end in one or more zeros.	16, 17
	Work a multiplication problem that can be simplified by crossing out zeros.	18
	Simplify fraction-multiplication problems by crossing out fractions that equal 1.	66
	Use simplification techniques to work problems that multiply fractions.	68, 69

	Objectives	Lessons
Reciprocals and Fraction Division	Express the relationship between the fraction for each part and the number of parts in a whole.	44, 45
	Write a multiplication equation to show the number of equal parts in a whole.	45
	Write the reciprocal for a fraction or a whole number.	46, 47
	Write an equation that starts with a given value and multiplies by its reciprocal.	47-49
	Rewrite an equation of the form: 75% ( ) = ■ = 1.	51
	Work a two-step word problem that involves reciprocals.	53-55
	Work a mixed set of problems involving the area of a figure divided into equal parts.	56, 57
	Work a division problem as a multiplication problem and vice versa.	81-84
	Rewrite a complex fraction as a division problem; then work a multiplication problem.	84

MIXED-NUMBER OPERATIONS

	Objectives	Lessons
	Use division to figure out the mixed number that equals an improper fraction.	4
	Add or subtract mixed numbers.	9, 10
	Work an addition or subtraction problem that involves a whole number and a mixed number.	13
	Work a renaming problem that involves a whole number and a fraction.	14, 15
	Solve a mixed-number addition problem and express the answer as a proper mixed number.	16, 17
	Multiply mixed numbers.	48, 49
	Add mixed numbers that have unlike denominators.	67, 68
	Add or subtract mixed numbers that have unlike denominators.	69
	Work a mixed-number subtraction problem that requires borrowing.	80, 81
	Work a mixed set of mixed-number problems that require addition or subtraction.	83

NUMBER FAMILIES

	Objectives	Lessons
	Make a complete fraction number family from a single fraction.	7
	Complete a fraction number family that has names.	8, 9
	Write a fraction number family for a sentence that refers to a decimal or percent value.	11

Objectives	Lessons
Make a fraction number family for a statement that compares two values.	31
Make a complete fraction number family for a statement that compares two values.	32
Identify the diagram that shows a specified fractional relationship.	33, 34, 49
Make percent number families for a set of sentences that compare or classify.	41-43, 59
Make fraction number families from sentences, some of which give a percent difference value.	48, 49, 51
Make a fraction number family that replaces percent values with simple fractions.	48
Construct two statements that compare values shown in a number family.	52-58

DECIMAL OPERATIONS

Add or subtract decimal values.	2-4
Add or subtract a whole number and a decimal value.	5
Multiply decimal values.	8, 10, 11
Work a mixed set of problems involving adding, multiplying and subtracting decimal values.	18
Write decimal answers to problems that divide by 10, 100 or 1,000.	26, 27
Work a decimal-multiplication problem as a fraction-multiplication problem.	27, 28, 29
Write a decimal answer to a division problem.	35, 36
Show the answer to a division problem as a mixed number and as a decimal value.	37, 39, 41
Show a fraction that is less than 1 as a decimal quotient in a division problem.	42, 43
Divide a decimal value by a whole number.	53, 54
Convert a fraction that has a decimal in the numerator into a division problem.	55, 56
Multiply a decimal value by 10, 100 or 1,000.	61
Work a decimal-multiplication problem that has a missing factor.	62
Work a mixed set of decimal-multiplication problems that have a missing factor or a missing product.	63, 64
Complete equivalent fractions that involve decimals.	65-68
Work a division problem based on a fraction that has a decimal denominator.	71-73
Work a division problem that has a decimal divisor.	74, 75, 77

COORDINATE SYSTEM	Objectives	Lessons
	Find the area of a complex figure shown on the coordinate system.	36-39, 48, 49
	Write the X and Y value for a point shown on the coordinate system.	87
	Refer to a line on the coordinate system to answer questions.	88, 89

PROBLEM SOLVING

	Objectives	Lessons
Ratio Equations	Set up and solve ratio problems that require a ratio equation with equivalent fractions.	2
	Work a ratio and proportion word problem that requires a complex fraction equal to 1.	13, 14
	Find the lengths of sides for similar triangles.	89
	Complete a ratio equation that uses a colon notation.	96
Ratio Tables	Complete a table that has the same multiplier for each row.	7, 8
	Complete a ratio table.	9
	Use the numerators from a fraction number family as values for the first column of a ratio table.	10
	Make a fraction number family and a ratio table to solve a word problem.	11
	Make a fraction number family and a ratio table to work a problem that involves decimals or percents.	12-15, 18, 19, 21
	Complete a ratio table that requires addition or subtraction of a mixed number.	16, 17
	Work a mixed set of problems, some of which require a ratio table.	22, 23, 26, 28
	Work a ratio-table problem that gives fractional information to compare two values.	33-35
	Work a ratio-table problem that uses percents to compare values.	36, 37, 56-58
	Work ratio-table percent problems that compare or classify.	43-46, 66
	Work ratio-table problems that compare or classify.	47, 57, 59
	Work a ratio-table problem that involves dollar-and-cent amounts.	69, 71
Probability	Compute the expected numbers for a probability problem involving a spinner.	81-83
	Match actual outcomes of a probability experiment with expected outcomes.	83-85
	Express probability as a fraction.	86
	Answer a question about probability by referring to a table.	87

	Objectives	Lessons
MultiplicationProblems	Use statements about probability to construct a table that shows ratio numbers and expected outcomes.	88
	Work a multiplication problem that refers to a fraction or percent **of** a value.	21-23
	Work a multiplication word problem that refers to a fraction or percent **of** a value.	24, 25
	Work a multiplication word problem that compares.	26, 27
	Determine whether a word problem can be solved by multiplication.	28-30
	Work a multiplication problem that tells about each like item and the number of items.	31-34
	Work a mixed set of problems that are solved by fraction multiplication or by a ratio table.	38, 39
	Work a word problem that involves multiplying a decimal by a fraction.	54
Multi-step Problems	Work a word problem that requires inverse operations.	5-8, 12
Inverse Operations	Write an equation with two missing values from a sentence that refers to doubling, tripling or twice.	6
	Solve a two-step word problem by figuring out the missing middle value in the second equation.	9
	Work a mixed set of word problems that require inverse operations.	12-17
	Use inverse operations to work a word problem that implies a starting value.	12
	Write an equation with three boxes for a sentence that refers to an operation but does not specify numbers.	18
	Work an inverse-operation problem, part of which refers to an operation without numbers.	21, 22
	Work a mixed set of inverse-operation problems.	23
Component Calculations	Work a word problem that involves component problems.	35
	Work a multi-step word problem that involves tax.	36-38
	Work a mixed set of multi-step problems that refer to area, perimeter and tax.	39
	Work a mixed set of multi-step problems that refer to area, circumference, perimeter or tax.	41, 42
	Work a multi-step problem.	43-47
	Find the area of a figure with a hole.	51, 52
	Find the area of a figure that has more than one hole.	53, 54
	Work a multi-step problem that involves complex area.	55-59
	Work a multi-step problem involving part of a figure.	58, 59, 68, 69

	Objectives	Lessons
Reciprocals	Express the relationship between the fraction for each part and the number of parts in a whole.	44, 45
	Work a word problem that involves finding the reciprocal of a common percent value.	52
	Work a two-step word problem that involves reciprocals.	53-55
	Work a mixed set of problems involving the area of a figure divided into equal parts.	56, 57
	Work an area-of-figure problem that asks about one or more than one equal part.	57
	Work a word problem that requires dividing by a fraction.	85, 86
Mixed-Number Problems	Work a word problem that requires multiplying by a mixed number.	51, 52
	Work a mixed set of measurement word problems.	57, 58
Time	Convert p.m. times to times on a 24-hour clock.	61
	Work an addition or subtraction word problem that involves clock time.	61-63
	Convert times on a 24-hour clock to a.m. and p.m. times.	62, 63
	Work a word problem that requires converting p.m. time to 24-hour time.	64-66
Coins and Money Amounts	Work a multiplication or division problem that involves coins.	73, 74
	Complete a rate-equation coin table.	75-77
	Construct a coin-table to solve a money problem.	77-79
Average	Compute the average for a set of data.	81, 82, 84
Circle Graphs	Make a table based on a circle graph.	72-75, 79, 81, 82
	Determine the degrees in a fraction or percent of a circle.	73, 75
	Make a table that has fractions of a circle in the first column and the corresponding number of degrees in the second.	76, 77
	Work a mixed set of problems that refer to a circle graph.	78, 79

MEASUREMENT

	Objectives	Lessons
	Make fractions that are based on a fact about related units.	7-9
	Write the unit name for a fraction that shows related units.	11-16
	Rewrite a fraction that refers to related units.	14-16
	Rewrite a mixed number as related units.	17-19
	Given a description of related units, students write a mixed number.	19, 21
	Write a mixed number and unit name for a description of related units.	22, 23

Objectives	Lessons
Complete an equation to show the names for related units.	24-26
Work a related-unit problem that asks about the smaller unit.	25-27
Complete an equation to show the names and numbers for related units.	27, 28
Construct an equation that shows related units based on a question.	29, 31, 32
Convert a fraction into the equivalent fraction that shows related units.	31-33
Make a complete equation for an item that asks about the smaller related unit.	33
Complete statements of the form: $1\frac{5}{12}$ minutes is ☐ minute and ☐ seconds.	34, 35
Work a mixed set of related-unit problems.	34-36, 41
Write an equation for related units that involves a mixed number.	37-39
Write an equation for a sentence that refers to nonconvertible units.	37
Solve a problem that involves nonconvertible units.	38, 39, 43, 44
Rewrite an incorrect equation that involves nonconvertible related units.	41, 42
Work a word problem that asks about the rate.	46
Work a mixed set of nonconvertible-unit problems, some of which ask about the rate.	47
Rewrite an "improper" expression that refers to related units.	49, 51, 77, 78
Add related units.	52-54
Rename values for related units.	54
Rename and subtract related units.	55, 56
Work a mixed set of related-unit problems involving addition or subtraction.	57, 58
Work a mixed set of measurement word problems.	57, 58
Work a related-unit word problem that requires addition or subtraction.	59, 60
Work a problem that multiplies related units.	62, 63
Work a word problem that requires multiplying related units.	63, 79
Work a mixed set of related-unit word problems that involve multiplication, addition or subtraction.	67
Work a problem that converts related units into the smaller unit.	68, 69

Objectives	Lessons
Work a mixed set of problems that refer to more than one unit.	87, 88

GEOMETRY

	Objectives	Lessons
Area, Perimeter, Circumference and Diameter	Use the equation $b \times h = A$ to find the area of a rectangle, parallelogram or square.	1, 2
	Find the perimeter of a triangle or rectangle.	2
	Find the area and perimeter of a parallelogram or rectangle.	3
	Use the equation: $\frac{b \times h}{2} = A$ to find the area of a triangle.	14
	Find the area of a parallelogram or triangle.	15
	Use the equation $\pi \times d = C$ to find the circumference of a circle.	24
	Work a mixed set of problems to find either the circumference or the diameter of circles.	25, 26
	Work a mixed set of problems to find either the circumference or the radius of circles.	27, 28
	Use the equation $\pi \times r \times r = A$ to calculate the area of a circle.	29, 31
	Find the area and circumference of a circle.	32, 33
	Find the area of a complex figure shown on the coordinate system.	36-39, 48, 49
	Work a mixed set of multi-step problems that refer to area, perimeter and tax.	39
	Work a mixed set of multi-step problems that refer to area, circumference, perimeter or tax.	41, 42
	Find the area of a figure with a hole.	51, 52
	Find the area of a figure that has more than one hole.	53, 54
	Work a multi-step problem that involves complex area.	55-59
	Work a complex-area problem that involves part of a circle.	55
	Work a fraction-of-an-area problem two ways.	56
	Work an area-of-figure problem that asks about one or more than one equal part.	57
	Work a multi-step problem involving part of a figure.	58, 59, 68, 69
	Work an area problem that involves mixed numbers.	77, 79
	Solve an area problem that involves more than one unit.	86

	Objectives	Lessons
Volume	Compute the volume of a rectangular prism.	71, 72
	Compute the volume of a triangular prism.	74
	Work a set of volume problems involving rectangular and triangular prisms.	75, 76
	Use the equation: **Area of b × h = V** to compute the volume of a cylinder.	83
	Work a mixed set of volume problems, some of which involve a cylinder.	84
	Use the equation: $\dfrac{\textbf{Area of b x h}}{3}$ to compute the volume of figures that come to a point.	85, 86
	Work a mixed set of volume problems including figures that come to a point and figures that have parallel sides.	87
Geometry Facts	Write the number of sides for common polygons.	44-46
	Given a set of common polygons, write the names.	47
	Answer a question about the degrees in a common angle.	47
	Work a mixed set of items that refer to angles and polygons.	48

SIGNED NUMBERS

	Objectives	Lessons
	Combine the values in a problem that adds and subtracts more than one value.	61, 62
	Rewrite and work a problem with signed terms in a different order.	63-65
	Work paired addition and subtraction problems on a number line that has positive and negative values.	64
	Write an equation for an arrow on a signed number line.	65, 66
	Indicate which of two signed numbers has the greater absolute value.	66, 67
	Complete the number part of the answer for signed-number combination problems.	67-69
	Combine signed numbers.	71-73
	Work a signed-number multiplication problem in which each value has a sign.	78, 79, 81
	Work multiplication problems by first combining the signed values on top.	82, 83
	Multiply by a negative value.	84
	Work a mixed set of problems that multiply by a positive or a negative value.	85, 86
	Work a signed-number multiplication problem of the form: -4×-3.	87, 88

Objectives	Lessons
Work a signed-number problem that has a large operational sign.	88, 89
Work a problem that divides by a signed value.	89, 90
Write a problem that has signed values and a large operational sign.	90

EXPONENTS

	Objectives	Lessons
	Write a base number and exponent for a repeated multiplication problem.	74
	Write complete equations for a set of exponent problems that show either the multiplication or the exponential notation.	75
	Figure out the value represented by an exponential notation.	76-78
	Show two groups of repeated multiplication in exponential notation.	83-85
	Rewrite a fraction that shows repeated multiplication as a base and exponent.	86, 87
Simple Machines	Work a lever problem.	88, 89, 91
	Work a set of problems that involve two types of levers.	90
	Solve a problem that involves a wheel and axle.	92, 94
	Solve a problem that asks about the amount of work that is done.	94

PROJECTS

Objectives	Lessons
Construct a symmetrical circle graph.	91
Use a rule to construct a circle graph that has slices of specified degrees.	92
Figure out the area of symmetrical figures.	92
Do an experiment that requires 72 trials at rolling a pair of dice.	93
Make letters on a coordinate system by using information about the X and Y values for the line segments.	94
Analyze an inclined plane and figure out how it works as a simple machine.	95
Find the sum of a series of numbers by "folding" the series in half.	95
Figure out a strategy for determining the sum of numbers in a series.	96
Figure out the amount of work required to move a weight to specified points along the incline.	96

Objectives	Lessons
Relate an inclined plane to a set of nested similar triangles.	96
Figure out a strategy for determining the sum of odd or even numbers in a series.	97
Figure out the relationship between an inclined plane and a screw.	97
Find the area of a figure that has a repeated pattern.	98
Determine the relationships between force and distance in a simple single-pulley system.	98
Solve problems that involve repeated patterns.	99, 100
Figure out the general rules for working division problems that require a whole-number answer.	99
Figure out the arrangement of string that requires a force that is 1/4 the amount of the weight that is being lifted.	99
Work out a strategy for finding the capacity of a box shape that has a figure inside.	100

Skills Profile

Student's
Name _____

Grade or
year in _____
school

Teacher's name _____

Starting
lesson _____   Date _____

Last lesson
Completed _____ Date _____

Number of
days absent _____

Summary of In-program Test Performance

	Part 1	Part 2	Part 3	Part 4	Part 5	Part 6	Part 7	Part 8	Part 9	Part 10	Part 11	Part 12
Test 1	+ −	+ −	+ −	+ −	+ −	+ −	+ −	+ −	+ −			
Test 2	+ −	+ −	+ −	+ −	+ −	+ −	+ −	+ −				
Test 3	+ −	+ −	+ −	+ −	+ −	+ −	+ −	+ −	+ −			
Test 4	+ −	+ −	+ −	+ −	+ −	+ −	+ −	+ −	+ −			
Test 5	+ −	+ −	+ −	+ −	+ −	+ −	+ −	+ −	+ −	+ −	+ −	+ −
Test 6	+ −	+ −	+ −	+ −	+ −	+ −	+ −	+ −	+ −			
Test 7	+ −	+ −	+ −	+ −	+ −	+ −	+ −	+ −	+ −	+ −	+ −	+ −
Test 8	+ −	+ −	+ −	+ −	+ −	+ −	+ −	+ −	+ −	+ −		
Test 9	+ −	+ −	+ −	+ −	+ −	+ −	+ −	+ −	+ −	+ −	+ −	+ −

Cummulative Test 1 Score _____ %

Cummulative Test 2 Score _____ %

Final Test Score _____ %

The charts on pages 145 to 153 may be reproduced to make a skills profile for each student. The charts summarize the skills presented in *Connecting Math Concepts, Level F* and provide space for indicating the date on which the student completes the lessons in which the skills are taught.

Skills	Taught in these Lessons	Date Lessons Completed
WHOLE-NUMBER OPERATIONS **Division**		
Works a long division problem that has a two-digit divisor and a two-digit quotient.	21-25	
Works a division problem in which both the dividend and divisor end in one or more zeros.	23, 24	
Uses "shortcuts" to work a mixed set of division problems.	28	
Writes mixed-number answers to problems that divide by 10, 100 or 1,000.	29	
Uses a calculator to work a division problem that does not have a whole-number answer.	44-46	
Combining Terms and Distributive Property		
Works a problem that requires distribution.	58-60	
Works a problem that subtracts more than one value.	59	
Combines the values in a problem that adds and subtracts more than one value.	61, 62	
NUMBER RELATIONSHIPS		
Writes an equation to show a mixed number and the improper fraction it equals.	1-3	
Writes an equation to show an improper mixed number and the proper mixed number it equals.	1-6	
Writes an equation to show a fraction and the decimal value it equals.	1-3	
Completes a table that shows mixed numbers and corresponding decimal values.	3	
Completes a table that shows mixed numbers and corresponding fractions.	4	

Skills	Taught in these Lessons	Date Lessons Completed
Completes a table to show fractions with denominators of 10, 100, 1,000; the corresponding decimal values; and corresponding mixed numbers.	4, 5	
Writes an equation to show the decimal value and the equivalent fraction.	6	
Completes a set of equations to show fractions and the equivalent mixed numbers.	6, 7	
Writes percents for a set of simple fractions.	41-44	
Derives a fraction from a percent that is related to a familiar percent.	42, 43	
Writes fractions for a set of common percents.	42	
Converts a fraction that does not have a denominator of 100 into a percent value.	71, 72	
OPERATIONAL RELATIONSHIPS **Inverse Operations**		
Uses inverse operations to solve a set of problems that have the first number missing.	1, 2	
Works a two-equation problem that requires inverse operations.	3	
Works a three-equation problem that requires inverse operations.	4	
Shows a missing factor as a fraction.	5	
Works a set of multiplication problems in which one of the factors is missing.	6	
Uses inverse operations to solve a problem in which the middle equation has three boxes.	18, 19	
Figures out the missing denominator in an equation that shows a whole number and the equivalent fraction.	45	

Skills	Taught in these Lessons	Date Lessons Completed
Completes a ratio table with more than three rows.	74, 75	
Works inverse-operation problems to find missing values in a ratio table.	76-80	
Solves an equation that has a single term on the left and the unknown on the right.	89	
Rewrites and solve four-value equations that have the unknown on the right.	89, 90	
Place Value		
Writes an equation to show a decimal value that ends in one or more zeros and the simplified decimal value.	1, 2	
Rounds a decimal value to the nearest hundredth.	24, 25	
FRACTION OPERATIONS		
Constructs a complex fraction that equals 1 to solve an equivalent-fraction problem.	11, 12	
Uses a calculator to work a problem that multiplies a fraction times a whole number.	51	
Uses a calculator to work a problem that multiplies a fraction times a whole number or decimal.	52	
Adds or subtracts fractions with unlike denominators.	61-64	
Works a mixed set of fraction problems with unlike denominators that require multiplication, addition or subtraction.	65	
Fraction Simplification		
Simplifies a fraction in which both the numerator and denominator end in one or more zeros.	16, 17	
Works a multiplication problem that can be simplified by crossing out zeros.	18	

Skills	Taught in these Lessons	Date Lessons Completed
Simplifies fraction-multiplication problems by crossing out fractions that equal 1.	66	
Uses simplification techniques to work problems that multiply fractions.	68, 69	
Reciprocals and Fraction Division		
Expresses the relationship between the fraction for each part and the number of parts in a whole.	44, 45	
Writes a multiplication equation to show the number of equal parts in a whole.	45	
Writes the reciprocal for a fraction or a whole number.	46, 47	
Writes an equation that starts with a given value and multiplies by its reciprocal.	47-49	
Rewrites an equation of the form: **75% ( ) = ▮ = 1.**	51	
Works a two-step word problem that involves reciprocals.	53-55	
Works a mixed set of problems involving the area of a figure divided into equal parts.	56, 57	
Works a division problem as a multiplication problem and vice versa.	81-84	
Rewrites a complex fraction as a division problem; then works a multiplication problem.	84	
MIXED-NUMBER OPERATIONS		
Uses division to figure out the mixed number that equals an improper fraction.	4	
Adds or subtracts mixed numbers.	9, 10	
Works an addition or subtraction problem that involves a whole number and a mixed number.	13	

Name _____

Skills	Taught in these Lessons	Date Lessons Completed
Works a renaming problem that involves a whole number and a fraction.	14, 15	
Solves a mixed-number addition problem and expresses the answer as a proper mixed number.	16, 17	
Multiplies mixed numbers.	48, 49	
Adds mixed numbers that have unlike denominators.	67, 68	
Adds or subtracts mixed numbers that have unlike denominators.	69	
Works a mixed-number subtraction problem that requires borrowing.	80, 81	
Works a mixed set of mixed-number problems that require addition or subtraction.	83	

NUMBER FAMILIES

Skills	Taught in these Lessons	Date Lessons Completed
Makes a complete fraction number family from a single fraction.	7	
Completes a fraction number family that has names.	8, 9	
Writes a fraction number family for a sentence that refers to a decimal or percent value.	11	
Makes a fraction number family for a statement that compares two values.	31	
Makes a complete fraction number family for a statement that compares two values.	32	
Identifies the diagram that shows a specified fractional relationship.	33-49	
Makes percent number families for a set of sentences that compare or classify.	41-59	
Makes fraction number families from sentences, some of which give a percent difference value.	48-51	
Makes a fraction number family that replaces percent values with simple fractions.	48	

Skills	Taught in these Lessons	Date Lessons Completed
Constructs two statements that compare values shown in a number family.	52-58	

DECIMAL OPERATIONS

Skills	Taught in these Lessons	Date Lessons Completed
Adds or subtracts decimal values.	2-4	
Adds or subtracts a whole number and a decimal value.	5	
Multiplies decimal values.	8-11	
Works a mixed set of problems involving adding, multiplying and subtracting decimal values.	18	
Writes decimal answers to problems that divide by 10, 100 or 1,000.	26, 27	
Works a decimal-multiplication problem as a fraction-multiplication problem.	27-29	
Writes a decimal answer to a division problem.	35, 36	
Shows the answer to a division problem as a mixed number and as a decimal value.	37-41	
Shows a fraction that is less than 1 as a decimal quotient in a division problem.	42, 43	
Divides a decimal value by a whole number.	53, 54	
Converts a fraction that has a decimal in the numerator into a division problem.	55, 56	
Multiplies a decimal value by 10, 100 or 1,000.	61	
Works a decimal-multiplication problem that has a missing factor.	62	
Works a mixed set of decimal-multiplication problems that have a missing factor or a missing product.	63, 64	
Completes equivalent fractions that involve decimals.	65-68	

Skills	Taught in these Lessons	Date Lessons Completed
Works a division problem based on a fraction that has a decimal denominator.	71-73	
Works a division problem that has a decimal divisor.	74-77	
COORDINATE SYSTEM		
Finds the area of a complex figure shown on the coordinate system.	36-49	
Writes the X and Y value for a point shown on the coordinate system.	87	
Refers to a line on the coordinate system to answer questions.	88, 89	
PROBLEM SOLVING		
Ratio Equations		
Sets up and solves ratio problems that require a ratio equation with equivalent fractions.	2	
Works a ratio and proportion word problem that requires a complex fraction equal to 1.	13, 14	
Finds the lengths of sides for similar triangles.	89	
Completes a ratio equation that uses a colon notation.	96	
Ratio Tables		
Completes a table that has the same multiplier for each row.	7, 8	
Completes a ratio table.	9	
Uses the numerators from a fraction number family as values for the first column of a ratio table.	10	
Makes a fraction number family and a ratio table to solve a word problem.	11	
Makes a fraction number family and a ratio table to work a problem that involves decimals or percents.	12-21	
Completes a ratio table that requires addition or subtraction of a mixed number.	16, 17	

Skills	Taught in these Lessons	Date Lessons Completed
Works a mixed set of problems, some of which require a ratio table.	22-28	
Works a ratio-table problem that gives fractional information to compare two values.	33-35	
Works a ratio-table problem that uses percents to compare values.	36-58	
Works ratio-table percent problems that compare or classify.	43-66	
Works ratio-table problems that compare or classify.	47-59	
Works a ratio-table problem that involves dollar-and-cent amounts.	69, 71	
Probability		
Computes the expected numbers for a probability problem involving a spinner.	81-83	
Matches actual outcomes of a probability experiment with expected outcomes.	83-85	
Expresses probability as a fraction.	86	
Answers a question about probability by referring to a table.	87	
Uses statements about probability to construct a table that shows ratio numbers and expected outcomes.	88	
Multiplication Problems		
Works a multiplication problem that refers to a fraction or percent **of** a value.	21-23	
Works a multiplication word problem that refers to a fraction or percent **of** a value.	24, 25	
Works a multiplication word problem that compares.	26, 27	
Determines whether a word problem can be solved by multiplication.	28-30	
Works a multiplication problem that tells about each like item and the number of items.	31-34	

Skills	Taught in these Lessons	Date Lessons Completed
Works a mixed set of problems that are solved by fraction multiplication or by a ratio table.	38, 39	
Works a word problem that involves multiplying a decimal by a fraction.	54	

MULTI-STEP PROBLEMS

Inverse Operations

Skills	Taught in these Lessons	Date Lessons Completed
Works a word problem that requires inverse operations.	5-12	
Writes an equation with two missing values from a sentence that refers to doubling, tripling or twice.	6	
Solves a two-step word problem by figuring out the missing middle value in the second equation.	9	
Works a mixed set of word problems that require inverse operations.	12-17	
Uses inverse operations to work a word problem that implies a starting value.	12	
Writes an equation with three boxes for a sentence that refers to an operation but does not specify numbers.	18	
Works an inverse-operation problem, part of which refers to an operation without numbers.	21, 22	
Works a mixed set of inverse-operation problems.	23	

Component Calculations

Skills	Taught in these Lessons	Date Lessons Completed
Works a word problem that involves component problems.	35	
Works a multi-step word problem that involves tax.	36-38	
Works a mixed set of multi-step problems that refer to area, perimeter and tax.	39	
Works a mixed set of multi-step problems that refer to area, circumference, perimeter or tax.	41, 42	

Skills	Taught in these Lessons	Date Lessons Completed
Works a multi-step problem.	43-47	
Finds the area of a figure with a hole.	51, 52	
Finds the area of a figure that has more than one hole.	53, 54	
Works a multi-step problem that involves complex area.	55-59	
Works a multi-step problem involving part of a figure.	58-69	

Reciprocals

Skills	Taught in these Lessons	Date Lessons Completed
Expresses the relationship between the fraction for each part and the number of parts in a whole.	44, 45	
Works a word problem that involves finding the reciprocal of a common percent value.	52	
Works a two-step word problem that involves reciprocals.	53-55	
Works a mixed set of problems involving the area of a figure divided into equal parts.	56, 57	
Works an area-of-figure problem that asks about one or more than one equal part.	57	
Works a word problem that requires dividing by a fraction.	85, 86	

Mixed-Number Problems

Skills	Taught in these Lessons	Date Lessons Completed
Works a word problem that requires multiplying by a mixed number.	51, 52	
Works a mixed set of measurement word problems.	57, 58	

Time

Skills	Taught in these Lessons	Date Lessons Completed
Converts p.m. times to times on a 24-hour clock.	61	
Works an addition or subtraction word problem that involves clock time.	61-63	
Converts times on a 24-hour clock to a.m. and p.m. times.	62, 63	

Name _____

Skills	Taught in these Lessons	Date Lessons Completed	Skills	Taught in these Lessons	Date Lessons Completed
Works a word problem that requires converting p.m. time to 24-hour time.	64-66		Works a related-unit problem that asks about the smaller unit.	25-27	
Coins and Money Amounts			Completes an equation to show the names and numbers for related units.	27, 28	
Works a multiplication or division problem that involves coins.	73, 74		Constructs an equation that shows related units based on a question.	29-32	
Completes a rate-equation coin table.	75-77		Converts a fraction into the equivalent fraction that shows related units.	31-33	
Constructs a coin-table to solve a money problem.	77-79		Makes a complete equation for an item that asks about the smaller related unit.	33	
Average			Completes statements of the form: $1\frac{5}{12}$ minutes is ☐ minute and ☐ seconds.	34, 35	
Computes the average for a set of data.	81-84		Works a mixed set of related-unit problems.	34-41	
Circle Graphs			Writes an equation for related units that involves a mixed number.	37-39	
Makes a table based on a circle graph.	72-82		Writes an equation for a sentence that refers to nonconvertible units.	37	
Determines the degrees in a fraction or percent of a circle.	73, 75		Solves a problem that involves nonconvertible units.	38-44	
Makes a table that has fractions of a circle in the first column and the corresponding number of degrees in the second.	76, 77		Rewrites an incorrect equation that involves nonconvertible related units.	41, 42	
Works a mixed set of problems that refer to a circle graph.	78, 79		Works a word problem that asks about the rate.	46	
MEASUREMENT			Works a mixed set of nonconvertible-unit problems, some of which ask about the rate.	47	
Makes fractions that are based on a fact about related units.	7-9		Rewrites an "improper" expression that refers to related units.	49-78	
Writes the unit name for a fraction that shows related units.	11-16		Adds related units.	52-54	
Rewrites a fraction that refers to related units.	14-16		Renames values for related units.	54	
Rewrites a mixed number as related units.	17-19		Renames and subtracts related units.	55, 56	
Given a description of related units, writes a mixed number.	19-21		Works a mixed set of related-unit problems involving addition or subtraction.	57, 58	
Writes a mixed number and unit name for a description of related units.	22, 23				
Completes an equation to show the names for related units.	24-26				

Connecting Math Concepts, Level F Guide

Skills	Taught in these Lessons	Date Lessons Completed
Works a mixed set of measurement word problems.	57, 58	
Works a related-unit word problem that requires addition or subtraction.	59, 60	
Works a problem that multiplies related units.	62, 63	
Works a word problem that requires multiplying related units.	63-79	
Works a mixed set of related-unit word problems that involve multiplication, addition or subtraction.	67	
Works a problem that converts related units into the smaller unit.	68, 69	
Works a mixed set of problems that refer to more than one unit.	87, 88	

GEOMETRY

Area, Perimeter, Circumference and Diameter

Skills	Taught in these Lessons	Date Lessons Completed
Uses the equation $b \times h = A$ to find the area of a rectangle, parallelogram or square.	1, 2	
Finds the perimeter of a triangle or rectangle.	2	
Finds the area and perimeter of a parallelogram or rectangle.	3	
Uses the equation $\frac{b \times h}{2} = A$ to find the area of a triangle.	14	
Finds the area of a parallelogram or triangle.	15	
Uses the equation $\pi \times d = C$ to find the circumference of a circle.	24	
Works a mixed set of problems to find either the circumference or the diameter of circles.	25, 26	
Works a mixed set of problems to find either the circumference or the radius of circles.	27, 28	
Uses the equation $\pi \times r \times r = A$ to calculate the area of a circle.	29-31	

Skills	Taught in these Lessons	Date Lessons Completed
Finds the area and circumference of a circle.	32, 33	
Finds the area of a complex figure shown on the coordinate system.	36-49	
Works a mixed set of multi-step problems that refer to area, perimeter and tax.	39	
Works a mixed set of multi-step problems that refer to area, circumference, perimeter or tax.	41, 42	
Finds the area of a figure with a hole.	51, 52	
Finds the area of a figure that has more than one hole.	53, 54	
Works a multi-step problem that involves complex area.	55-59	
Works a complex-area problem that involves part of a circle.	55	
Works a fraction-of-an-area problem two ways.	56	
Works an area-of-figure problem that asks about one or more than one equal part.	57	
Works a multi-step problem involving part of a figure.	58-69	
Works an area problem that involves mixed numbers.	77-79	
Solves an area problem that involves more than one unit.	86	

Volume

Skills	Taught in these Lessons	Date Lessons Completed
Computes the volume of a rectangular prism.	71, 72	
Computes the volume of a triangular prism.	74	
Works a set of volume problems involving rectangular and triangular prisms.	75, 76	
Uses the equation **Area of $b \times h = V$** to compute the volume of a cylinder.	83	

Skills	Taught in these Lessons	Date Lessons Completed
Works a mixed set of volume problems, some of which involve a cylinder.	84	
Uses the equation $\frac{\text{Area of b x h}}{3} = v$ to compute the volume of figures that come to a point.	85, 86	
Works a mixed set of volume problems including figures that come to a point and figures that have parallel sides.	87	
Geometry Facts		
Writes the number of sides for common polygons.	44-46	
Given a set of common polygons, writes the names.	47	
Answers a question about the degrees in a common angle.	47	
Works a mixed set of items that refer to angles and polygons.	48	
SIGNED NUMBERS		
Combines the values in a problem that adds and subtracts more than one value.	61, 62	
Rewrites and work a problem with signed terms in a different order.	63-65	
Works paired addition and subtraction problems on a number line that has positive and negative values.	64	
Writes an equation for an arrow on a signed number line.	65, 66	
Indicates which of two signed numbers has the greater absolute value.	66, 67	
Completes the number part of the answer for signed-number combination problems.	67-69	
Combines signed numbers.	71-73	
Works a signed-number multiplication problem in which each value has a sign.	78-81	

Skills	Taught in these Lessons	Date Lessons Completed
Works multiplication problems by first combining the signed values on top.	82, 83	
Multiplies by a negative value.	84	
Works a mixed set of problems that multiply by a positive or a negative value.	85, 86	
Works a signed-number multiplication problem of the form: -4×-3.	87, 88	
Works a signed-number problem that has a large operational sign.	88, 89	
Works a problem that divides by a signed value.	89, 90	
Writes a problem that has signed values and a large operational sign.	90	
EXPONENTS		
Writes a base number and exponent for a repeated multiplication problem.	74	
Writes complete equations for a set of exponent problems that show either the multiplication or the exponential notation.	75	
Figures out the value represented by an exponential notation.	76-78	
Shows two groups of repeated multiplication in exponential notation.	83-85	
Rewrites a fraction that shows repeated multiplication as a base and exponent.	86, 87	
Simple Machines		
Works a lever problem.	88-91	
Works a set of problems that involve two types of levers.	90	
Solves a problem that involves a wheel and axle.	92-94	
Solves a problem that asks about the amount of work that is done.	94	

Skills	Taught in these Lessons	Date Lessons Completed
PROJECTS		
Constructs a symmetrical circle graph.	91	
Uses a rule to construct a circle graph that has slices of specified degrees.	92	
Figures out the area of symmetrical figures.	92	
Does an experiment that requires 72 trials at rolling a pair of dice.	93	
Makes letters on a coordinate system by using information about the X and Y values for the line segments.	94	
Analyzes an inclined plane and figures out how it works as a simple machine.	95	
Finds the sum of a series of numbers by "folding" the series in half.	95	
Figures out a strategy for determining the sum of numbers in a series.	96	
Figures out the amount of work required to move a weight to specified points along the incline.	96	

Skills	Taught in these Lessons	Date Lessons Completed
Relates an inclined plane to a set of nested similar triangles.	96	
Figures out a strategy for determining the sum of odd or even numbers in a series.	97	
Figures out the relationship between an inclined plane and a screw.	97	
Finds the area of a figure that has a repeated pattern.	98	
Determines the relationships between force and distance in a simple single-pulley system.	98	
Solves problems that involve repeated patterns.	99, 100	
Figures out the general rules for working division problems that require a whole-number answer.	99	
Figures out the arrangement of string that requires a force that is 1/4 the amount of the weight that is being lifted.	99	
Works out a strategy for finding the capacity of a box shape that has a figure inside.	100	

Remedy Summary—Group Summary of Test Performance

Note: Test remedies are specified in the *Answer Key.* Percent Summary is also specified in the *Answer Key.*

Name	Test 1										Test 2										Test 3									
	Check parts not passed									Total %	Check parts not passed									Total %	Check parts not passed									Total %
	1	2	3	4	5	6	7	8	9		1	2	3	4	5	6	7	8			1	2	3	4	5	6	7	8	9	
1.																														
2.																														
3.																														
4.																														
5.																														
6.																														
7.																														
8.																														
9.																														
10.																														
11.																														
12.																														
13.																														
14.																														
15.																														
16.																														
17.																														
18.																														
19.																														
20.																														
21.																														
22.																														
23.																														
24.																														
25.																														
26.																														
27.																														
28.																														
29.																														
30.																														

Number of students Not Passed = NP

Total number of students = T

Remedy needed if NP/T = 25% or more

Remedy Summary—Group Summary of Test Performance

Name	Test 4 Check parts not passed									Total %	Test 5 Check parts not passed												Total %	Test 6 Check parts not passed									Total %
	1	2	3	4	5	6	7	8	9		1	2	3	4	5	6	7	8	9	10	11	12		1	2	3	4	5	6	7	8	9	
1.																																	
2.																																	
3.																																	
4.																																	
5.																																	
6.																																	
7.																																	
8.																																	
9.																																	
10.																																	
11.																																	
12.																																	
13.																																	
14.																																	
15.																																	
16.																																	
17.																																	
18.																																	
19.																																	
20.																																	
21.																																	
22.																																	
23.																																	
24.																																	
25.																																	
26.																																	
27.																																	
28.																																	
29.																																	
30.																																	

Number of students Not Passed = NP

Total number of students = T

Remedy needed if NP/T = 25% or more

Remedy Summary—Group Summary of Test Performance

Name	Test 7 — Check parts not passed												Total %	Test 8 — Check parts not passed										Total %	Test 9 — Check parts not passed												Total %
	1	2	3	4	5	6	7	8	9	10	11	12		1	2	3	4	5	6	7	8	9	10		1	2	3	4	5	6	7	8	9	10	11	12	
1.																																					
2.																																					
3.																																					
4.																																					
5.																																					
6.																																					
7.																																					
8.																																					
9.																																					
10.																																					
11.																																					
12.																																					
13.																																					
14.																																					
15.																																					
16.																																					
17.																																					
18.																																					
19.																																					
20.																																					
21.																																					
22.																																					
23.																																					
24.																																					
25.																																					
26.																																					
27.																																					
28.																																					
29.																																					
30.																																					
Number of students Not Passed = NP																																					
Total number of students = T																																					
Remedy needed if NP/T = 25% or more																																					

Graph A

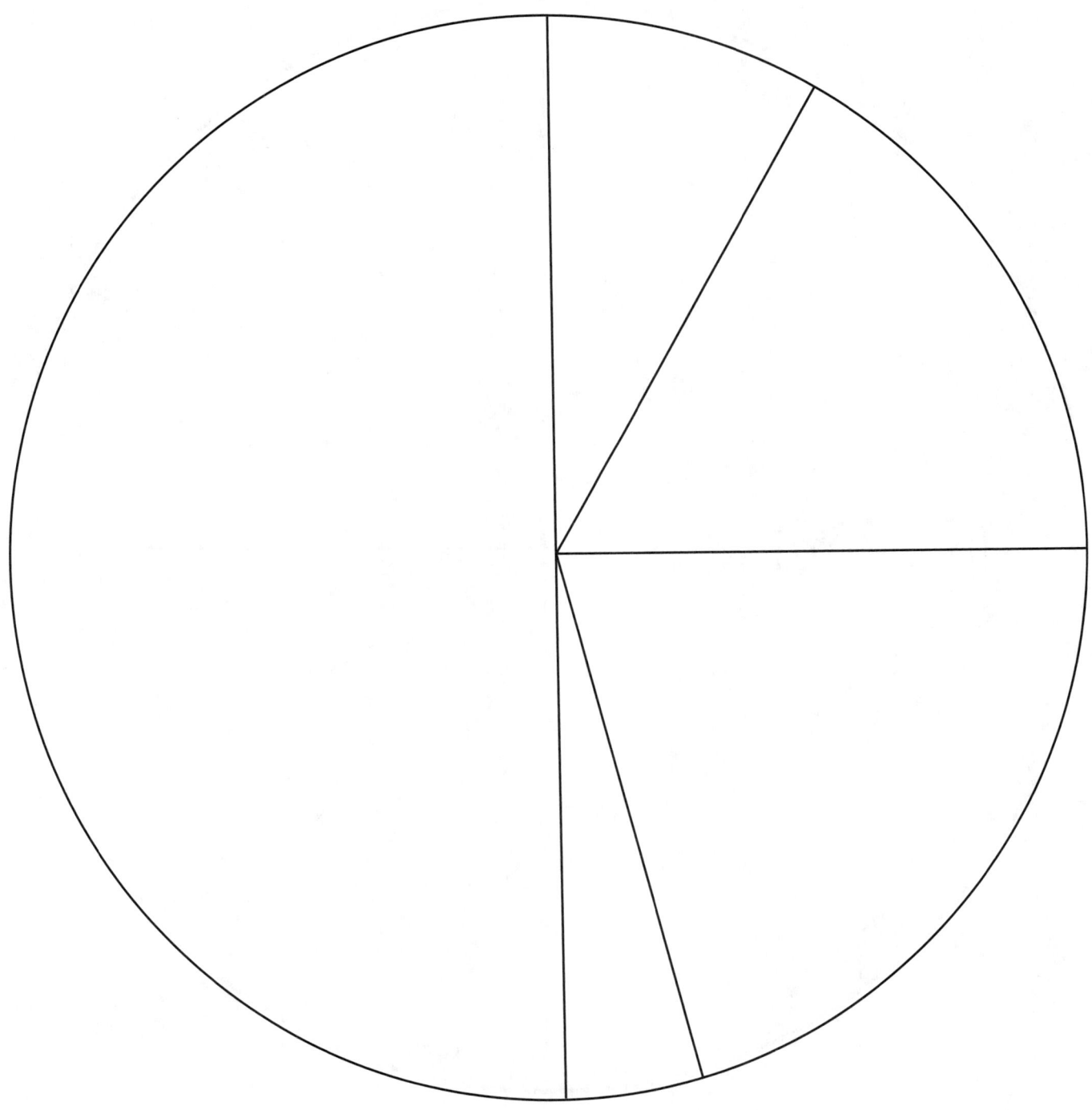

Graph B

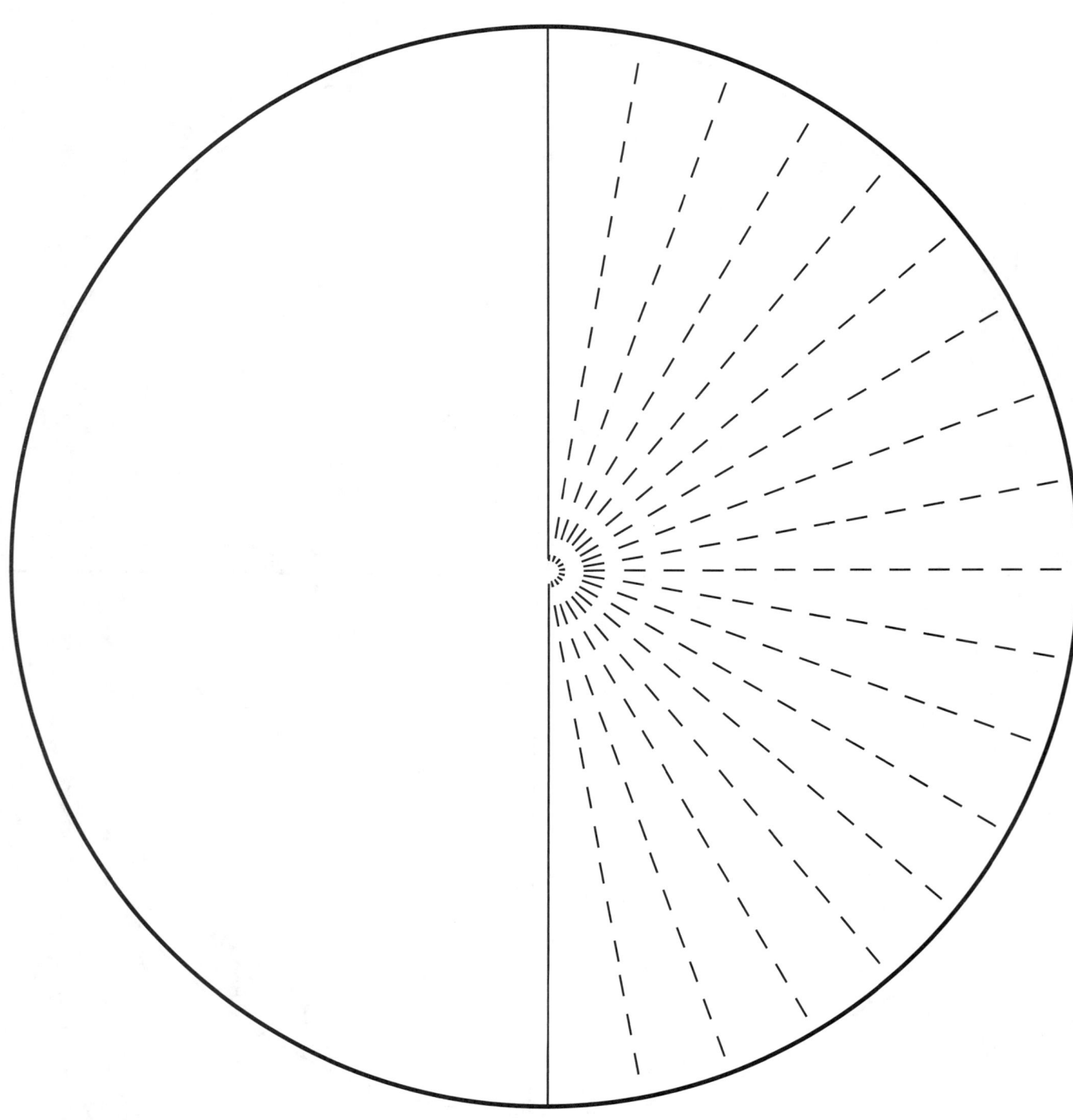

Table 1

# of dots.	Combinations = left + right	possibilities	degrees	expected #	tally	actual #
2	1 ¦ 1	1				
3						
4	1 ¦ 3 2 ¦ 2 3 ¦ 1	3				
5						
6						
7	1 ¦ 6 2 ¦ 5 3 ¦ 4 4 ¦ 3 5 ¦ 2 6 ¦ 1	6				
8						
9						
10						
11	5 ¦ 6 6 ¦ 5	2				
12						
total		36	360	72	72	72

Coordinate System

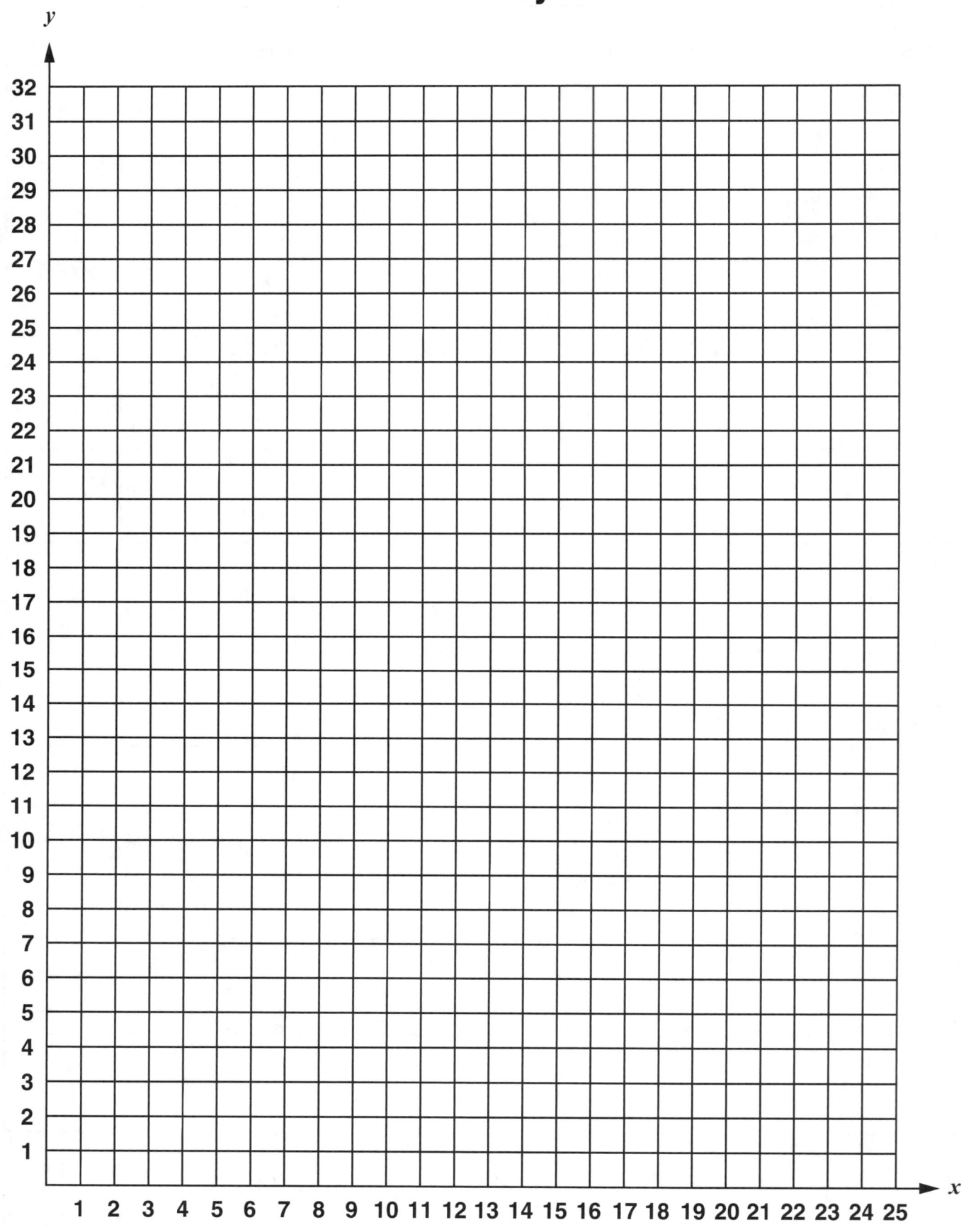

Connecting Math Concepts, Level F Guide